Blowing the Bridge

Sun Valley, Idaho, 1940: Ernest Hemingway and Gary Cooper (star of Para-mount Studio's *For Whom the Bell Tolls*). Photo by Lloyd Arnold, used by permission of Erma O. Arnold.

BLOWING THE BRIDGE

Essays on Hemingway and *For Whom the Bell Tolls*

Edited by
Rena Sanderson

CONTRIBUTIONS IN AMERICAN STUDIES, NUMBER 101
Robert H. Walker, *Series Editor*

GREENWOOD PRESS
NEW YORK • WESTPORT, CONNECTICUT • LONDON

Library of Congress Cataloging-in-Publication Data

Blowing the bridge : essays on Hemingway and For whom the bell tolls /
   edited by Rena Sanderson.
        p.   cm.—(Contributions in American studies, ISSN 0084–9227
; no. 101)
    Includes bibliographical references and index.
    ISBN 0–313–28451–2
    1. Hemingway, Ernest, 1899–1961—Criticism and interpretation.
    2. Hemingway, Ernest, 1899–1961. For whom the bell tolls.
    3. Spain—History—Civil War, 1936–1939—Literature and the war.
    I. Sanderson, Rena.   II. Series.
    PS3515.E37Z5825   1992
    813'.52—dc20   92–3307

British Library Cataloguing in Publication Data is available.

Library of Congress Catalog Card Number: 92–3307
ISBN: 0–313–28451–2
ISSN: 0084–9227

First published in 1992

Greenwood Press, 88 Post Road West, Westport, CT 06881
An imprint of Greenwood Publishing Group, Inc.

Printed in the United States of America

The paper used in this book complies with the
Permanent Paper Standard issued by the National
Information Standards Organization (Z39.48–1984).

10 9 8 7 6 5 4 3 2 1

Copyright Acknowledgments

This book is dedicated to my mother, Berta Kennedy.

Contents

Preface

Most of the pieces in this collection first took shape at the "Hemingway in Idaho" Conference (June 1989), which was funded in part by the Idaho Humanities Council, a state-based program of the National Endowment for the Humanities; by the Boise State University (BSU) Student Programs Board; by the BSU Foundation; and by the BSU Hemingway Western Studies Center. As director of that conference, I had the pleasure of working with many enthusiastic friends and colleagues, including Jim Maguire (who first had the idea for the conference), Betty Maguire, Carol Martin, Gwen Kimball, Helen Lojek, Glenn Selander, Tom Trusky, Jim and Joni Hadden, Nina Ray, Alan Virta, Jim Baker, and Larry Burke.

In addition, John de Groot, Tillie Arnold, the Hemingway Society, the Nature Conservancy, the Sun Valley Company, the Ketchum Public Library, and the John Fitzgerald Kennedy Library in Boston deserve recognition for variously facilitating the conference, and thus indirectly this book.

I want to thank my contributing authors for their confidence in this project and for their many helpful suggestions. For their continuing support of scholarship, I thank John, Patrick, and Gregory Hemingway. I am also grateful to Cynthia Harris of Greenwood Press for her accessibility, patience, and editorial expertise. Special thanks go to Susan Beegel, Ruth Prigozy, Jackson R. Bryer, and Robert Lewis for their invaluable advice and encouragement.

Most of all, however, I want to thank my husband, Ken, who has been a constant helpmate through it all.

Blowing the Bridge

1   Introduction

Rena Sanderson

The plot of Hemingway's *For Whom the Bell Tolls* centers on the task assigned to Robert Jordan—the blowing of a bridge controlled by the Spanish Fascists. Though destroying the bridge is Jordan's goal, he has been warned by the Loyalist General Golz that "to blow the bridge is nothing. . . . Merely to blow the bridge is a failure. . . . To blow the bridge at a stated hour based on the time set for the attack is how it should be done" (Hemingway, *FWBT* 4–5). The underlying idea—that individual acts are meaningful only when coordinated with the acts of others—is of course consistent with the lines of John Donne from which Hemingway chose the title and the epigraph for this novel: "No man is an *Iland*, intire of it selfe; every man is a peece of the *Continent*, a part of the *maine*."

To blow the literal bridge in the right way—as part of a communal, cooperative effort—thus entails the *building* of metaphoric bridges: between men and women, between the International Brigades and the Spanish Republic, between the hero and his past, and, not least, between the author and his readers. Hemingway's novel in this sense *is* a bridge; the essays in this volume (contributions to the collective enterprise of literature and criticism) all add to our understanding of how bridges are strengthened or weakened, created or destroyed. *For Whom the Bell Tolls* has been the most neglected of Hemingway's major novels. Now that fifty years have passed since its publication, it is fitting that we take a fresh look both at the text and at that other self-consciously created text, the author's life.

COMPOSITION

Hemingway has made it easy for us to reconstruct his composing process. In a note attached to the manuscript folder, he left the following record: "This, the original manuscript of For Whom the Bell Tolls, was written in Cuba in the Hotel Sevilla Biltmore and at San Francisco de Paula in the Finca Vigia from March 1939 until late August 1939, at Sun Valley, Idaho from September 20, 1939 until December 6, 1939 and was written at the Finca Vigia from Christmas 1939 until July 21, 1940 when the first draft was completed."[1] Charles Scribner's Sons published the novel on October 21, 1940.

For Hemingway, the novel was the culmination of his four-year involvement in the Spanish Civil War.[2] In 1936, General Franco led the revolt of the Spanish army against the Republic, initiating the war that would later be seen as a dress rehearsal for World War II. In a letter of September 26, 1936, Hemingway told Maxwell Perkins of his "hope to go to Spain" (*Selected Letters* 454); his interest marked the beginning of a serious commitment. Early in 1937, Hemingway joined John Dos Passos, Archibald MacLeish, and Lillian Hellman as a board member of Contemporary Historians, the organization set up to produce films on the war. During his January visit to New York City, Hemingway prepared the subtitles for the pro-Loyalist propaganda film, *Spain in Flames*. In addition, he agreed to write the dialogue for a documentary, *The Spanish Earth*, which was being planned by the Dutch film-maker Joris Ivens. Hemingway's participation in the film projects and his association with Ivens strongly influenced his understanding of the war and of his own role in it (see William Braasch Watson's essay in this volume).

During the spring and fall of 1937 and 1938, Hemingway made four extended visits as a correspondent in Spain. After his stay in Spain from March to May, 1937, he returned to the United States to address a gathering of 3,500 people at the Second American Writers' Congress (sponsored by the Communist-dominated League of American Writers) at Carnegie Hall on the evening of June 4, 1937. Many, from Albert Einstein to Thomas Mann, sent messages expressing their support of the congress. "From Madrid came this cable: 'Militant writers in the International Brigade, defending world democracy in Spain, salute the Congress of American writers. It is a writer's duty to fight for democracy; fascism is the enemy of the liberty of the artist'" (Hart 200). After Ivens showed the silent version of *The Spanish Earth*, Hemingway gave his first public address and declared his support of the anti-Fascist cause. That same summer, Hemingway returned to New York City to complete the script for *The*

Spanish Earth and ended up replacing Orson Welles as narrator. On July 8, Hemingway, Martha Gellhorn, and Joris Ivens had dinner at the White House and showed *The Spanish Earth* to the Roosevelts. Also in July, Hemingway and Ivens showed the documentary in the Los Angeles region and raised several thousand dollars to support the Spanish Loyalist cause. Carlos Baker describes the success of the undertaking: although the film was still incomplete and without sound, Hemingway read off "a speech that he had written out on fifteen sheets of hotel stationery." His fame, "obvious sincerity," and the film's effect combined to bring in "enough money [for] twenty ambulances" (Baker, *EH: Life Story* 316).[3]

In addition to the film script, Hemingway produced a considerable amount of writing between 1937 and 1939. During his four visits to Spain in 1937 and 1938, he wrote thirty-one dispatches for the North American Newspaper Alliance (NANA), several of which were reprinted in such magazines as *Time* and the British *Fact*.[4] In addition, he wrote diverse pieces for *Ken* magazine (including "The Old Man at the Bridge" in the May 1938 issue), for *New Masses*, and one article for *Pravda*.

In the fall of 1937, Hemingway composed a play, *The Fifth Column*, reflecting his Spanish Civil War experience. Together with earlier short stories, it appeared in print as *The Fifth Column and the First Forty-Nine Stories* in October 1938, and it was variously criticized for its wooden characters, melodrama, and didacticism. An adaptation, prepared by Hollywood scriptwriter Benjamin Glazer, was eventually performed on Broadway in March 1940 and received mixed reviews.

Between May 1938 and March 1939, Hemingway also wrote five short stories, which were individually published: in *Esquire*, "The Denunciation" (November 1938), "The Butterfly and the Tank" (December 1938), and "Night before Battle" (February 1939); in *Cosmopolitan*, "Nobody Ever Dies" (March 1939) and "Under the Ridge" (October 1939). With the exception of "Nobody Ever Dies" (set in Cuba rather than Spain), the stories were eventually collected in *The Fifth Column and Four Stories of the Spanish Civil War* (1969).[5] Taken together, the film script, the journalistic pieces, the play, and the short stories of the late thirties may be seen as valuable preparation or pre-writing for the subsequent Spanish Civil War novel.[6]

Hemingway returned from Spain in February 1939. The end of the Spanish Civil War coincided with the end of Hemingway's homelessness, his marital conflicts, and his preparatory writings. In the summer of 1939, he finally decided to break up for good with his second wife Pauline (Pfeiffer) and to have his future third wife Martha (Gellhorn) join him on his way to Idaho. He gradually committed himself to new people, new places, new productivity. At forty, he was settling into the identity of his prime: he was a popular, photogenic, and pampered writer-in-residence at Suite 206 of Sun Valley Lodge. The promotional pictures show him at his best—vigorous, exuberant, and apparently pleased with his new daily routine of writing, outdoorsmanship, romancing, and socializing.

Relocating a couple of times between his two paradises in Idaho and Cuba, he was making good progress on his book. On his forty–first birthday (July 21, 1940), he finished the first draft (Hemingway, *Selected Letters* 510). By late July, he was staying at the Hotel Barclay in New York City, correcting the manuscript and delivering it "piecemeal by runner boy at the rate of 200 pages a day" to Scribner's (Baker, *EH: Life Story* 350). By August 26, he sent from Havana the first 123 galley pages of the book; by September, 1940, he was back in Sun Valley, proofreading and sending out his final corrections. That fall he declared it "the best goddamn book" he had ever written (*Selected Letters* 511).

CRITICAL RECEPTION

On October 21, 1940, Charles Scribner's Sons published a first printing of 75,000 copies of *For Whom the Bell Tolls*, at a price of $2.75 each. It was an immediate popular and critical success. By April 4, 1941, less than six months after publication, 491,000 copies had been sold. "At the end of 1943 the cumulative sales figures stood at 785,000, plus another 100,000 in England, thus making the novel the biggest seller in American fiction since *Gone With the Wind*" (Lynn 484). *For Whom the Bell Tolls* was chosen as the Book-of-the-Month-Club selection for November 1940; it was awarded the Limited Editions Club Gold Medal in the following year; it was published by Overseas Editions in 1945; and it would eventually be translated into more than twenty-five languages. The third volume of Asa Don Dickinson's *The Best Books of Our Time* (1948) lists *For Whom the Bell Tolls* in first place in the table of the "Best American Fiction" of the decade 1936–45. It "was rated the best of the 'Fifty Best Books,' . . . [and] also tops in the lists of the 'Twenty Best Novels' and the 'Twenty Best American Books.' It was given 680 points, the maximum possible. . . . the highest [score] on record" up to that time (Hubbell 298).

With a "sense of relief and . . . celebration," most reviewers welcomed Hemingway's new novel of 1940 as "fulfillment of the long-delayed promise and one of the major American books of the century" (Stephens, *EH: The Critical Reception* xxiii). Henry Seidel Canby, Dorothy Parker, Edmund Wilson, J. Donald Adams, John Chamberlain, Clifton Fadiman, and many others whose opinions counted most hailed the novel's merits.

In October 1940, John Chamberlain asserted that *For Whom the Bell Tolls* "redeem[ed] a decade"—that is, the thirties (227).[7]

The book carried Hemingway's reputation through the forties until the publication of *The Old Man and the Sea* (1952). Indeed, *For Whom the Bell Tolls* helped to save Hemingway's reputation: in August 1944, the *Saturday Review of Literature* published a poll of critics, in which Hemingway won "hands down as the leading novelist" of the previous twenty years (Stephens, *EH: The Critical Reception* 269). Looking back, we can see that *For Whom The Bell Tolls* was the only true critical success during a creative lull that lasted from 1929 (*A Farewell to Arms*) until 1952 (*The Old Man and the Sea*).

Nevertheless, a survey of the criticism over the past half century (much of it conveniently reprinted in Stephens and in Meyers) shows the reputation of the book rising and falling with changes in critical tastes and historical circumstances. Five general developments mark the critical reception of *For Whom the Bell Tolls* during the last fifty years. First, a debate between realists and symbolists in the forties. Second, the attention paid to biography, the Hemingway Hero, and the "code" during the fifties. Third, the effect of Hemingway's suicide, the prominence of sensational media coverage, and the decline of scholarly interest during the sixties. Fourth, during the seventies, the reappearance of more varied criticism of Hemingway's work generally, but a disproportionate lack of interest in *For Whom the Bell Tolls*. And fifth, during the eighties, a strong revival of Hemingway scholarship, with the establishment of the Hemingway collection at the Kennedy Library, the founding of the Hemingway Society, and the spread of new critical theories.

Criticism of Hemingway's Spanish Civil War novel in the forties generally took one of two approaches: realist and symbolist. In a review of October 26, 1940, Howard Mumford Jones outlined the positions of the two critical camps when he insisted on the distinction between naturalistic, representational art and lasting, "true" art. Jones rejected "mere reporting, mere realism, mere enlistment on the right side" and expressed his appreciation of "imagination" that creates a lasting legend:

I wish we had in criticism the phrase, "occasional novel." I refer to those books which, produced by such an event as the Spanish Civil War, are impassioned and journalistic, and no more. . . . But somehow, sometime, somebody comes along and lifts the occasional novel out of contentiousness into the world of Humanity. Such a book is "Uncle Tom's Cabin." There is a small library of fiction on Negro slavery—who reads it today? But who doesn't know the story of Little Eva and Uncle Tom? . . . I think it at least possible that "For Whom the Bell Tolls" may be . . . the "Uncle Tom's Cabin" of the Spanish Civil War. . . . The book will last . . . because it rises out of partisanship into imaginative comprehensiveness. (238)

On the realist side, however, *For Whom the Bell Tolls* was read as a historical war novel. J. Donald Adams, Dorothy Parker, and many lesser known reviewers agreed with John Chamberlain's generous praise for Hemingway, "the chronicler of warring man" (Chamberlain 227). Ralph Thompson, in a 1940 review in the *New York Times*, called the book "our finest major novel of the Second World War and the most impressive work to date on the Spanish Civil War" (230).

Other critics just as extravagantly criticized Hemingway's social and political representation. Alvah Bessie, writing for *New Masses* in 1940, charged that it was "not a book about Spain at all!" (27) and that it betrayed the cause because it was not sympathetic enough to the Russians' role in Spain. Arturo Barea, in 1941, also sharply disagreed with those who praised Hemingway's knowledge of Spain, its people, and the Spanish language. Yet others thought it was not political enough. Dwight Macdonald, in the 1941 *Partisan Review*, ascribed the failure of the novel to Hemingway's "moral and intellectual" inability to handle "the great political event [of] the Spanish Civil War" (327).

An alternative to political readings was offered by Edmund Wilson's 1940 review in the *New Republic*. Wilson appreciated *For Whom the Bell Tolls* as "not so much a social analysis as a criticism of moral qualities" (320). Graham Greene, in 1941, applauded it as "a record more truthful than history" (343). Finally, in his introduction to the *Viking Portable Hemingway* (1944), Malcolm Cowley effectively influenced the general direction of Hemingway research by promoting Hemingway as a symbolist. According to Stephens, this collection

was important, as Granville Hicks and Max Lerner indicated, because Cowley established a new view of Hemingway as nocturnal symbolist and ritualist in the tradition of Hawthorne and Melville, rather than as a literary naturalist. The new interpretation became important in the post-war years as criticism based on archetypes became dominant, and despite the failure of *Across the River and into the Trees* in 1950, the new approach helped keep Hemingway under consideration by the Nobel Prize committee. (*EH: The Critical Reception* xxvi).

Diverse explorations of the "mythic, pre-discursive, pre-political level of comprehension" soon followed and continue today (Stephens, "Language Magic . . ." 153).[8]

After World War II, Hemingway critics were disappointed in their expectation of "a literary renaissance following the Second World War to match the one following the First." In addition, the "taste for an intellectualized and complex vision of the artist's role helped turn the verdict against Hemingway" after the critical disaster of *Across the River and into the Trees* in 1950 (Stephens, *EH: The Critical Reception* xxvii). Nevertheless, *The Old Man and the Sea* (1952) was both a popular and critical success, and finally won Hemingway the Nobel Prize. The clever marketing strategy of publishing the work in a single issue of *Life* magazine also signaled an increasing promotion of Hemingway's popular appeal throughout the fifties.

Indeed, this sketch of the critical reception is complicated by the related fortunes of the Hemingway myth. Already during the late 1920s, Hemingway's early success and the convergence of biographic, fictive, and cultural components produced the myth of Hemingway himself as hero. It was during the 1930s, however, as John Raeburn suggests, that Hemingway started consciously to shape his public personality in *Death in the Afternoon* (1932). Writing monthly contributions for *Esquire*, the new how-to magazine for men, Hemingway subsequently stressed the virility of his public persona (Raeburn 38–57). As early as 1933, Clifton Fadiman claimed that Hemingway "triumphed more as a hero than as an artist" because he provided a Romantic "hero myth" necessary during historical crises, much as Lord Byron had done a hundred years earlier. Like Byron, Hemingway—emblematic of "violence, waywardness, and independence"—fulfilled a social function as a model of behavior, "embodying to perfection the mute longings and confused ideals of a large segment of his own and the succeeding generation" (125, 128).

By the mid-thirties, "several magazines published caricatures of the virile Hemingway. A 'paper doll' satire in *Vanity Fair* offered costumes representing aspects of his public personality which the reader could cut out and paste on a body figure" (Raeburn 59). It is not clear if Hemingway's subsequent involvement in the Spanish Civil War redeemed the legend of the Hemingway Hero by proving its manly substance or if it simply intensified the caricature.

Starting in the fall of 1940, Hemingway's association with Gary Cooper helped to Americanize and Westernize the Byronic Hero. Publicity photographs of Hemingway and Cooper promoted the resort of Sun Valley, Idaho; incidentally, they also promoted the qualities represented by the two men. One September 1940 picture shows the two tall handsome men on a dirt road next to their car; they are sporting shotguns and gazing off into the distance of the open range (see frontispiece). Together, Cooper and Hemingway represented not only good looks, the manhood of few words, and Western outdoorsmanship, but also the glamor associated with Hollywood, the intelligence and sensitivity associated with writing, and the ease and success enjoyed by both men. Recalling the fall of 1940, Hemingway's son Gregory said that both men "were great actors (yes, my father was one) who had forged, consciously or otherwise, two of the most successful hero images of this century. There was never rivalry between them, and there was no reason for any. They were both at their peak then" (44–45). The film rights to *For Whom the Bell Tolls* were reportedly sold for $110,000, thought to be the most ever paid for a novel. During the winter of 1943–44, the movie version, which starred Gary Cooper as Robert Jordan, Ingrid Bergman as Maria, Katina Paxinou as Pilar, and Akim Tamiroff as Pablo, broke box-office records.

While the name of Hemingway achieved popular fame, serious critics thought it essential to separate the myth of the Hemingway Hero from the writing. Hemingway's literary reputation rose and fell at least partly in response to the changing definition and fluctuating prominence of the legendary figure.

The 1950s mark the beginning of a biographic flood that has both promoted and hurt Hemingway's literary reputation. In 1949, *Life* published Malcolm Cowley's minibiography, "A Portrait of Mister Papa." Cowley wrote out of the conviction that Hemingway had "created for himself a persona, like Byron," and Cowley's portrait promoted that myth of Hemingway as a larger-than-life figure of exceptional abilities, stature, and privilege (Brian 199). Other biographic sketches were less flattering. There was a fictive parody of Hemingway, as a reporter making a study of fear, in Irwin Shaw's novel, *The Young Lions* (1949). In her piece, "How Do You Like It Now, Gentlemen?" (*New Yorker*, May 1950), Lillian Ross presented what some have called a realistic portrait and what others have called a caricature of a swaggering Hemingway (Brian 204–9). In 1952, Philip Young's biography helped to redefine the Hemingway Hero. Stressing the importance of Hemingway's shell shock, Young explored the consequences of the traumatic neurosis inflicted on Hemingway by his World War I experience. Young also coined the expression Hemingway Code Hero. The image of the more vulnerable, but experienced and stoic Hemingway Hero was reinforced not only by pictures of an aging, white-haired Hemingway but also by his last best-seller, *The Old Man and the Sea* (1952). The attention given to this work and to Hemingway's life throughout the fifties contributed to the neglect of *For Whom the Bell Tolls*, a work that was of course too political and time-bound for the 1950s.

During the 1960s, *For Whom the Bell Tolls* was not the only Hemingway work that was ignored. In October 1970, Joseph Epstein commented on the decline of Hemingway's reputation since 1961:

Such are the sweeping swings of critical opinion that in less than a decade Hemingway's reputation appears to have gone from that of a major (if not *the* major) American novelist to that of a writer of little consequence: from—to use a boxing analogy of the sort he was so fond of—the heavyweight champ to just another bum. (557–58)

Epstein attributes the "swing from champ to bum" most of all to "the manner of Hemingway's death":

[While the suicide of other writers] authenticated their pain and enhanced the stature of their work, [Hemingway's suicide] seemed to throw into doubt, if not utterly to disqualify, almost every word he had ever written. . . . As the shotgun went off it was as if all those bullfighters, big-game hunters, fishermen, ambulance drivers, and soldiers were blown to smithereens. Not merely Ernest Hemingway but the Hemingway hero seemed to die that morning in Ketchum, Idaho. (558)

While alive, Hemingway was his own best press agent; but his suicide and the subsequent lawsuit between Mary Hemingway and A. E. Hotchner drew the kind of sensational press coverage that did little to promote his literature. After Mary Hemingway's failed attempt to block its publication, Hotchner's revealing biography, *Papa Hemingway: A Personal Memoir*, came out in 1966. Hotchner's book helped to initiate what Denis Brian, in his 1988 biography, has called the "second wave" of biographers. As Frederick J. Hoffman noted with regret, in 1967, it was perhaps to be expected that Hemingway would be "re-evaluated in terms of the character and circumstances of his life's conclusion" (96).

Also responsible for the decline of Hemingway's reputation during the sixties was the posthumous publication of *A Moveable Feast* (1964). Hemingway's memoir of the expatriate 1920s, like his other posthumously published works—*Islands in the Stream* (1970) and *The Garden of Eden* (1986)—provided material for critics but disappointed many.

By the 1970s, postmodernist literary theories, and most of all the introduction of new research tools, greatly revived Hemingway scholarship and criticism. As early as 1972, Mary Hemingway began to deposit the materials for the Hemingway Collection at the Kennedy Library in Boston. On July 18, 1980, the Kennedy Library officially opened the Hemingway Room, which houses this extensive accumulation of miscellaneous documents, newspaper clippings, pictures, letters, rough drafts, and manuscripts, including the 1,147–page manuscript of *For Whom the Bell Tolls*. On the same day, the Hemingway Society was formed. As Bernard Oldsey remarked at the time, these events signalled "a new beginning" (xii). Early access to the collection allowed Carlos Baker to edit *Ernest Hemingway: Selected Letters, 1917–1961* (1981), one of several important contributions to research during the 1980s. The international conferences of the Hemingway Society and its publications, the *Hemingway Newsletter* and the *Hemingway Review*, have promoted and stimulated work on the author.

Also during the 1980s, new biographic information created controversy. In the summers of 1986 and 1987, the *New York Review of Books* featured two review articles that drew attention to a rich crop of biographies. In 1986, Wilfrid Sheed reviewed the posthumous publication of *The Garden of Eden*, as well as *Dateline Toronto: The Complete "Toronto Star" Dispatches, 1920–1924* and recent biographies by Jeffrey Meyers, Peter Griffin, Michael Reynolds, and Anthony Burgess. In 1987, Frederick Crews reviewed the controversial life-study by Kenneth S. Lynn. The two reviews proved, if nothing else, that enough time had passed since Hemingway's suicide to mention the unmentionable and to bring back from the infamous dead Hemingway's name and work. The drawing by David Levine that accompanied Crews's review depicts a naked Hemingway, endowed with an oversized head and an undersized fig leaf, and propped on a shotgun that points upward into his armpit. The picture captures the irreverence of criticism that stresses Hemingway's sexual ambivalence and that sets out to demystify the Hemingway legend.

Crews makes the hefty claim that "nothing will be the same in any branch of Hemingway studies" after Lynn's biography (30). In one respect the claim is accurate: as a consequence of the controversy that was stirred up by Lynn's biography, and promoted by Sheed's and Crews's reviews, new attention has been paid to the importance of gender issues in Hemingway's life and work. The author's masculinity and sexual preferences are the subject of new inquiry. And although his works have received relatively few feminist readings, this pattern is changing.[9]

Thanks to the Hemingway Collection, the Hemingway Society, and new critical and theoretical considerations, Hemingway research during the last twenty years has become more diverse and more sophisticated. Yet *For Whom the Bell Tolls* has remained relatively neglected. The Modern Language Association bibliographies published between 1972 and 1990 list 112 critical pieces on *The Sun Also Rises* and 81 on *A Farewell to Arms*, but only 54 on *For Whom the Bell Tolls*.

The novel's later critical neglect may be traced, in part, to its early enthusiastic reception. Two consequences of that reception are of special interest. First, the plentiful early reviews and analyses by recognized public figures (Lionel Trilling, Edmund Wilson, Alvah C. Bessie, Leo Gurko, Carlos Baker) subsequently encouraged the publication of critical anthologies, which offered primarily reprints rather than original, fresh essays.[10] Second, the many reprints in turn reinforced the impression that everything of importance had been said. Actually, however, following its initial critical acclaim, the book received less attention (and more biased attention) than the other major Hemingway novels. And while there have been individual pieces of exceptional quality, there has been neither a book-length study nor an updated critical anthology dedicated to *For Whom the Bell Tolls*.

The fiftieth anniversary of the Spanish Civil War may, in part, account for the recent publications on that war and on Hemingway's involvement in it, including several books and special journal issues, such as *Salmagundi* 76–77 (Fall 1987–Winter 1988) and the *Hemingway Review* (Spring 1988).[11] It is time that Hemingway's novel be given similar attention.

A REASSESSMENT

The present collection evolved from the "Hemingway in Idaho" conference that was held in Boise and Sun Valley on June 9–11, 1989. Over 130 scholars, book-dealers, and Hemingway enthusiasts from 26 states and Canada gathered to celebrate the fiftieth anniversary of Hemingway's arrival in Idaho and to reassess *For Whom the Bell Tolls*, the book he partly composed in Sun Valley. This anthology contains the keynote address by novelist Kurt Vonnegut, seven articles by Hemingway scholars that were first presented at the conference, and three additional pieces (two of them previously published) on Hemingway's Spanish Civil War novel.

Vonnegut's remarks on Hemingway, first delivered to an audience of 1,200 people, should not be evaluated on the same terms as the scholarly studies. Vonnegut begins by setting himself apart from the scholars: "they all know a hell of a lot more about Hemingway than I do." Perhaps in this concession there is the practicing writer's disdain for academics as well as a boast: he can tell us more than they.

In fact, Vonnegut's talk invites a dialogue with literary scholars who, for better or worse, largely determine what is read in and out of the classroom. While none of the other pieces directly responds to Vonnegut's speech, his provocative view that Hemingway was not really an American writer and his comments on Hemingway's relation to patriarchal values have particular relevance to the rest of the anthology. Equally important are the questions Vonnegut raises about Hemingway's work and popular reputation. Since Vonnegut's presentation reveals as much about himself as about Hemingway, it should be of interest to readers of both authors.

Of the ten scholarly articles, the first two are largely biographical. Hemingway biographer Michael Reynolds links the author's long-standing fascination with the American West to the development of his central male characters. Reynolds points to a sharp break between the passive men of Hemingway's early fiction and the self-reliant males who populate his books after 1928. This latter group, epitomized by Robert Jordan of *For Whom the Bell Tolls*, realizes the Western spirit of a mythical time and place.

William Braasch Watson presents circumstantial evidence that the film director Joris Ivens took steps—either under orders or on his own initiative—to develop Hemingway into an effective instrument of Communist propaganda on the war in Spain. Without revealing to Hemingway his objectives, Ivens served in this manner as Hemingway's secret "case officer." This speculative study implies that the political ambivalence expressed in *For Whom the Bell Tolls* might have been caused by Hemingway's resentment at having been manipulated.

The remaining eight articles take a variety of approaches, which might be described loosely (and too simply) as political, ethical, religious, mythic, feminist, generic, textual, and poststructuralist.

In a seemingly old-fashioned source-study, Robert A. Martin demonstrates the journalistic cast of Hemingway's imagination. Martin shows how Hemingway derived some of the novel's primary characters and many of its dramatic incidents from actual persons and events he encountered while on assignment in Spain for the North American Newspaper Alliance. *For Whom the Bell Tolls* thus has "an authentic sense of time, place, and history" that still speaks to us today.

Closely examining the original manuscript of *For Whom the Bell Tolls*, Thomas E. Gould shows that Hemingway's manuscript revisions reflect his struggle against a climate of censorship. Hemingway strove to include as much daring "truth" as possible without violating the rules governing the written portrayal of sexual activity and the use of profane language. This study shows, incidentally, the importance for American literary scholarship of the Hemingway collection established in 1980 at the Kennedy Library.

Charles Molesworth examines the nexus between the political struggles of the thirties and Hemingway's own notions of meaningful personal action, shedding light on both the Spanish Civil War and on the somewhat overworked idea of the "Hemingway code." He argues for a moral and political reading of "grace under pressure," a phrase commonly understood as referring to "an essentially aesthetic model of human agency." For Molesworth, *For Whom the Bell Tolls* embodies the complex blend of "high ideals and low behavior" found in the Spanish Civil War. He argues that the novel's strength is the poise it maintains between blind support for the Republican cause and a defeatist individualism arising from the awareness that the cause has been betrayed by the Soviets. Molesworth's close reading of Robert Jordan's meditations refutes the various critics who fail to perceive this balance: those who see the Republic as nothing but a Comintern front and those who denounce Robert Jordan (and Hemingway) for harboring Fascist sympathies. This essay brings fresh insight to old debates about the Civil War and about Hemingway's politics.

H. R. Stoneback reminds us of Hemingway's complex attitude toward religion. He studies the author's views on the Roman Catholic Church and on the Spanish Left in relation both to Hemingway biography and to the treatment of religion and politics in *For Whom the Bell Tolls*.

Robert E. Gajdusek explores, via Jungian analysis, the mythic and metaphoric significance of the psychodynamics in Pilar's tale. His reading challenges historical/political interpretations of Pilar's famous tale and shows that the tale's form and details are more determined by carefully structured levels of meaning developed throughout the novel than by narrative or historical/political needs.

Gerry Brenner presents a creative/feminist reading in the form of an imaginary interview between a critic and the fictive Maria of the novel. The interviewer invokes the language of feminist criticism to express her dislike of Maria's stereotypical aspects and her disapproval of Robert Jordan's ideological chauvinism. Maria wins over her interviewer, getting her to collaborate in assessing the evidence of Jordan's homoeroticism and feminized sympathies that link him to Walt Whitman and T. E. Lawrence. This unusual piece of fictive criticism links *For Whom the Bell Tolls* with the current debate over Hemingway's androgyny.

Mark C. Van Gunten offers a postmodernist analysis that explores the structures of difference—Fascist/Loyalist, history/fiction, religion/politics, the individual/the collective body—in *For Whom the Bell Tolls* to demonstrate that warfare in the novel becomes a pretext for a discourse preoccupied with the threat of self-destruction. The importance and power of language and signification in the text are examined to show that warfare itself is a language comprising many texts; thus the difficulties of Robert Jordan's bridge-blowing mission are analogous to Hemingway's efforts to write "a true book" that transcends the difficulties of historical/fictional representation and originality.

In the concluding essay, Dean Rehberger argues for a dialectic understanding of genre as an ever-shifting cultural construction. He examines how Hemingway's writing evolved within the same social, political, and cultural matrix that produced the genre of the Western. Analyzing the significance in American life and literature of the "adventure ethos" as promoted by such men as Owen Wister and Theodore Roosevelt, he shows how contradictions within the adventure ethos play out in Hemingway's Spanish Civil War novel. He discusses the rhetorical and narrative strategies of *For Whom the Bell Tolls*, revealing Hemingway's reinscription of American (especially Western) legends such as Custer's Last Stand. The Western motif, initiated in this collection by the essay of Michael Reynolds, comes full circle.

Lionel Trilling's observation, made a long time ago, that "criticism of one kind or another has played an unusually important part in Hemingway's career" (Meyers 280) was disputed by later critics who sought to defend Hemingway's artistic integrity. But current critical thought tends to play down the image of the artist as heroic individual; it sees the literary work not as the product of one person working in isolation but rather as a communal artifact. We show no disrespect to Hemingway when we say that *For Whom the Bell Tolls* is part of a creative process that he initiated and that is still being completed by others—scholars, critics, film-makers, actors, readers, and movie-goers. The bridge between Hemingway and his audience is not permanently created once for all time but is constantly under construction.

NOTES

1. *Catalog of the Ernest Hemingway Collection at the John F. Kennedy Library* (Boston: G. K. Hall, 1982), 1:11.

2. His involvement may have been greater than has been previously recognized. According to a recent article by William Braasch Watson, there is some reason to believe that Hemingway was part of a guerrilla operation that blew up a train behind Fascist lines.

3. See also Richard Allan Davison, "The Publication of Hemingway's *The Spanish Earth*: An Untold Story." Davison tells of the seriocomic misunderstandings that occurred in the summer of 1938 when the author granted Jasper Wood, a high-school-aged Hemingway fan, permission to print 1,000 copies of his narration to *The Spanish Earth*.

4. See the special Spanish Civil War issue of *The Hemingway Review* 7.2 (Spring 1988) for reprints of Hemingway's NANA dispatches and for informative editorial commentary.

5. For reviews of the 1969 publication, see Ray Lewis White.

6. For three careful analyses of these "pre-writings," see Martin Light, "Of Wasteful Deaths: Hemingway's Stories about the Spanish War"; Linda W. Wagner, "The Marinating of *For Whom the Bell Tolls*"; and Allen Josephs, "Hemingway's Spanish Civil War Stories, or the Spanish Civil War as Reality."

7. Starting in the mid-thirties, the general critical consensus found Hemingway's work wanting in social sensitivity. *Death in the Afternoon* (1932), *Winner Take Nothing* (1933), and *Green Hills of Africa* (1935) kept most critics waiting for yet another major work, but Hemingway's return to the novel with the publication of *To Have and Have Not* (1937) disappointed many. The depiction of violent human nature without social consciousness was especially criticized. Only later commentators read the ending as an enforcement of collective action related to Hemingway's sympathies with Spanish leftist politics.

8. See also John J. Teunissen, "*For Whom the Bell Tolls* as Mythic Narrative" and Michael J. B. Allen, "The Unspanish War in *For Whom the Bell Tolls*."

9. Useful examinations of gender questions in Hemingway's work will be found in Robert W. Lewis, Jr., *Hemingway on Love*; Charles J. Nolan, Jr., "Hemingway's Women's Movement"; Robert D. Grozier, S.J., "The Mask of Death, the Face of Life: Hemingway's Feminique"; and Mark Spilka, *Hemingway's Quarrel with Androgyny*.

10. Examples of this tendency will be found in Carlos Baker, ed., *Ernest Hemingway: Critiques of Four Major Novels*; John K. M. McCaffery, ed., *Ernest Hemingway: The Man and His Work*; Sheldon Norman Grebstein, ed., *The Merrill Studies in "For Whom the Bell Tolls."*

11. Especially helpful are book-length reassessments of Hemingway's political orientation and of his relationship to Spain: Stephen Cooper, *The Politics of Ernest Hemingway*, and Angel Capellán, *Hemingway and the Hispanic World*.

WORKS CITED

Allen, Michael J. B. "The Unspanish War in *For Whom the Bell Tolls*." *Contemporary Literature* 13.2 (1972): 204–12.

Baker, Carlos, ed. *Ernest Hemingway: Critiques of Four Major Novels*. NY: Scribner's, 1962.

————. *Ernest Hemingway: A Life Story*. NY: Scribner's, 1969.

————, ed. *Hemingway and His Critics: An International Anthology*. NY: Hill and Wang, 1961.

Barea, Arturo. "Not Spain but Hemingway." *Horizon* 3 (May 1941): 350–61.

Bessie, Alvah. Rev. of *For Whom the Bell Tolls*. *New Masses* 5 November 1940: 25–29.

Brian, Denis. *The True Gen*. NY: Grove, 1988.

Capellán, Angel. *Hemingway and the Hispanic World*. Ann Arbor: UMI Research P, 1985.

Chamberlain, John. "Hemingway Tells How Men Meet Death." Rev. of *For Whom the Bell Tolls. New York Herald Tribune Books* 20 October 1940: 1–2. Rpt. in Stephens, ed. 226–27.

Cooper, Stephen. *The Politics of Ernest Hemingway.* Ann Arbor: UMI Research P, 1987.

Crews, Frederick. "Pressure under Grace." Rev. of *Hemingway*, by Kenneth S. Lynn. *New York Review of Books* 13 August 1987: 30–37.

Davison, Richard Allan. "The Publication of Hemingway's *The Spanish Earth*: An Untold Story." *Hemingway Review* 7.2 (Spring 1988): 122–30.

Epstein, Joseph. *Washington Post Book World* 11 Oct. 1970: 1+. Rpt. in Meyers 557–562.

Fadiman, Clifton. "Ernest Hemingway: An American Byron." *Nation*, 18 January 1933: 63–64. Rpt. in Stephens, ed. 124–28.

Grebstein, Sheldon Norman, ed. *The Merrill Studies in "For Whom the Bell Tolls."* Columbus, OH: Charles E. Merrill, 1971.

Greene, Graham. Rev. of *For Whom the Bell Tolls. Spectator* 7 (March 1941): 258. Rpt. in Meyers 341–44.

Grozier, Robert D., S.J. "The Mask of Death, the Face of Life: Hemingway's Feminique." Wagner, *Six Decades* 239–57.

Hart, Henry, ed. *The Writer in a Changing World.* NY: Equinox Cooperative Press, 1937.

Hemingway, Ernest. *Ernest Hemingway: Selected Letters, 1917–1961.* Carlos Baker. NY: Scribner's, 1981.

———. *For Whom the Bell Tolls.* NY: Scribner's, 1940.

Hemingway, Gregory. *Papa.* Boston: Houghton Mifflin, 1976.

Hoffman, Frederick J. "Hemingway and Fitzgerald." *American Literary Scholarship: An Annual:1965.* Ed. James Woodress. Durham, NC: Duke UP, 1967. 90–103.

Hubbell, Jay B. *Who Are the Major American Writers?* Durham, NC: Duke UP, 1972.

Jones, Howard Mumford. "The Soul of Spain." *Saturday Review of Literature* 26 October 1940: 5, 19. Rpt. in Stephens, ed. 236–38.

Josephs, Allen. "Hemingway's Spanish Civil War Stories, or the Spanish Civil War as Reality." *Hemingway's Neglected Short Fiction: New Perspectives.* Ed. Susan F. Beegel. Ann Arbor: UMI Research P, 1989. 313–27.

Lewis, Robert W., Jr. *Hemingway on Love.* NY: Haskell House, 1973.

Light, Martin. "Of Wasteful Deaths: Hemingway's Stories about the Spanish War." *Western Humanities Review* 23 (1969): 29–42.

Lynn, Kenneth S. *Hemingway.* NY: Simon and Schuster, 1987.

McCaffery, John K. M., ed. *Ernest Hemingway: The Man and His Work.* Cleveland: World, 1950.

Macdonald, Dwight. *Partisan Review* 8 (January 1941): 24–28. Rpt. in Meyers 326–31.

Meyers, Jeffrey. *Hemingway: The Critical Heritage.* London: Routledge & Kegan Paul, 1982.

Nolan, Charles J., Jr. "Hemingway's Women's Movement." Wagner, *Six Decades* 209–21.

Oldsey, Bernard, ed. *Ernest Hemingway: The Papers of a Writer.* NY: Garland Publishing, 1981.

Raeburn, John. *Fame Became of Him: Hemingway as Public Writer.* Bloomington: Indiana UP, 1984.

Sheed, Wilfrid. "A Farewell to Hemingstein." *New York Review of Books* 12 June 1986: 5–12.

Spilka, Mark. *Hemingway's Quarrel with Androgyny.* Lincoln: U of Nebraska P, 1990.

Stephens, Robert O., ed. *Ernest Hemingway: The Critical Reception.* NY: Burt Franklin & Co., 1977.

————. "Language Magic and Reality in *For Whom the Bell Tolls.*" *Criticism* 14 (1972): 151–64.

Teunissen, John J. "*For Whom the Bell Tolls* as Mythic Narrative." Wagner, *Six Decades* 221–37.

Thompson, Ralph. "Books of the Times." Rev. of *For Whom the Bell Tolls. New York Times* 21 October 1940: 15. Rpt. in Stephens, ed. 230.

Trilling, Lionel. "Hemingway and His Critics." *Partisan Review* 6 (Winter 1939): 52–60. Rpt. in Meyers 278–88.

————. "An American in Spain." *Partisan Review* 8 (January 1941): 63–67. Rpt. in Meyers 330–36.

Wagner, Linda W., ed. *Ernest Hemingway: Six Decades of Criticism.* East Lansing: Michigan State UP, 1987.

————. "The Marinating of *For Whom the Bell Tolls.*" *Journal of Modern Literature* 2 (1972): 533–46.

Watson, William Braasch. "Investigating Hemingway." *North Dakota Quarterly* 59.1 (Winter 1991): 36–68. Parts 2 and 3 of this article forthcoming in *North Dakota Quarterly* 59.3 (1991) and 60.1 (1992).

White, Ray Lewis. "*The Fifth Column and Four Stories of the Spanish Civil War*: 38 Additional Reviews." *Fitzgerald/Hemingway Annual 1978.* Ed. Matthew J. Bruccoli and Richard Layman. Detroit: Gale Research, 1979. 273–82.

Wilson, Edmund. "Return of Ernest Hemingway." Rev. of *For Whom the Bell Tolls. New Republic.* 28 October 1940: 591–92. Rpt. in Meyers 320–23.

Young, Philip. *Ernest Hemingway.* NY: Rinehart, 1952.

2   Kurt Vonnegut on Ernest Hemingway

Kurt Vonnegut

Hello. There are about 150 real Hemingway scholars present here, and they all know a hell of a lot more about Hemingway than I do, and so, much of this may be wrong.

Hemingway was an exile, as much as we talk of him as though he were an American writer. But he was as much an exile as James Joyce was and really knew very little about us, ostensibly his people. About the only time he spent here [in Idaho] was in Ketchum, where I don't think you meet a hell of a lot of Americans—you don't come across a cross-section of the population, at any rate. Wilfrid Sheed, writing disrespectfully of him, said that a lot of his style might have to do with the fact that he no longer knew how Americans spoke. Of course, he spent most of his time in New York. Hence, Sheed suggested, he invented "explosive babytalk" in order to fake the speech of Americans with which he wasn't familiar.

This is a conference of very little interest to most Americans because most Americans are not interested in literature, and we are among the least literate nations in the world. The most literate nation is Iceland, which has the same population as Rochester, New York. When only one American in twenty during the course of a year takes a book out of the public library or buys one, that's not a hell of a lot of people. We have forty million people, according to the *New York Times*, who can't read and write; so there are a whole lot of Americans who are not prepared to be interested in whatever we have to say about Ernest Hemingway as they can't read him anyway.

[At this point, Vonnegut asked the audience of some 1,200 people to indicate by a show of hands how many had read something by Hemingway. Although he evidently expected a small response, almost everyone raised a hand.]

Some others and I were going to put on a musical based on F. Scott Fitzgerald's *Scott and Zelda* (the plan fell through, thank God). I was picked out to call up Scottie McClanahan, F. Scott Fitzgerald's only child, and ask her if she would interfere with this production in any way, and she said, "O God, won't people ever get sick of this story? Go ahead." And she hung up. Now Hemingway's story and Fitzgerald's story continued to be well known even to young people just because of the orchestration of these two guys. They were as interesting as Laurel and Hardy; I don't mean they were as foolish, but they are quite memorable, and they are like twin stars that orbit around each other, and [there are] very few couples like that in literary history, I think, of two authors whose reputations both lived because they both existed, and it continues to be an interesting story, and Zelda, of course, is all mixed up in it.

Now, I did not know Ernest Hemingway. He was 23 years older than myself; I doubt that he ever heard of me. He would now be 90. We have some things in common. He was from the Cornbelt; so was I. He was from Chicago, I was from Indianapolis. We both set out to be reporters; that's what we wanted to be. Our fathers were both gun-nuts; we both expressed gratitude to Mark Twain, as our literary ancestor, and of course Mark Twain is the literary ancestor of all American writers because he showed that it was possible to be a writer and yet not write in the European manner; that did not seem possible until Twain came along and wrote, by God, as an American. And it was perfectly acceptable and terribly interesting, and he finally got a degree from Oxford for writing like an American and not like a European. He cried incidentally, Mark Twain did, when he got a degree from Oxford, and so will I certainly.

I'm not aware that Hemingway thought much about my own generation of American novelists, the class of 1922 roughly. Norman Mailer, I know, sent him a copy of *The Naked and the Dead* soon after it was published, asking for his comments, and the package was returned unopened. He scolded the late Irwin Shaw for having, as he put it, dared to go into the ring with Tolstoy by writing a novel which tried to view a war from both sides of the battle lines, *The Young Lions*. I know of only two members of my own generation who were praised by Hemingway: Nelson Algren, the Chicago toughguy, and pal of boxers and gamblers, and Vance Bourjaily, the hunting enthusiast who had been in the Second World War what Hemingway had been in the first one, a civilian ambulance driver attached to a combat unit. Now the late James Jones, by the way, the author of *From Here to Eternity*, and a rifleman in peace time and then in the war, told me at one time that he could not consider Hemingway a fellow soldier since Hemingway had never submitted to Army training or discipline. Scribner's published both men and thought they had the great American war heroes from the First World War and then from the Second World War as writers, and Jones politely declined to pose with Hemingway, because Hemingway was not a soldier.

Now in the Spanish Civil War and then in World War II, Hemingway took no orders and gave no orders, and came and went wherever he pleased, which Jones was not allowed to do. He actually hunted German submarines for a while in the Caribbean, within his own boat and of his own accord. He was a reporter of war, and truly one of the best the world has ever known. So was Tolstoy—who was also a real soldier. During the First World War, the United States got into the fighting so late that an American with true war stories to tell, and a wound besides, was something of a rarity. Such, of course, was Hemingway's situation. He was an even rarer sort of American when he wrote about the Spanish Civil War during the 1930s. Few Americans had seen war. But then the coinage of true war stories by Americans was utterly debased by World War Two, when millions upon millions of us fought overseas and came home, no longer needing a Hemingway to say what war was like. Joseph Heller told me that he would have been in the drycleaning business if it hadn't been for World War II. Heller, of course, is the author of *Catch-22*, a far more influential book nowadays than Hemingway's *A Farewell to Arms*, and *The Sun Also Rises*, and *For Whom the Bell Tolls*.

The key word in my speech is "nowadays." Hemingway was unquestionably an artist of the first rank, with an admirable soul the size of Kilimanjaro. His choice of subject matter, though, bullfighting and nearly forgotten wars and shooting big animals for sport, often makes him a little hard to read *nowadays*. Conservation and humane treatment of animals and contempt for the so-called arts of war rank high on most of our agendas *nowadays*. How many of us can find pleasure *nowadays* in these words from Hemingway's *Green Hills of Africa*, reportage not fiction, describing a lion hunt fifty-three years ago: "I knew that if I could kill one alone, I would feel good about it for a long time. I had in my mind absolutely not to shoot unless I knew I could kill him. I had killed three and knew what it consisted in, but I was getting more excitement from this one than the whole trip." Imagine boasting of killing three lions and reporting delight at the prospect of killing a fourth one, *nowadays*. As for bullfighting, it is a so-called sport so little admired in this country by most people that it is in fact against the law here—I don't have to say "nowadays" about a revulsion against that gory form of entertainment or whatever you want to call it—it was against the law here long before Hemingway was born. But I find that Hemingway's bullfighting stories remain among my favorites. This could be because they are so alien to my own passions and experiences that I can accept them as ethnography, as accounts by an explorer of a society which had nothing to do with me.

Let me hasten to say that no matter how much his choice of subject matter bothers me nowadays, I'm always amazed and delighted by the power he discovered in the simplest language. A sample chosen almost at random from his short story, "Big Two-Hearted River":

Nick sat down against the charred stump and smoked a cigarette. His pack balanced on the top of the stump, harness holding ready. . . . Nick sat smoking, looking out over the country. He did not need to get his map out. He knew where he was from the position of the river. As he smoked, his legs stretched out in front of him, he noticed a grasshopper walk along the ground and up onto his woolen sock. The grasshopper was black. As he had walked along the road, climbing, he had started many grasshoppers from the dust. They were all black.

They are all black incidentally because this whole area has been burned over, and it is protective coloring that the grasshoppers have. The thing with this passage, which I really did just pick at random, is that there is certainly no fear of repeating words. How many of you had teachers who told you that you must never use the same word twice in a paragraph, or even in adjacent paragraphs? Clearly that's poor advice. The longest word in that passage, incidentally, is "grasshopper," a big enough word. The strongest word is "black," a strong enough word. Now I myself when I teach writing say that you can't have a story which people will read and like if nothing much happens. Two of Hemingway's most thrilling stories have almost nothing happening: "A Clean Well-Lighted Place" is one, and again, "The Big Two-Hearted River." Nothing happens, and these are marvelous stories. If Hemingway were a painter, I would say of him that while I often don't like the subjects he celebrates, I sure as hell respect his brush work.

Let me hasten to say, too, that we can all expect in this volatile century to find enthusiasms and passions of our years as young adults to become somehow obsolescent. What happened to Hemingway has happened, or will happen, to all of us, writers or not—it simply can't be helped; no person should be scorned when that happens to her or him. The sharks almost always get the big fish, the big truths we reeled in so proudly when we were young.

Now, I have named one of the sharks which took a bite out of Hemingway's big fish: the conservation movement. Another one, of course, is feminism. I don't think I need to expand on that. The ladies auxiliary for men engaged in blood sports has pretty much disappeared. He is still quite famous although he is not taught much anymore in colleges and universities. For a while there, he was as famous as General Motors and the *New York Times*. Think of that: just one human being, without even an assistant usually, somehow becoming as imposing as great institutions. Such can be the power, sometimes, of written words. We have seen that power demonstrated very recently, and very tragically too. I refer to the case of Salman Rushdie, who with one book made himself the second most famous Moslem in the world and had an entire nation declare war on him. Well, he is now [i.e., after the death of the Ayatollah Khomeini] the most famous Moslem. A couple of decades ago, just one person, again a novelist, embarrassed the Soviet Union as profoundly as would have a great military defeat. I speak, of course, of Aleksandr Solzhenitsyn.

Let me insert something here which I intended to say when I was talking about the vanishing glamor of big game hunting. It is now predicted that the last East African elephant will die of starvation or be killed for its ivory in about eight years. It will miss all the fireworks we will surely shoot off when the year 2000 comes. As long as I've back-tracked like that and come back to the subject of killing wild animals, let me tell you what the great anthropologist Margaret Mead replied, when she was asked when adult male human beings of any society she had observed seemed to be most happy. She had to think a while and then she said, "When they're starting out on a hunt with no women along." Back when war was also kind of a hunt, going on the war-path must have induced the same sort of purely male happiness. I will guess, too, that the permission for males to bond with one another, to love themselves and one another, which was given to such an expedition, was the principal ingredient of that happiness. Now then, please understand that I am not talking about homosexuality, nor suggesting that Ernest Hemingway was a homosexual when I say that male bonding, the freedom of one man to somehow express love for another one in the neighborhood of danger or bloodshed, is very often the greatest reward for a viewpoint-character in a Hemingway story.

The last time I was in Boise I met a very nice woman with a sense of humor. Hunting was very important to her husband, who was then out hunting with some heavy-duty equipment and pals. She laughed, and without any cue from me, she said men had to get off by themselves in the out-of-doors and try to kill something and have a few drinks before they could show how much they loved each other. Again, I'm not talking about homosexuality in the clinical sense, and neither was she. She laughed, I think, because men had to go to such ridiculous trouble and expense before they could express something as simple and natural as love. Which reminds me of something Vance Bourjaily—and, of course, he was one of two members of my generation praised by Hemingway—said about duck hunting: he said it was like standing in a cold shower with all your clothes on and tearing up twenty-dollar bills. Now I say parenthetically that I myself was an infantryman in time of war and experienced the kind of love I just talked about—and, believe me, it is terrific.

Few writers in mid-life have had as clear an idea as Hemingway did of what, God willing, they had yet to do. In 1938, when Hemingway was thirty-nine and had twenty-three more years to live, he said that he hoped to live long enough to write three more novels and twenty-five more stories. He had by then published all of the forty-nine superb short stories which nowadays appear to be his most durable contribution to our culture. He would not give us twenty-five more. I've been told that he actually gave us something on the order of three, four, or five. He had by then published four novels, *The Torrents of Spring*, *The Sun Also Rises*, which made him a world figure, *A Farewell to Arms*, which confirmed his planetary importance, and *To Have and Have Not*, a much weaker book. Incidentally, I've got several kids who went to college, and the Hemingway book that broke a couple of their hearts was *A Farewell to Arms*. That may turn out to be the most durable of all the novels. Well, he would honor the contract he made with himself in 1938 by actually delivering three more novels: *For Whom the Bell Tolls*, *Across the River and into the Trees*, and a very a short book which won him the Nobel Prize, *The Old Man and the Sea*. The last one, of course, is about what sharks do to the old man's big fish. Eight years of literary silence, pretty much, would follow his deserved Nobel Prize in 1954.

And then came what he may have considered yet another work of art, although perfectly horrible, his self-inflicted death by gunshot in this clean and handsome state. His life itself, after all, was the most memorable of all his stories. I myself, a cornbelt free-thinker like Hemingway, with no strong feelings about the sinfulness of suicide, regard his death as a punctuation mark, as a period. The story is told, the end. I'm reminded of the suicide of another American genius, George Eastman, the inventor of the Kodak camera and roll film, the founder of the Eastman-Kodak Company. He shot himself in 1932. Eastman said in his suicide note what I think Hemingway must have felt when he himself felt very close to the end: "My work is done." As a piece of literary trivia, Hemingway died on the same day as the French novelist and fascist maniac and world-class writer, Louis Ferdinand Céline. Céline also was a real soldier during the First World War.

Hemingway's hero and mine—Mark Twain—also died a bitterly un-
happy man. And that seems to be a quite ordinary way for things to go.

[Vonnegut then gave a variation of a seriocomic lecture about fiction
that he has delivered on other occasions; he described various stories, from
fairy tales to *Hamlet*, plotting them on a blackboard graph, with "Begin-
ning-to-Ending" as a horizontal axis and "Good-Fortune-to-Ill-Fortune"
as a vertical axis. A version of this talk can be found in his *Palm Sunday:
An Autobiographical Collage* (New York: Dell, 1981) 312–16.]

What's the connection between this [blackboard talk] and Hemingway?
Let me tell you first, as a therapeutic matter, you should understand that
lives are not supposed to be stories. Only stories are supposed to be stories.
They are artificial constructions. Like a diamond tiara, like a ballet, they
are purely artifacts and have no relation to life except they are entertaining.
And yet there are a certain number of people, and Hemingway was one of
them, who believe that their lives have to be good stories or are not worth
living. Again, only stories are supposed to be stories. And Hemingway
made a serious mistake thinking that his life had to be a good story and
that, when it ceased to be one, it was over.

3   Hemingway's West: Another Country of the Heart

Michael Reynolds

It's a puzzle, Hemingway's West. A strange collection of contradictions. No one can doubt that he loved the open, wild country of Wyoming and Montana, yet he almost never wrote about it. His two short stories—"Wine of Wyoming" and "The Gambler, the Nun, and the Radio"—barely scratch the surface of his Western experiences. His dying writer in "The Snows of Kilimanjaro" thinks of all the stories he did not write, the ones he was saving for a good day. He remembers the ranch and the "silvered gray of the sage brush," the cattle grazing in the hills, "and behind the mountains, the clear sharpness of the peak in the evening light and, riding down along the trail in the moonlight, bright across the valley" (71). He chides himself for the Western story he never wrote.

Paris, Pamplona, Key West, Africa, Italy, all the haunts he knew so well became his fiction. Only two places remained ever pristine in his mind: the village of Oak Park and the Western spaces. His biographers become perplexed, skipping over the terrain uneasily, misplacing parts of it, ignoring others, never at ease with Hemingway's life in the West. Maybe it's the distances. A painter friend of mine, on first coming West, said he understood why there was so much bad painting of the Western landscape: the vista was too big, too much to handle even on a large canvas. None of the traditional modes of landscape painting were of any use. The same could be said about Eastern biographers coming West. Unaccustomed to vast distances and constant reminders of deep geological time, they are uncomfortable with Hemingway's West. But that does not explain why Hemingway never wrote about this country that he clearly loved.

We've seen the pictures so often—Ernest beside the lovely dead pheasants, Ernest measuring the spread of the buck's horns, Ernest in his leather vest. We've seen these pictures and read what the memoirists have told us about Hemingway riding the pack horse into the hunting grounds, shooting the bear in the snow, and afterward drinking his whiskey with only a little water. We have even heard him say in his cups or dotage that he was part Indian. And we know he came finally West to die in Ketchum. But that is not where his West began. The Western landscape and topography he loved were part of his life before he ever saw them, part of his dreams before he smelled sage, heard the creak of saddle leather, or pulled tight his first cinch strap.

Like so many 1890s cowboys from New Jersey or the Bronx, Ernest Hemingway first went West in his imagination, transported by books into that far country where a suburban boy could still vicariously lead the strenuous life Teddy Roosevelt espoused and Owen Wister immortalized. As a child in Oak Park, Hemingway grew up enamored with the fiction and factual books of Stewart Edward White. At age fifteen, he listed White as one of his three favorite writers.[1] It was in the pages of White that young Hemingway first traveled to the High Sierras, and wandered the north country of Hudson Bay.

From White's detailed supply lists for Western camping Hemingway constructed his own youthful dreams for exploring the wilderness. For the imaginary Moose River trip, which he never made, he wrote out elaborate lists for four-man and two-man expeditions: they would need food, of course, and maps, a rifle, ammunition, and axes. Soap was necessary, as well as laxative and quinine pills. They'd take along two cameras and ten rolls of film to record it all. If he could not get companions for the journey, he'd go it alone. There in the notebook he records an individual outfit to carry in on his back: socks, underwear, and shirts of wool, two blankets and a heavy sweater. He'd take matches in a sealed bottle, a watch, a pipe and tobacco, a .32 revolver with a box of shells. Last and perhaps most important on the list: one notebook and two pencils. As explorer, natural historian, and writer, he would need to take notes.[2]

That's what Teddy Roosevelt did on his adventures, and young Ernest was steeped in Roosevelt's philosophy of the strenuous life. Every school-boy knew of Teddy living in the Dakota Badlands, where the intrepid politician-turned-rancher was as handy with a gun as with his pen. Teddy's iron jaw and steely visage were part of the air surrounding young Hemingway in Oak Park. Like his hero, Hemingway wanted to become an explorer and naturalist.[3]

Through instinct, early training, and much of his reading, young Hemingway was raised to be a natural historian, an observer and cataloger of animal behavior. Buried within *Death in the Afternoon* is his manifesto,

"The Natural History of the Dead," a story whose title has yet to be fully appreciated. For in his fiction he was continually tracing out the natural history of that most interesting animal, his fellow man. He may never have written the book on the marlin, but he gave us *The Old Man and the Sea*. And isn't most of his fiction a study in animal behavior: how man the animal behaves under pressure, where and how he feeds, his mating habits, and how he faces death. Like his mentor, Joseph Conrad, Hemingway's basic laboratory experiment first isolated the specimen and then observed him with a detached and sometimes ironic eye. It was, of course, a self-study as well, and its conclusions were not always uplifting, as his parents were wont to remind him. But that was his trade, his métier as he called it. And where better to practice his study of man at the crisis point than in the West?

But he never did, and nothing this biographer can do can change that fact; nor can I ignore it, for its very absence requires explanation. Much of his life, early and late, points toward the West. For Christmas and birthdays, he received books about the West: gold prospectors, Indian raids, and natural history.[4] As a young boy he devoured the monthly magazine, *St. Nicholas*, which brought him fact and fiction out of the American West. In those stories, a boy's life was continually in danger but never lost, and quick wit and courage always won the day. Young Hemingway spent many an afternoon reading stories like "The Black Hero of the Ranges," where the hard lean riders of the Diamond H Ranch try to capture a wild stallion (Mills). Or while reading "A Strange Refuge," he could learn how a beaver lodge might provide safety during a forest fire (Haworth).

Even better than the stories were the factual essays in *St. Nicholas* that took him, through text and photographs, to Glacier National Park in Montana, with Little Chief Mountain and Gunsight Lake. "The region," he was told, "is wild and mountainous, the last resort of the Indian in his natural state, before he surrendered himself wholly to the guardianship of the white man's government. Excepting a few ranches which lie in the river valley, the whole region remains today as it has been from the beginning" (Christy). When he wasn't reading the serialized version of Mark Twain's life in the West, he could travel in the magazine pages to Mesa Verde with its mysterious ruins (Chapman) or be with Lone Wolf on the prairie risking his life in a buffalo stampede (Olaf Baker). As Clarence Rowe asked his readers in his essay "Out in the Big-Game Country": "Is there a healthy, red-blooded American boy who does not feel a thrill of excitement at the thought" of stalking bighorn sheep, elk and black bear, maybe even a grizzly? (Rowe).

In all of the Western stories and essays, there was adventure and danger, risk and recompense. Heady stuff for a young boy. As Owen Wister's Virginian said, "You must do a thing well in this country." A lesson to memorize: in that far country beyond the law where the social contract no longer binds or protects, a man, to be a man, must do a thing well. It was a Western lesson that Hemingway first read in high school and would remember all his life. He might not write about the West, but like so many American boys, he grew up knowing its myths and maxims as part of his inheritance.

Yet when one looks at his early fiction, few of the characteristics associated with Western individualism can be found. Nick Adams, Jake Barnes, and Frederic Henry are essentially passive men to whom unpleasant things happen. They do not initiate action, nor do they behave particularly well under pressure. Nick Adams, in pre-1928 stories, is a vulnerable young man growing up without strong male role models. He is neither sexually confident nor physically sure of himself. Jake Barnes is a denatured war victim incapable of satisfying a woman. Frederic Henry is more forceful in love but no more active in life. Under the pressure of the Caporetto retreat, Frederic botches his orders by losing his ambulances and his men before deserting himself. He is neither a leader of men, nor a solitary hero. Like Nick and Jake, Frederic is a survivor, no better than most of us. Heroes should be made of sterner stuff, the right stuff, such stuff as dreams are made on.

Had Hemingway stopped writing in 1928, the influence of the American West upon his work would never have come to question, for his twenties fiction contains little of Western attitudes or virtues. His early male characters with whom we can identify are not self-reliant; they do not take responsibility for their lives. They are stoic in pain, but with little of the inner fortitude associated with the Western hero. They have little sense of duty and are not competitive. Victims of outside forces, these early central characters have little in common with the violent, confident, self-reliant men who pushed the edge of civilization West and who later became the heroes of pulp fiction, Western novels, and all the Saturday morning movies I ever watched as a kid. In fact there is little in the pre-1930 Hemingway that prepares the reader for the fiction and nonfiction of his middle and later periods.

For years we pretended that there was a continuum—something we called the Hemingway Hero. Let me say it as clearly as possible: the Hemingway Hero is a figment of our collective imaginations. The difference between Jake Barnes and Harry Morgan is not one of degree but of kind. Frederic Henry is no more than a distant third cousin to Robert

Jordan. For Hemingway, 1928–30 was a turning point, an enormous break with the fiction that established his popularity. After 1928 Hemingway's central characters became everything his twenties men were not. In paleontological terms, it is as if one species died out almost overnight, to be replaced by a new and more vital species. Such radical change, whether in biology or in fiction, is not easily explained, but we can begin to assemble the data points that may lead to understanding.

Several events took place, each of which, separately and in conjunction, contributed to this change in Hemingway's fiction. First, he and his second wife Pauline, newly married, returned to the United States, ending his seven years of expatriation. Second, the economy at home and abroad plunged into the Great Depression. Third, his father committed suicide. And finally, Hemingway visited for the first time the American West. Neither he nor his fiction were ever the same afterwards.

In 1928, as he was finishing *A Farewell to Arms*, Hemingway made his first trip West. While Frederic Henry and Catherine Barkley wintered in the cold fastness above Montreux, Hemingway was summering outside of Sheridan, Wyoming, not far from Owen Wister's ranch retreat at Shell. When he was as done as he could get with his novel, Ernest and Pauline visited the older and more successful writer, beginning a short but intense friendship. Wister was Hemingway's major link to the previous generation of American writers and doers. Classmate of Teddy Roosevelt and friend of Henry James, Wister recognized Hemingway's talent and tried to influence its direction with avuncular advice and moral support.[5]

In December 1928, following Hemingway's Wyoming summer, his father, Clarence Hemingway, put a bullet into his brain. Ernest took on his father's role of family patriarch and provider. After his second summer on the L-Bar-T Ranch outside of Cooke City, Montana, in 1930, Hemingway's reading began to change and his fiction with it. Between 1930 and 1936, we know he bought several western histories, memoirs, and biographies, including works such as *Apache Agent*, *A Journal of the Santa Fe Expedition*, *Emigrant's Guide to Oregon and California*, and *James Pike: Scout and Ranger*. He bought a biography of Wyatt Earp and a book called *Triggernometry*, a gathering of the legendary Western gunfighters. He also bought two books about George Armstrong Custer, American folk hero and centerpiece of the famous barroom lithograph. By the time he died, Hemingway's Cuban library contained at least fifty books of nonfiction about the American West, including five about Custer. He had also accumulated a fair library of Western fiction by Luke Short, Peter Dawson, and Max Brand, as well as the collected works of Owen Wister.[6]

This mid-life reading course reinforced Western fantasies and myths laid down years before in Oak Park. The Western experience demanded fortitude and endurance, determination and self-reliance—the frontier virtues. Middle-class, urban softness swathed in vague Christian rhetoric never pushed the frontier West. Hemingway first learned that lesson in Owen Wister's *The Virginian*, where the self-reliant, shrewd Southerner goes West after the Civil War to meet the New England blue-blood schoolteacher. In the West, he teaches her to ride and shoot; she teaches him to read Shakespeare and Dostoyevski. She saves his life; he revitalizes her Eastern bloodline grown effete since the Revolutionary War. There in the violent West, Southern valor weds Eastern intellect, a prescription for the country as a whole, which Wister and Roosevelt, to whom the novel was dedicated, both felt needed saving.

The effect of Hemingway's Western experience combined with his reading to produce changes in his fiction and nonfiction. His 1933 African safari was not merely an escape into another country; it was more like a trip backward in time. British East Africa, with its barely civilized natives, its plenitude of wild game, and its frontier conditions, was, for Hemingway, like going back to the early Western experience. The black natives were not Indians, but they were a close approximation. Hunting dangerous game in difficult terrain gave him that blood thrill no longer available to urban Americans. Teddy Roosevelt in 1909 perceived that same terrain as potentially belonging to the white man. (*African Game Trails*). Similar thoughts must have motivated mountain men, buffalo hunters, Indian fighters, and cattlemen as they moved our frontier West. In 1933, Africa still had that magic for Hemingway. The Serengeti, with its seemingly unlimited wild game, was a natural resource that exceeded his imagination. After the experience of Africa, Wyoming, and Montana, his fictive characters changed. No longer the passive man of the 1920s, the new Hemingway protagonist created his own violence, sought it out, faced it with his gun in his hand.

Harry Morgan, the film-noir hero of *To Have and Have Not*, is not a Westerner, but only by chance of birth. In Key West, Harry rides the open sea like his pirate namesake rather than the open plain, but he is just as violent as the Western gunslingers out of Hemingway's reading. Like them, Harry is adept with weapons, kills easily and without passion, has no respect for the law, and looks to no one for favors. He is Hemingway's self-reliant man, set down in the Great Depression to learn that "a man alone ain't got no bloody fucking chance" (225). That's what he says, gut-shot and dying. Some have taken this statement to mean that the dying Morgan has seen the light of cooperation and brotherhood. But having watched him wring the Chinaman's neck and coolly contemplate killing his own drunken mate to shut his mouth, I rather doubt this analysis. I think Harry meant that one man alone was not enough to take on four armed Cubans—that what he needed was at least one more gunfighter on his side. Wyatt Earp did not take on the Clantons singlehanded at the O.K. Corral.

Harry Morgan, with few redeeming virtues, has never been taken seriously by Hemingway watchers, who haven't spilled enough ink over him to float a toothpick. He is not a man one could either admire or wish to emulate. Robert Jordan, of *For Whom the Bell Tolls*, is a different matter. Born in Red Cloud, Montana, and educated in Billings, Jordan brings to the Spanish Civil War all the virtues his grandfather perfected in the War between the States and in the Indian wars that followed. Jordan may be living dangerously in another country, but he is a man out of our West. He knows horses, rides well, reads terrain clearly, and goes armed at all times. Into that mountain cave of Spanish partisans, he walks tall, confident, and self-reliant. There, where there is no law, Robert Jordan establishes his own rules. He displaces Pablo, the old leader gone soft in his trade, and claims the beautiful Maria for his own. He and she cavort in the timeless fifth dimension of sexual ecstasy, but not to the point that he loses sight of his purpose. Like the hired gun that he is, Jordan lets nothing interfere with his mission: blowing the bridge. At the end, belly down on the pine needle floor, badly wounded, he keeps the rear guard, laying down his life to help Maria and the others escape. At that sticking place, he calls on the memory of his grandfather's feats to sustain him in his death. Jordan behaves as well as we have come to expect of Western heroes. Compared with Frederic Henry, who sacrifices nothing and gains nothing, Jordan lives in a rare and heady atmosphere. He dies alone, but feels a part of something larger.

And like Harry Morgan, Colonel Cantwell, and Thomas Hudson, his brothers in arms, Jordan takes pride in his trade, is a good tactician, and does little by the book. None of these men live in the West, but all four are Westerners at their core, embodying virtues we associate with the American frontier. All of these men are warriors, gunmen, enforcers, men with the ability to kill dispassionately. None smells of city life. They are all a bit uncivilized, informal, and basic. They could not have been created by James Joyce or Henry James. They could not have come from the books of city boys like Cheever or Updike. None has the least connection with our East Coast. So if the New York critics did not much care for them as a group, we shouldn't be surprised. Once you've said that, then our initial question becomes less puzzling: Hemingway may never have used a

Western setting for a novel, but after 1928, he was always writing about the West, searching for wholeness of purpose, for the illusive quality you can still sometimes find in the eyes of men west of the Brazos and east of Los Angeles.

Thomas Hudson, on his long and mortal submarine patrol, receives this final message from headquarters: "CONTINUE SEARCHING CARE-FULLY WESTWARD" (Hemingway, *Islands* 368). As Carlos Baker tells us, "It is not only a military but a moral directive. It is precisely what Hudson and all others like him must do until the end" (408). More than that, searching westward is the history of our country, a history that Hemingway fully understood, embodying it in his fiction and in his life.

NOTES

1. High-school notebook dated 1915, on loan from a private collection to the Alderman Library, University of Virginia, in 1977 for an exhibit, "In Their Time: 1920–1940."
2. Hemingway high-school notebooks, Hemingway Collection, John F. Kennedy Library, Boston.
3. For the influence of Roosevelt on Hemingway, see Michael Reynolds, *The Young Hemingway* 23–25, 27–30, 230–33.
4. For more details, see Michael Reynolds, *Hemingway's Reading, 1910–1940* and "A Supplement to Hemingway's Reading."
5. For the most complete version of Hemingway's relationship with Wister, see Alan Price, " 'I'm Not an Old Fogey.' "
6. For complete information see Michael Reynolds, *Hemingway's Reading, 1910–1940*, and James Brasch and Joseph Sigman, *Hemingway's Library*.

WORKS CITED

Baker, Carlos. *Hemingway: The Writer as Artist*. 4th ed. Princeton: Princeton UP, 1972.
Baker, Olaf. "Where the Buffaloes Begin." *St. Nicholas* 42 (February 1915): 291–96.
Brasch, James, and Joseph Sigman. *Hemingway's Library*. NY: Garland Publishing, 1981.
Chapman, Arthur. "Where the Cliff Dweller Children Lived." *St. Nicholas* 41 (September 1914): 1036–39.
Christy, Bayard H. "The Roof Tree of the Continent." *St. Nicholas* 43 (June 1916): 744.
Haworth, Paul L. "A Strange Refuge." *St. Nicholas* 43 (June 1916): 689–95.
Hemingway, Ernest. *Islands in the Stream*. NY: Scribner's, 1970.

————. "The Snows of Kilimanjaro." *The Short Stories of Ernest Hemingway.* NY: Scribner's, 1938.

————. *To Have and Have Not.* 1937. NY: Macmillan, 1987.

Mills, Enoch J. "The Black Hero of the Ranges." *St. Nicholas* 42 (November 1914): 16–24.

Price, Alan. " 'I'm Not an Old Fogey and You're Not a Young Ass': Owen Wister and Ernest Hemingway." *Hemingway Review* 9.1 (Fall 1989): 82–90.

Reynolds, Michael. *Hemingway's Reading, 1910–1940.* Princeton: Princeton UP, 1981.

————. "A Supplement to Hemingway's Reading." *Studies in American Fiction* 14 (1986): 99–108.

————. *The Young Hemingway.* NY: Basil Blackwell, 1986.

Roosevelt, Theodore. *African Game Trails.* NY: Scribner's, 1910.

Rowe, Clarence H. "Out in the Big-Game Country." *St. Nicholas* 37 (September 1910): 970.

4 Joris Ivens and the Communists: Bringing Hemingway into the Spanish Civil War

William Braasch Watson

When Ernest Hemingway marched onto the stage of Carnegie Hall at 10:30 on the steamy night of 4 June 1937, the audience of writers and activists in the jam-packed hall must have sensed they were about to witness an historic moment in American letters. Before the thunderous ovation that followed his introduction by Archibald MacLeish died down, a nervous and sweating Hemingway lunged from his chair and quickly began to read, as if to get it over with, a speech he had modestly titled "A Writer in War Time."

A writer's problem does not change. He himself changes, but his problem remains the same. It is always how to write truly and, having found what is true, to project it in such a way that it becomes a part of the experience of the person who reads it.[1]

How true this was and how difficult it would be to carry out nobody in the audience, not even the speaker himself, could have fully appreciated. It was obvious that Hemingway had changed, and it would become even more obvious in the weeks and months that followed as he prepared the narration for Joris Ivens's film, gave another speech in Hollywood a month later, and raised tens of thousands of dollars for the purchase of ambulances for the Spanish Loyalists.

The Carnegie Hall speech marked the beginning of a sustained commitment to the war against fascism that Hemingway and thousands of others saw unfolding on the battlefields of Spain, but the transformation of Ernest Hemingway into an active and at times outspoken partisan and propagandist did not take place on the stage of Carnegie Hall in New York. It had taken place over the weeks and months of his first visit to the war in the spring of 1937, and it was the product not only of his own personal reaction to the events he witnessed there, but also of the careful political nurturing and guidance provided by various members of the Communist movement.

Since the details of this transformation have been generally overlooked and the factors contributing to it largely unknown—although not its most obvious manifestations, such as the Carnegie Hall speech—it is worthwhile taking a closer look at how Hemingway got involved in the Spanish Civil War. His entrance into the war shaped his views of the war, shaped his political orientation during the war, shaped the roles he would undertake both in Spain and in the United States, and in the end shaped the manner in which he tried to extricate himself from the dilemmas his political involvement had created for him.

Contrary to what many thought at the time and have since, Hemingway did not go to the war in Spain a political innocent or a strictly neutral observer. Before he left for Spain he made a commitment of sorts by agreeing to sponsor an ambulance unit for the Loyalist side, and we have learned subsequently that he secretly contributed $3,000 of his own money (a third of which he borrowed from his publisher, Charles Scribner, Jr.) for the purchase of two ambulances.[2]

Once he got to Europe, moreover, his views on the war in Spain took on another dimension. In Europe, and especially in France, the Spanish war was more passionately felt and its political ramifications more sharply drawn than had seemed the case in the United States. During the week he was in Paris preparing to go into Spain, Hemingway made a number of contacts, among them various members of the Communist movement. By the late fall of 1936, because of their superior commitment and resources and their widespread international organizations, the Communists had virtually taken over the leadership of the international campaign to defend the Spanish Republic. Under the direction of the Communist International, or the Comintern as it was then known, and including a variety of associated front organizations, the Communists had not only recruited thousands of volunteers to fight in Spain and had supplied tens of thousands of dollars of relief funds and weapons to the beleaguered Republic, they had also become the principal organ of pro-Loyalist propaganda throughout the world. It was only natural, therefore, that they would take great interest in the celebrated American writer, whose pro-Loyalist views they must have been aware of.[3] They would have wanted to recruit him as a propagandist, not just for the Loyalist cause in general, but for the particular version of that cause being promoted by the Communist International throughout the world.

After a careful examination of Hemingway's activities and of those associated with him as he was entering into the Spanish Civil War in the spring of 1937, I am convinced that the Communists began recruiting Hemingway in Paris and continued doing so in Spain in order that he would become a contributor, witting or unwitting, to the propaganda objectives of the Comintern. The person primarily responsible for carrying out this task, the person who was in effect to become Hemingway's "case officer" during his entry into the Spanish Civil War, was none other than Joris Ivens.

"Case officer," for those unfamiliar with the term, is what the present-day espionage community calls that person designated by an organization to develop an agent or an asset. The case officer provides guidance and support in order that the recruited person will produce the desired ends or carry out a specific task for the organization. So far as I know, "case officer" was not a term used by the espionage and propaganda communities in the 1930s, but the practice of developing agents or assets through a contact or source within the organization whose full identity and real functions were never revealed was widespread in the Comintern and in the Communist movement at large in the Popular Front period of the 1930s. There is no evidence that I know of—nor is there likely to be any, given the clandestine nature of the inner workings of Communist organizations in this period—that Joris Ivens was detailed by the Comintern or by any other Communist controlled organization, such as Willi Münzenberg's AGITPROP Department, to be Hemingway's "case officer." There is, however, ample evidence that Ivens took every step he could to develop Hemingway into an effective instrument of Communist propaganda on the war in Spain and that he did so without revealing to Hemingway his real motives or objectives. In this sense, Ivens served, whether independently or not, as Hemingway's secret case officer.[4]

Much of the story of how Ernest Hemingway became involved in the Spanish Civil War centers less on the writing of his dispatches, as might be expected, than on the making of *The Spanish Earth*. It was his involvement with the film and his close and creative association with Ivens during its filming in Spain that more than anything else shaped his understanding of the war and of the role he would play in it for many months thereafter. The story begins the day before Hemingway was to leave for Spain.

On 26 February 1937, Joris Ivens, who was then in Paris, cabled Archibald MacLeish in New York—MacLeish was then president of Contemporary Historians, the film's production company—that he was planning to return to Spain the next week (Ivens to MacLeish, 26 February 1937). He had already shot one film in and around Madrid in January and February, a short *reportage* film on the defense of Madrid, and now, after a week in Paris, he wanted to get back and start work on a planned second film, what he called the "documentary" or longer film that would show why the Spanish people, the villagers of Spain, were fighting to defend their land and their country. This was to be his premier film, the one that would unite his artistic talents with his political convictions into a coherent statement on the Spanish Civil War.

Several days later Ivens, who was still in Paris, suddenly changed his mind about returning to Spain. He cabled his friend Wenceslau Roces in the Ministry of Public Instruction and Fine Arts in Valencia—the propaganda bureau of the Spanish Republican government—that he had found an excellent village near Madrid in which to begin shooting his second film. He wanted Roces to get a car for two weeks beginning on March 3rd, not for *himself*, however, but only for his cameraman, John Fernhout (Ivens to Roces).

This abrupt change in Ivens's plans is curious, because it means that he was now delegating a major responsibility to his young cameraman. Although Ivens was someone who sometimes did assign important responsibilities to other people while making his films, the village shots he had planned to take would be of critical importance to the artistic success of the documentary film, and it was this film, not the *reportage* film he had just shot, to which Ivens attached the most importance.[5] No doubt he had confidence in the ability of his cameraman, but to leave the first shooting in the village of Fuentidueña entirely in the hands of Fernhout was not something Ivens would have done without some extraordinary reason. Why then the sudden change in plans? What happened between February 26th and March 1st or 2nd to make Ivens change his mind about returning to Spain?

Sometime in the few days between his cabling MacLeish and his telegram to Roces, Ivens found out, probably from MacLeish, that Hemingway had sailed from New York on 27 February and was on his way to France and Spain to report on the Spanish Civil War. Ivens, it seems apparent, decided to stay on in Paris in order to receive Hemingway, a decision that was to have major consequences, both for Ivens and, even more, for Hemingway.

Ivens did not know Hemingway, and it is doubtful that he had even read him (*mémoire* 146). But he certainly knew who Ernest Hemingway was, and he knew as well as anyone what an asset the presence of Hemingway could mean for the success of his film projects.

Having Hemingway on your side, publicly and visibly committed to the projects and causes you were trying to promote, was definitely an asset, no question about it, for Hemingway was not just another famous writer on his way to the Spanish Civil War. He was among the half dozen most celebrated figures in America, certainly its most celebrated writer. His actions and words got the kind of press coverage no publicist or campaign manager could hope to arrange or buy. He enjoyed, in short, the kind of celebrity that in the late 1930s only the most famous movie stars, aviators, and prize fighters could command (Raeburn 5–7).

It would seem natural, therefore, that Ivens would want to stay behind in Paris in order to enlist Hemingway's participation in his film projects. In this respect Ivens was no different from Jack Wheeler of the North American Newspaper Alliance, who signed up Hemingway to report on the Spanish Civil War for his news agency, or from Arnold Gingrich and David Smart of *Esquire* magazine, who corralled Hemingway to write a bi-weekly article for their new political magazine *Ken*, or from the directors of the American Friends of Spanish Democracy, who, before Hemingway went to Spain, got him to sponsor an ambulance unit for its Medical Bureau.

But Ivens differed in one respect from most of the others who had recruited Hemingway for their projects during the Spanish Civil War: his cause was not his alone. His cause was part of a larger international undertaking then being supported and directed by the Communist International out of its office in Paris. Since the fall of 1936, one of the Comintern's principal objectives had been to mobilize international support for the Spanish Republican government in its struggle against Spanish and international fascism. The ultimate objective of the Comintern, which was guided by the foreign policy objectives of the Soviet Union, was to organize a united popular front movement under Communist leadership in the western democracies strong enough to resist the rising aggressiveness of fascism.

Ivens was not then a member of the Communist Party, but he was so closely allied with the international Communist movement in his views and in his personal friendships that he might as well have been one. Indeed, as he explained to me, there was an advantage in his not being a member of the party, for it allowed him to make contacts with other groups and individuals who might otherwise, had he been a Communist, have kept their distance (Personal interview with WBW, 24 June 1982).

In much this same spirit of an independent artist who happened to have strong political views but would never seek to impose them on someone else, especially another artist, Ivens in his two memoirs, *The Camera and I* and his more recent *Ou la mémoire d'un regard*, consistently minimizes any role he might have had in the development of Hemingway's political views or of his function as a propagandist. For example, although Hemingway's impending arrival was an important enough event for Ivens to alter his filming plans in Spain, there is no mention of his sudden decision to stay on in Paris. Just the opposite. His meeting with Hemingway in Paris the first week in March is presented as a casual encounter, a kind of fortuitous piece of good luck (*Camera* 111; *mémoire* 146).[6] They ran into each other at the café *Deux Magots*, Ivens reports, had some drinks and a few meals together, and although they naturally talked about the war, Ivens did not try to recruit Hemingway for his second film project and did not try, he says, to influence Hemingway's views on the war in Spain.

Ivens says that in Paris Hemingway offered to help the film projects in any way he could and that in Spain he just showed up one day and became a member of the film crew (*Camera* 111, 113; *mémoire* 146, 148). This off-hand picture of Hemingway's casual incorporation into the film projects does not correspond with the evidence. Hemingway did not just happen to come on the scene and offer to be of help. He had already been recruited for the film projects of Contemporary Historians by his friends John Dos Passos and Archibald MacLeish before he left for Spain.

Sometime in mid-January, when in New York, Hemingway agreed to serve on the Board of Directors of Contemporary Historians, the film project's newly formed production company.[7] He also stepped in at the last minute to write the subtitles for the second part of "Spain in Flames," a newsreel-type film hastily put together in December and January by Helen van Dongen, the wife of Ivens, and Dos Passos (Pereda to Hemingway).[8] This newsreel montage, composed of available film footage from the Spanish government and a Soviet film agency in New York, was the first of three projected film projects of Contemporary Historians. It was intended as a kind of stop-gap rebuttal to the commercial newsreels on the war then playing in theaters across the country. It would make the case for Republican Spain until Contemporary Historians could present its own films shot by Ivens in Spain.

Nor was this to be the end of Hemingway's planned involvement in the film projects, for he had also agreed with MacLeish to do the dialogue on the longer documentary that Ivens was now preparing to shoot in the village of Fuentidueña (MacLeish to Hemingway, 8 February 1937). Ivens may not have been wholly aware of all of these developments when he met Hemingway in Paris, as he had been in Spain for most of this time shooting the short film on the defense of Madrid, but it would have taken only a few minutes of conversation at the *Deux Magots* to bring Ivens up to date.[9] Hemingway, in short, was involved in Ivens's film projects even before they met for the first time in Paris.

And what about Hemingway's views on the war in Spain those early March days in Paris? As Ivens reports it, Hemingway's views were quite simple and naïve. "War is always evil," he quotes Hemingway as saying. "There's no need to do it more than once. Men have already shed enough blood like that" (*mémoire* 146). As Ivens recorded in his earlier memoirs, "he saw no particularly deep implications in this war and was pretty sceptical when I described it as the first test of fascism in Europe, fascism on its first battlefield" (*Camera* 111). Ivens could see that Hemingway's ideas on the subject were quite fixed and that neither words nor theories could convince him. He had to touch and see things for himself. Ivens was confident that Hemingway would find out for himself when he got to Spain what the war was all about (*mémoire* 146).

Although it is not hard to detect the stereotype of a politically naïve and bull-headed Hemingway in all of this, there is nonetheless some foundation for this impression, and it comes from Hemingway himself. In his well-publicized departure from New York on 27 February, Hemingway made it clear that he was going to cover the war in Spain so that Americans would know what "this modern, new style war looks like, so that they can see it and hate it as much as any man who has ever seen it hates it."

Everybody is trying to push us into the next war, the new style war, the kind of war they fought in Ethiopia and are fighting in Spain, the total war, where there is no such thing as a non-combatant, where everybody who lives across a line on the map is a target. The horror of that kind of war hasn't been brought home enough.

He was, he said, going to be "an anti-war correspondent for the home folks," because "if enough people get fear-knots tied into their guts, then we just are not going to get into the next war" (Wolfert).

This fulsome dockside report by NANA correspondent Ira Wolfert unquestionably recorded Hemingway's anti-war sentiments accurately, for it was a position he had already staked out three weeks earlier in one of his letters to the Pfeiffer family. "This is the dress rehearsal for the inevitable European war," he wrote, explaining why he was leaving his wife and children to go to Spain, "and I would like to try to write anti-war correspondence that would help to keep us out of it when it comes" (Hemingway to the Pfeiffer family).

Although Hemingway knew that his anxious in-laws and most Americans would find these anti-war sentiments more acceptable than some other, more partisan views he might have expressed, he held them sincerely. The Spanish Civil War *was* a cruel and violent war, and the horror of another world war was the common overriding emotion of a generation that had witnessed the first one.[10] There was also a practical reason for taking such a stance. As a correspondent expected to report objectively on the war in Spain, it would have been unwise to openly express a partisan attitude from the outset, regardless of what his political views might have been.[11]

These anti-war sentiments did not represent, however, the full range of Hemingway's views on the war in Spain. A better and fuller sense of what he really thought about the war comes from the narrative comments he secretly wrote for the second part of *Spain in Flames* in mid-January. Although this part of the film has been lost, Hemingway's manuscript notes for the film's subtitles survive, and in them one can see that although he drives home the horrors of war, this is not just an anti-war film. He says the film is a true picture of modern war in which there are no neutrals and no escape. he likens war to a lottery of death in which there is a prize for everyone, and those who are waging the war keep drawing until everyone gets their prize.

The subtitles continue in much the same vein until the last two; they are hardly nonpolitical. The thirteenth subtitle must have accompanied shots of dead children. Hemingway declares them to be the viewers' children, a dramatic way of warning the audience what will happen if the Fascist bombers are not stopped. In the next subtitle, accompanying scenes of Madrid burning, Hemingway explicitly notes that Madrid is being burned by the Fascists of both Germany and Italy ("Amkino Presents"). Hemingway did not need Joris Ivens to convince him that the war in Spain was "the first test of fascism in Europe" (Ivens, *Camera* 111).

But what, if anything, did Ivens contribute to the political education of Ernest Hemingway? In his first memoirs Ivens reconstructed his relationship with Hemingway in such a way as to suggest that he had nothing to do with the development of Hemingway's views. "Two weeks later," Ivens writes, referring to two weeks after meeting Hemingway in Paris, "I met Hemingway in his Madrid hotel *The Florida*. He had found out a lot in that time, and, being Hemingway, you could be sure he had found it out *personally*" (*Camera* 111). "Personally" is italicized. This account, which goes on to show how quickly Hemingway learned about fascism and its danger for the world, conforms to Ivens's view of the politically innocent Hemingway, but not to much else, and least of all to the documents in Ivens's own archives.

Hemingway, we know, stayed in Paris until 13 March, when he took the train to Toulouse and the French border before flying into Spain on 16 March ("Dispatches" 13–18; *New York Herald Tribune* 11 March 1937). Ivens did not leave Paris until the 17th, arriving in Valencia later that day, where he again met up with Hemingway, although he makes no mention of this fact in his memoirs. Since this was Hemingway's first visit to wartime Spain and Ivens was already an old hand who knew his way around the government ministries and party headquarters now relocated in Valencia because of the danger in Madrid, Ivens could have been, and probably was, a willing and useful guide. Three days later, on 20 March, Ivens and Hemingway travelled together in a chauffeur-driven car to Madrid (Ivens cable to MacLeish, [27 March 1937]; shooting log).

Why in his memoirs Ivens is so diffident about his meeting with Hemingway in Paris and so inventive about his reunion with him in Spain is a little puzzling. It was no secret that Hemingway and Ivens were frequently together in Spain and that Hemingway became, if not exactly a member of the film crew, at least deeply involved in the project. What was there to hide, or to forget? We do not know for sure, and probably never will, but it would seem that even decades after the events in Spain Ivens still felt he could not reveal what some others had known all along.

In 1951, when Carlos Baker was poking around in the biographical fragments of Hemingway's life, he received a letter from Donald Ogden Stewart. Stewart wrote that he presumed Baker had the details of Hemingway's education in anti-Francoism, especially Hemingway's friendship with Joris Ivens, details which would be essential for any biography. Stewart, a former member of the Communist Party, president of the League of American Writers, and later a friend of Ivens in Hollywood in the 1940s, knew, I am sure, just how important Ivens had been in the development of Hemingway as a propagandist. Hemingway, however, needed no education in anti-Francoism.

Hemingway's commitment to the Loyalist, anti-Francoist cause was immediately recognized by the political and governmental people who saw him in New York and Paris before he went to Spain. They regarded him as a comrade in arms and a person in whom they had complete confidence, as the letters of introduction they wrote for him indicate. Ogier Preteceille, the right-hand man of the Spanish ambassador in Paris and a friend of Ivens, wrote three such letters to various functionaries of the Spanish government in Barcelona and Valencia on 13 March, the day Hemingway left Paris. They all presented him as a great friend of the Loyalist cause and pointed out that he was about to undertake a propaganda mission that would be of great help to the cause (Preteceille).

Another letter Hemingway carried with him to Spain was dashed off by the French writer and former commander of the España Squadron in Spain, André Malraux, whom Hemingway had met in New York just before he sailed (Madsen 194–95). Addressed to the comrades of the Alliance of Antifascist Intellectuals in Valencia, it explained that of all their American friends it was Hemingway who carried the greatest weight in the United States and could do the greatest good for Spain, even more than the considerable amount he had already done (Malraux).[12] Malraux, who was just starting a fund-raising tour of the States for the Loyalists at the request of Louis Fischer, also knew what he was talking about. In short, there was no sudden transformation in Hemingway's views on the war in Spain.

But if he did not need an education in anti-fascism by the time he got to Paris, he was certainly open to suggestions on how to use his talents and his celebrity status for the benefit of the Republican cause. It was not Hemingway's views on the war or anti-fascism that changed, but rather his understanding of the role he would now play in that war. It happened rather quickly too, in just a couple of weeks, and it happened before he even got to Spain and could see for himself what was going on there. The evidence for this transformation comes from his own words.

When Hemingway left for Spain at the end of February, his clearly stated intention, as we have seen, was to be an anti-war correspondent, a Cassandra warning the American people of the horrors of war and of the folly of getting involved. Now in the middle of March, just as he was about to fly into Spain, he cabled NANA a dispatch from the Franco-Spanish border that sharply attacked those very policies designed to keep Europeans and Americans out of the war in Spain ("Dispatches" 14–16). Yes, he said, "the French border is closed up and airtight," but while the French are preventing a Swiss woman from delivering "supplies and canned milk for undernourished refugee children from Madrid," the Germans and Italians are pouring troops and war material into Spain for the Franco army. The details Hemingway provided in this dispatch on the character and scale of German and Italian intervention—details he may have picked up along the border, as he claimed, but could just as easily have been given him in Paris—serve as an ironic indictment of the ineffective and dangerous hypocrisy of nonintervention.

This was a very useful service he was rendering, for in mid-March, before the Loyalist victory over the Italians at Brihuega had been known, the only real hope the Spanish Republic seemed to have of surviving and overcoming such massive intervention was to win the support of the western democracies, and in order to do that, the Loyalists had first to discredit the policy of nonintervention.[13]

Hemingway's vigorous attack on that policy also serves to mark the conversion of the anti-war correspondent into an articulate exponent of intervention to save the Republic, just the opposite of his stance in New York. It may be too much to say that Hemingway had received his marching orders in Paris and was now faithfully carrying them out, but it is not too much to suggest that with the help of Ivens and others he did acquire there a clearer understanding of how he could be most helpful.

That understanding developed further during Hemingway's first weeks in Spain. Beginning on March 20th, the day Hemingway arrived in Madrid with Ivens, and continuing for the next three weeks, the friendship between Ivens and Hemingway ripened during the filming of *The Spanish Earth*. That friendship in turn laid the foundation for Hemingway's increasing involvement in the Spanish Civil War, an involvement that enmeshed him more and more in the unanticipated and, I believe for him, the unsettling complications of being a loyal propagandist.

Ivens writes in his memoirs that he did not remember "making any particular arrangement with Hemingway—nothing of the I-do-this-you-do-that—but one day he was part of our crew, helping in every way he could." The impression of this casual arrangement is, I am sure, as misleading as his account of the casual encounter with Hemingway at the *Deux Magots* in Paris or of his meeting Hemingway at his hotel in Madrid. Ivens knew too well the importance of having Hemingway attached to his film projects not to have urged him in Paris to become involved in the actual filming in Spain. This advantage to his own projects aside, Ivens also knew that he had an even more important responsibility to make sure that after his arrival Hemingway was properly introduced to the right people, correctly oriented around the battlefields of the Madrid sector, and guided through the labyrinthine politics of the Loyalist side. Filming in and around Madrid, rather than in the village where Ivens had originally intended to go at this time, would provide the proper environment for Hemingway's orientation, for it was in and around Madrid that the Communist political and military leadership had its greatest strength.

Ivens kept a film log, detailing where he went and what subjects he shot every day, even days when he could not go anywhere because "wagon kaput" (car broke down) ("Reprise"). From the comparison of this log with what we know of Hemingway's comings and goings we can see that in the first weeks of their time together in Madrid, wherever Ivens and Fernhout went, Hemingway (and often Martha Gellhorn) usually went as well. The comparison of their activities confirms in general what Ivens reported in his earlier memoirs:

Hemingway went everywhere with us. He felt that if he was participating in the making of a documentary film, he had to stay with the crew no matter where they went or how dull it might be at times. (*Camera* 113)

The day after their arrival in Madrid, for instance, they went in the rain to the Guadalajara/Brihuega battlefield for an inspection tour led by Hans Kahle, one of the Communist leaders of the International Brigades. The next two days, March 22nd and 23rd, Ivens and Fernhout were in Valdesas filming the French and Garibaldi Battalions of the International Brigades. On the first of these two days Hemingway may have stayed in his room at the Hotel Florida, working on his fourth dispatch, filed later that night, and waiting for the arrival of Martha Gellhorn and Sidney Franklin. The next day, however, he apparently did go with Ivens and Fernhout to Valdesas, because Fernhout took a photograph of Hemingway talking with the commander of the Garibaldi Battalion. On the 24th Ivens and Fernhout returned to the Guadalajara front, with or without Hemingway we do not know. On the 25th the car broke down and nobody went anywhere.

The next day, the 26th, witnessed a full-scale expedition of sorts to the Guadalajara front: Ivens, Fernhout, Hemingway, Gellhorn, perhaps Franklin and others. Ivens notes in his film log that they took shots of the llth International Brigade as they were shown around the battlefield by the commander of the Thaelmann Battalion, Ludwig Renn. Again Fernhout took along his Leica camera to record the day's highlights. He took some gruesome shots of dead Italian soldiers, including one of Hemingway looking down at two of them, and there are also shots of Hemingway and Renn together (Fernhout).[14]

Over the next days and into the next couple of weeks Ivens remained in Madrid at Hemingway's side, delaying even further his shooting in the village of Fuentidueña. It was not until 13 April, when he began filming the village in earnest, that he and Hemingway now went their more or less separate ways. But by then it had been almost an entire month since they had both arrived in Spain, and it was now a month-and-a-half later than Ivens had originally planned to start shooting in the village. From a comparison of their itineraries alone it would seem that Hemingway, rather than the village of Fuentidueña, had for a while become Ivens's main project.

And it was not just that they were together all this time visiting various sectors of the Madrid front, but also that they shared some frightening and dangerous combat experiences. This more than anything else confirmed their friendship.

The first of these experiences came ten days after inspecting the Guadalajara front. On 5 April Hemingway accompanied Ivens and Fernhout in filming a tank and infantry attack of the 12th International Brigade near Morata de Tajuña not far from Madrid. It was Hemingway's first combat experience of the war, and it made quite an impression on him. He described the experience briefly in his sixth dispatch four days later and at some length in "The Heat and the Cold," an article he wrote later for *Verve*.

The second experience, on April 9th, was a fierce battle in the Casa de Campo on the outskirts of Madrid, during which the film crew had to flee incoming shells in the West Park and climb up above the park to the Paseo de Rosales in order to set up the telephoto camera in a ruined house overlooking the battle. Later that night Hemingway filed a vivid account of the battle and of their dramatic experiences, and two days later, as though not entirely through with the experience, he returned with Fernhout and some friends (Ivens was off to the village of Fuentidueña with Dos Passos) and filed yet another dispatch on the continuing battle ("Dispatches" 26–29).

The development of their friendship was, as I believe the experienced Ivens knew it would be, the natural product of shared risks for a cause they both believed in. In his second interview with me in 1982 Ivens developed this point at some length:

You know yourself that if you are on the front line with a man, even for one day, you come to know who he is. We saw each other and we held each other in high regard. . . . So this friendship grew out of mutual respect between two people who had dignity and character and personality. I was very politically involved; he wasn't. The first two weeks in Spain we spent getting to know one another, each of us seeing what kind of man the other was. At the front these preliminaries go very quickly. For myself I set the task to make Hemingway understand the anti-fascist cause. I felt he would be an asset to our cause because he wrote such good articles.

Ivens has also acknowledged that he was able to be of considerable help to Hemingway, although again, as in so much else he has written and said about his relationship with Hemingway, the reasons are not quite what he would have us believe they are (*Camera* 118).

These military expeditions [to Morata de Tajuña and the Casa de Campo in Madrid] were the only part of our film-making over which any government supervision was exerted—and it was entirely local and military supervision. Apparently the government trusted us to do what we said we wanted to do: make these trips to the front line to see everything. This was also a help to Hemingway, because as part of our crew he was given more confidence and could go much closer and oftener to the front than other correspondents.

What Ivens neglected to say was that because he was trusted by the Comintern and by the Communist commanders of the International Brigades in charge of important sectors of the Madrid front, he had unusually privileged access to what was happening around Madrid. Nor does he indicate that the principal reason for including Hemingway in his film crew was not to give Hemingway an advantage over other correspondents, although his association with Ivens undoubtedly did that, but to integrate him into a network of contacts, experiences, and even friendships that would gradually bring Hemingway into the framework of the Comintern propaganda apparatus in Spain and, later, in the United States.

As a result of these experiences and of his growing friendship with Ivens, Hemingway came to see and understand the Spanish Civil War almost wholly within the context of its international participants, most of whom on the Madrid front were associated with international Communist organizations. He had very little contact with the Spaniards, and most of those whom he did get to know, such as Enrique Lister or Gustavo Durán, were also Communists.

In his second interview with me Ivens was quite explicit about the kind of introductions he was able to give Hemingway.

Also I knew, for example, Koltsov of Pravda and some of the Russians. They were living in the Gaylord Hotel and I introduced Hemingway to them so that he would know some other communists. That gave him an edge and with it came more confidence, which for him was very important, because other correspondents did not have this access. So through me he was able to get accurate, first-hand information. I didn't keep any secrets from him. "Yes, here are Russians," [I said.] For many people the Gaylord Hotel was some kind of secret center. I had a plan for Hemingway, and I think I used the right tactics. For this kind of man, I knew how far he could go and that he was not [would not become] a traitor. I didn't introduce him to the Russians when he first asked me. But after four weeks, I thought, now, he is ready to make that step, and it worked.

Much of the rest of Hemingway's time in Spain that first trip was taken up with his courting of Martha Gellhorn. While Ivens was off with Fernhout and Dos Passos in the village of Fuentidueña during the second half of April, Hemingway took off on a ten-day trip into the Guadarrama Mountains with Gellhorn, not returning until the last day of April, by which time Ivens had left Madrid with Dos Passos and was on his way to Paris and eventually to the United States.

Before Ivens departed Spain, however, he left a set of instructions with Hemingway on completing the film and some other matters (Ivens to Hemingway, 26 April [1937]). These instructions reveal as well as anything what kind of relationship Ivens had developed with Hemingway during those four weeks together in Spain. The details on transferring money into Spain, on getting a radio to the blind comrade in the American hospital (Robert J. Raven, upon whom Hemingway focused one of his dispatches), and on making sure that Fernhout and Sidney Franklin finished the filming in the village in two or three days show that Ivens had come to trust Hemingway completely on virtually all matters related to the film. Ivens also confided in Hemingway his concern that Dos Passos, who was now on his way out of Spain and in a very disillusioned frame of mind, might say something that would damage the film projects.

Dos was planning to talk in interviews about the picture. I told him to say a minimum. You agree? I spoke with him about dialogue and talk in the picture. You do that with me; he agrees with that. (Ivens to Hemingway, 26 April [1937])

The most interesting part of these instructions, however, does not concern the film at all, but Ivens's strong recommendation that Hemingway write an article on political commissars. Political commissars had been introduced into the International Brigades and were just now being introduced into the unified "Popular Army" under the direction of the Communists. Their model was the political commissar system used by the Soviet armies. Commissars held a rank equal to the military commanders of the brigades and battalions, and their function was to give their troops political indoctrination as well as to deal with morale problems in their units. Outside of Communist circles the functions of the political commissars were not well understood. Ivens thought that Hemingway could explain how valuable they really were in Spain.

Could you write in one of your articles about the great and human function of the political commissar on the front? It is important that the public knows how important their work is, specially in *this* war. Some people think we could do it now [win the war, that is] . . . without political commissars. Therefore I ask you to write about them if it is possible and if you find the right form. (You will go to the front, comrade.) (Ivens to Hemingway, 26 April [1937])

Hemingway never did publish an article on the political commissars, but he did try to write a short story on one of them, his friend Gustav

Regler, who was political commissar of the 12th International Brigade ("Gustav"). Whether Hemingway was following Ivens's suggestion or not is of less interest here than the fact that these instructions from Ivens convey a sense of assured control and confident command, just the kind of attitude, one might imagine, appropriate to a political commissar or, as I would rather maintain, to a case officer. Ivens knew his man by now and knew that he could ask him to do things that no one else could, so fully had he won Hemingway's confidence. And now that they were both leaving Spain, that confidence in Ivens would play an important role in getting Hemingway further involved in the propaganda battles of the Spanish Republic.

When Hemingway landed in New York on 18 May aboard the French liner *Normandie*, he was met by a crowd of reporters and photographers eager to record the famous correspondent's thoughts on the war in Spain. His views, as reported in *The New York Times*, bore little resemblance to the anti-war sentiments he expressed on leaving for the war back in February (19 May 1937). Then he was going to show how horrible war was so Americans could stay out of it; now he was predicting the war would last another year, with the Loyalists the ultimate victor. Although he did not say so, he knew that such optimism was essential if the campaign to repeal the Embargo Act in the United States and to overcome the policy of nonintervention in Europe were to succeed.

The objective of international propaganda on the Loyalist side was not to keep everybody out of the war—that had proved impossible—but to get the French and the British and the American people sufficiently aroused by the fate of Spain to pressure their governments into abandoning their isolationist and noninterventionist policies. Over and over again the message had to be driven home: the war in Spain was not someone else's war; it was our war too. What was going on in Spain was certain to engulf the whole of Europe, and if Europe went up in flames, the rest of the world was sure to follow. In this broad international campaign to convince the western democracies that the first battles of World War II had already begun in Spain Hemingway now became an ardent participant.

Perhaps he would have become so without the encouragement and guidance of Ivens and the Communists—many others did—but it is doubtful that without their efforts to bring his views into alignment with those of the Communist International Hemingway would have become, not just a champion of the Loyalist cause, but a defender and supporter of the Communists in their political campaigns as well. He supported their campaign to get rid of the politically based militias and to reorganize the military under a unified command. He joined them in their attacks on the

anarchists and the anti-Stalinist Communists as Gestapo-infiltrated trai-
tors. He saw the war, as they did, as an international conflict—a war of
resistance against foreign invasion, a war against international fascism—
and virtually ignored, even denied, the social and political conflicts in
Spain itself that had provoked it and now fueled its most bitter passions.
He suppressed certain realities he knew to be true and he promoted as
realities things he must have known to be false, all in the name of winning
a war whose character the Communists had largely defined.

In this respect Hemingway had become an effective propagandist. For
someone who had spent as much time in Spain as Hemingway had and for
someone who had previously avoided political action as assiduously as he
had, his transformation into an active propagandist willing to ignore some
of the war's most fundamental realities in order to promote others requires
some explanation. Partly it was a matter of temperament—a desire to be
helpful and a deep personal loyalty and sense of responsibility to those he
had come to know during the war. He genuinely admired the Communists
for their commitment and for their proven ability to organize and fight the
war. But partly too his transformation was the product of a conscious effort
on the part of the Communists to gain his confidence and to enlist his support.

The central figure in this effort was Joris Ivens, whose strong character
and political skills were effective agents in bringing about Hemingway's
transformation. Joris Ivens may not have been assigned the task of serving
as Hemingway's case officer in Spain, but he certainly served that function
well in the spring of 1937, and he did his best to help keep Hemingway in
the Communist fold in the months following as well. In August 1937, after
they had finished their work on *The Spanish Earth* and as Hemingway was
preparing to return to Spain, Ivens wrote two letters of introduction for
Hemingway to Communist friends of his: one to Wenceslau Roces, an
undersecretary in the propaganda bureau in Valencia, and the other to Paul
Vaillant Couturier, editor of *L'Humanité*, the newspaper of the French
Communist Party. To the latter he wrote as follows:

I have never written a letter of introduction to you for a friend of mine, but today
I make an exception for Ernest Hemingway. He is a very good friend of ours [i.e.,
of the communists]. He has done and will do a great deal for our cause, for the
cause of Spain here in America and in England. He will show you our film on
Spain. I am counting on you to help Ernest Hemingway if he needs anything. A
letter for Díaz [José Díaz, head of the Spanish Communist Party] would be good.

How much good such letters would do to keep Hemingway "a very good
friend of ours" remained to be seen, for without the reinforcing presence

of Ivens's personality it was not hard to imagine that the artist and writer Ernest Hemingway would eventually seek to establish a position independent of Ernest Hemingway the propagandist. "I am very far away, too far away, from all my actions in France," Ivens ended his letter to Couturier. Nonetheless, he did what he could, even from a distance, to make sure that the relationships he had carefully nurtured between Hemingway and the Communists in France and Spain in the spring of 1937 would not be undone in the fall.

NOTES

1. Carlos Baker (313) gives a good description of the Carnegie Hall setting and of Hemingway's obvious discomfort. Several eye-witnesses (Murphy, Powell, Romaine) all agree on the emotional impact of his powerful speech (Hemingway, "Fascism").

2. "Hemingway Sponsors Ambulance Unit," *New York Times* 12 January 1937: sec 4:7; Hemingway to Chase regarding the payment of $3,000 for two ambulances. On the loan of $1,000 from Scribner's made on 19 February 1937, see Perkins to Hemingway, 4 February 1938 and c. 25 October 1940.

3. André Malraux and Louis Fischer, both of whom signed letters of introduction for Hemingway shortly before he left for Spain, would have likely alerted their Communist associates in Paris that Hemingway was clearly committed to the Loyalists.

4. In response to an earlier draft of this article, the Dutch film scholar and Ivens expert, Bert Hogenkamp, asserted that he would "*never* regard Ivens as working for the Comintern during the Spanish war" (letter to author, 4 August 1989). He may be right about this, and I share with him his regard for the independence and integrity of Ivens. Yet I think the nature of Ivens's relationships with Communist organizations involved in the Spanish war, including the Comintern, is not that easily resolved. Given Ivens's deep involvement in the Communist movement and considering the way in which Communist organizations usually operated in those days, I have preferred to leave the matter of an *organized* effort to recruit Hemingway an open question. What is not an open question, in my view, is the considerable effort made by Ivens to guide and develop Hemingway into a propaganda asset for the Communists.

5. The importance Ivens attached to the longer documentary film is evident throughout his preparatory notes and the correspondence he had on the subject while making the film.

6. *The Camera and I*, although published in 1969, was actually written in 1943–44 while Ivens was in Hollywood. *Ou la mémoire d'un regard* was published in 1982.

7. For Hemingway's membership in the Board of Directors of Contemporary Historians, see three telegrams and a letter of MacLeish to Hemingway, 8,

15, 16 February 1937. The first indication that Hemingway was a member of Contemporary Historians, Inc., comes from the typed letterhead on a letter MacLeish sent to Reissig on 19 January 1937.

8. Hemingway's narration or subtitles for *No Pasaran*, the film based on Soviet footage that formed the second part of *Spain in Flames*, survive in a ms. note, "Amkino Presents, 'Madrid in Flames.'"

9. Ivens's recollection in both of his memoirs that Hemingway only stepped into the film project after Dos Passos had left it is contradicted by his own documents and by other evidence cited above. In *Ou la mémoire* Ivens says that after Dos Passos left the project, the committee in New York cabled Ivens: "There is a man you can work with in complete confidence; it is Hemingway" (146). Although I was unable to find this cable in the Ivens archives in Amsterdam, it is quite probable, as I suggest above, that MacLeish cabled Ivens of Hemingway's imminent arrival in Paris. He may also have told him that Dos Passos would soon be there as well, for Dos Passos arrived in Paris just a few days after Hemingway.

10. Hemingway's conviction on this matter was often clearly expressed in his dispatches and in his short story "Old Man at the Bridge."

11. Hemingway was quite emphatic that the Medical Bureau of the American Friends of Spanish Democracy not reveal his ambulance purchases. He had to borrow the money to buy the ambulances, he reminded Chase, and he had to risk his life covering the war in Madrid for the North American Newspaper Alliance in order to pay it back. He also reminded Chase of their prior agreement that his name would not be used and that nothing would be said to the press in any way about him other than that he was a sponsor of an Ambulance Unit. Hemingway stressed the importance of keeping that agreement at that particular time (Hemingway to Chase, 11 February 1937).

12. Malraux's note, written on stationery of The Mayflower in New York, is not dated, but a similar letter of introduction written by Louis Fischer, also on Mayflower stationery, is dated 25 February 1937. I would like to thank Marcia and John Goin for letting me see the Fischer letter from their collection.

13. The headlines in the *New York Herald Tribune*, European ed., 13 and 14 March 1937, as Hemingway was leaving for Spain, were full of alarming news of the imminent capture of Madrid by mechanized Italian forces.

14. In March, 1989, the author was able to inspect the photographs of John Fernhout in the Haags Gemeentemuseum, Den Haag, thanks to the then curator of modern painting, Flip Bool.

WORKS CITED

Baker, Carlos. *Ernest Hemingway: A Life Story*. NY: Scribner's, 1969.

Fernhout, John. Photographs from the Spanish Civil War. Fernhout Collection. Haags Gemeentemuseum, Den Haag, Netherlands. Courtesy of Flip Bool.

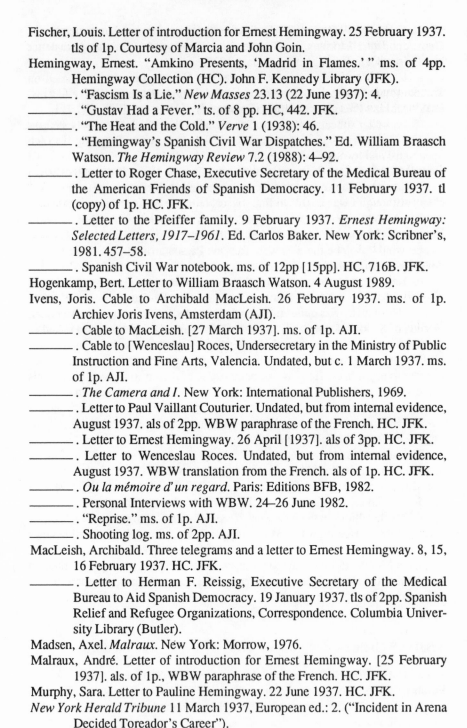

Fischer, Louis. Letter of introduction for Ernest Hemingway. 25 February 1937. tls of 1p. Courtesy of Marcia and John Goin.

Hemingway, Ernest. "Amkino Presents, 'Madrid in Flames.' " ms. of 4pp. Hemingway Collection (HC). John F. Kennedy Library (JFK).

———. "Fascism Is a Lie." *New Masses* 23.13 (22 June 1937): 4.

———. "Gustav Had a Fever." ts. of 8 pp. HC, 442. JFK.

———. "The Heat and the Cold." *Verve* 1 (1938): 46.

———. "Hemingway's Spanish Civil War Dispatches." Ed. William Braasch Watson. *The Hemingway Review* 7.2 (1988): 4–92.

———. Letter to Roger Chase, Executive Secretary of the Medical Bureau of the American Friends of Spanish Democracy. 11 February 1937. tl (copy) of 1p. HC. JFK.

———. Letter to the Pfeiffer family. 9 February 1937. *Ernest Hemingway: Selected Letters, 1917–1961*. Ed. Carlos Baker. New York: Scribner's, 1981. 457–58.

———. Spanish Civil War notebook. ms. of 12pp [15pp]. HC, 716B. JFK.

Hogenkamp, Bert. Letter to William Braasch Watson. 4 August 1989.

Ivens, Joris. Cable to Archibald MacLeish. 26 February 1937. ms. of 1p. Archiev Joris Ivens, Amsterdam (AJI).

———. Cable to MacLeish. [27 March 1937]. ms. of 1p. AJI.

———. Cable to [Wenceslau] Roces, Undersecretary in the Ministry of Public Instruction and Fine Arts, Valencia. Undated, but c. 1 March 1937. ms. of 1p. AJI.

———. *The Camera and I*. New York: International Publishers, 1969.

———. Letter to Paul Vaillant Couturier. Undated, but from internal evidence, August 1937. als of 2pp. WBW paraphrase of the French. HC. JFK.

———. Letter to Ernest Hemingway. 26 April [1937]. als of 3pp. HC. JFK.

———. Letter to Wenceslau Roces. Undated, but from internal evidence, August 1937. WBW translation from the French. als of 1p. HC. JFK.

———. *Ou la mémoire d'un regard*. Paris: Editions BFB, 1982.

———. Personal Interviews with WBW. 24–26 June 1982.

———. "Reprise." ms. of 1p. AJI.

———. Shooting log. ms. of 2pp. AJI.

MacLeish, Archibald. Three telegrams and a letter to Ernest Hemingway. 8, 15, 16 February 1937. HC. JFK.

———. Letter to Herman F. Reissig, Executive Secretary of the Medical Bureau to Aid Spanish Democracy. 19 January 1937. tls of 2pp. Spanish Relief and Refugee Organizations, Correspondence. Columbia University Library (Butler).

Madsen, Axel. *Malraux*. New York: Morrow, 1976.

Malraux, André. Letter of introduction for Ernest Hemingway. [25 February 1937]. als. of 1p., WBW paraphrase of the French. HC. JFK.

Murphy, Sara. Letter to Pauline Hemingway. 22 June 1937. HC. JFK.

New York Herald Tribune 11 March 1937, European ed.: 2. ("Incident in Arena Decided Toreador's Career").

————. 13 & 14 March 1937, European ed. (front page headline articles).

New York Times 12 January 1937: sec. 4:7 ("Hemingway Sponsors Ambulance Unit").

————. 19 May 1937: 10 ("Hemingway Sees Defeat of Franco").

Pereda, Prudencio de. Letter to Ernest Hemingway. 9 February 1937. HC. JFK.

Perkins, Maxwell. Letter to Ernest Hemingway. 4 February 1938. HC. JFK.

————. Letter to Ernest Hemingway. c. 25 October 1940. Scribner's Archive I, Hemingway Correspondence, 4/22/unnumbered. Princeton University Library (PUL).

Powell, Dawn. Letter to John Dos Passos. c. 8 June 1937. Dos Passos Papers, 5950–AA, box 4. University of Virginia Library.

Preteceille, M. E. Ogier. Three letters of introduction for Ernest Hemingway. 13 March 1937. tls, WBW paraphrase of the Spanish. HC. JFK.

Raeburn, John. *Fame Became of Him: Hemingway as Public Writer*. Bloomington: Indiana UP, 1984.

Romaine, Paul. Letter to Carlos Baker. 4 February 1963. Carlos Baker Files. PUL.

Stewart, Donald Ogden. Letter to Carlos Baker. 20 February 1951. Carlos Baker Files. PUL.

Wolfert, Ira. "Hemingway Off to Spain to Write About the War." 28 February 1937, for release on 1 March. NANA Release. HC. JFK.

5 Hemingway's *For Whom the Bell Tolls*: Fact into Fiction

Robert A. Martin

In writing *For Whom the Bell Tolls*, Ernest Hemingway drew upon his experiences as a war correspondent during the Spanish Civil War much more extensively than is generally recognized. Many of the characters, as well as the events and places of the novel, are based on historical fact and on the exploits of people Hemingway knew or heard of while he was covering the war. It is in this masterful blend of fact and fiction that *For Whom the Bell Tolls* achieves the status of a classic war novel.

The most obvious example of Hemingway's transformational blending process is the model for Robert Jordan, who is based on the life and adventures of a young American from California named Robert Merriman. A graduate student in economics at the University of California at Berkeley, Merriman had left his teaching fellowship to spend a year in Moscow in 1935–36 after winning a Newton Booth Traveling Scholarship of nine hundred dollars (Merriman 28). According to Merriman's wife, Marion, who accompanied him to Moscow and later to Spain, his interests were primarily in Soviet economics rather than the politics of revolutionary Russia (Merriman 51–52). Wounded in March of 1936, Merriman early became one of the better-known American volunteers in the International Brigades. He eventually achieved the rank of Major in the Abraham Lincoln Battalion, during which time in 1937 he met and became a casual acquaintance of Hemingway. Mrs. Merriman recalls their first meeting with Hemingway in his room at the Hotel Florida in Madrid.

I studied Bob and Hemingway. They got along. Each talked for a moment, then listened to the other. How different they were, I thought. Bob at twenty-eight, Hemingway at least a good ten years older. Hemingway seems complex. He was big and bluff and macho. He didn't appear to be a braggart but he got across the message, through an air of self-assurance, that he could handle what he took on. (Merriman 132)

In nearly all first-hand accounts of Hemingway in Spain during the Civil War, his careful questioning of combat veterans in the Brigades is remarkably consistent. Hemingway went to Spain four times as a correspondent for the North American Newspaper Alliance (NANA): from March to May, 1937; from August, 1937 to January, 1938; from March to May, 1938; and from August to November, 1938. On the morning of April 2, 1938, somewhere near Corbera, Merriman disappeared during a nighttime retreat and was never seen again.

Like Merriman, Robert Jordan has been a college instructor in the United States, is a volunteer fighting for the Loyalists, is a natural leader, and, at the end of his life behind enemy lines, may be said to also disappear from all official information and records. It was, in Wyden's view, Merriman's exploits during the war that led him "to become in the most significant respects, the prototype for the best-known hero of the Spanish war, Ernest Hemingway's fictional Robert Jordan in *For Whom the Bell Tolls*, and portrayed in the movie by Gary Cooper, playing opposite Ingrid Bergman" (Wyden 100). Hemingway, however, could not resist writing himself and his troubled family into the novel. When Jordan thinks about his father's suicide near the end of the book (338–40), he is as far from Robert Merriman as he could possibly be and as close to Hemingway's own preoccupation with his father's death as any of his characters would ever be again.

Further confirmation of sources has appeared from José Castillo-Puche's book, in which he says "I had questioned Ernesto closely about the material he had used, in particular the models for the Spanish characters. According to Ernesto, these characters had been drawn from life" (Castillo-Puche 50). Another main character of the novel, Maria, originated in a conversation Hemingway had with Fred Keller, a Battalion commissioner in the Lincoln Battalion. When Hemingway visited Keller in the hospital after his wounding during the Ebro retreat, he persuaded Keller to recount his recent experiences. As told by Wyden,

Over his usual map, Hemingway got Keller to sketch his adventures. Then Fred told Ernest they should all do something special for two young Spanish *sanitarias*, the two nurse's aides who had been taking care of him. The prettier one was Maria: shy, serene, about 24. She was a Communist, like her father, who had been executed in Andalusia when the war broke out. Maria had been imprisoned and, over the months, raped 24 times. (468)

While Keller's capsule summary of his nurse's unfortunate experience clearly gave Hemingway the idea for Maria, the characters of Pilar and El Sordo came directly from people he knew in Spain during the war. Castillo-Puche recounts that when Hemingway "decided in 1953 that it would be all right for him to return to Spain, he had discovered that Pilar was still alive in Galicia. When I asked him, 'What about El Sordo?' "

"El Sordo died," he answered. "But not the way he did in the novel."

"Was he shot by a firing squad?"

"No, he was killed on the Guadalajara front."

(Castillo-Puche 50–51)

Although Hemingway decided to incorporate into his novel representative officers of the Republican army, he did not bother to change the names of four of the most important: André Marty, El Campesino, Enrique Lister, and Juan Modesto. In the novel, Hemingway says that El Campesino, whose real name was Valentin Gonzalez and who was also called The Peasant, "had never been a peasant but was an ex-sergeant in the Spanish Foreign Legion who had deserted and fought with Abd el Krim,"[1] which fact is also noted by Peter Wyden in his history of the war, as are the backgrounds of Lister and Modesto (Wyden 327–28). Wyden also comments that Hemingway was surprised that many of the Loyalist commanders spoke Russian and had been trained in the Soviet Union, a fact that Hemingway worked into Robert Jordan's reflections on Gaylord's hotel in Madrid:

Gaylord's was the place where you met famous peasant and worker Spanish commanders who had sprung to arms from the people at the start of the war without any previous military training and found that many of them spoke Russian. That had been the first big disillusion to him a few months back and he had started to be cynical to himself about it. But when he realized how it had happened it was all right. They *were* peasants and workers. They had been active in the 1934 revolution and had to flee the country when it failed and in Russia they had sent them to the military academy and to the Lenin Institute the Comintern maintained so they would be ready to fight the next time and have the necessary military education to command. (229)

The fourth of these men, André Marty, was the chief commissar of the International Brigades, for whom Hemingway had an intense personal animosity, and whom he characterizes in the novel as being crazy and paranoid about the dangers of infiltration by Fascist spies (418–21). Hugh Thomas supports this view of Marty in *The Spanish Civil War* by noting

that "Marty was obsessed by spies" and that he "was only narrowly
forestalled in an attempt to shoot a number of his old staff at Albacete,
who might, so he feared in his nervous insanity, tell the world of some of
his maniacal acts" (492, 881). Gustav Regler, a political commissioner of
the Twelfth International Brigade, once told Hemingway of an incident in
which Marty had two volunteers executed when they panicked during
combat. Hemingway reacted strongly by calling Marty a "swine" and
spitting on the ground in contempt. Afterward, according to Regler,

I gave him secret material relating to the Party which he respected, because it was
fighting more actively than any other body, although he despised it as Marty's.
He used my material later in *For Whom the Bell Tolls*. . . . He depicted the spy
disease, that Russian Syphilis, in all its shameful, murderously studied workings,
writing with hatred of the huntsman for the poacher. (Bolloten 294–95)

Two other important characterizations based on Hemingway's circle of
acquaintances in Madrid are those of General Golz and the Russian
newspaper correspondent Karkov. Golz was modeled after a "Polish
colonel in the Russian service known as Walter," according to Hugh
Thomas (455–56), while Peter Wyden states that " 'Walter,' a Polish
officer named Karol Swierczewski, was memorialized by Hemingway as
the brave General Golz in *For Whom the Bell Tolls*" (Wyden 408).
Although the character of Karkov is not expanded by Hemingway, he is
obviously a portrait of a brilliant Russian journalist from *Pravda*, Mikhail
Koltsov, who was simultaneously Stalin's personal agent to spy on other
Russians and important political figures in the military hierarchy (Beever
122). As one of Russia's most influential journalists, Koltsov easily was
transformed into Karkov, who insolently confronts Marty concerning the
dispatch from Golz, which Marty has held up from delivery:

Marty stood up. He did not like Karkov, but Karkov, coming from *Pravda* and in
direct communication with Stalin, was at this moment one of the three most
important men in Spain. . . . Karkov always punctured him. The French word is
dégonfler and Marty was worried and made wary by him. It was hard, when
Karkov spoke, to remember with what importance he, André Marty, came from
the Central Committee of the French Communist Party. It was hard to remember,
too, that he was untouchable. Karkov seemed always to touch him so lightly and
whenever he wished. (424)

The most dramatic event in *For Whom the Bell Tolls* is the blowing of
the bridge. Hemingway based this central event on military action that
took place at the Arganda bridge, which spanned the Jarama River. The

Arganda bridge soon became a key link in the supply line to Madrid, and the battle for Madrid—the battle of Jarama—was fought for its control and possession. After the battle, Hemingway talked with many of the survivors and later went to see it. It impressed him immensely, as Wyden notes, in that the "Arganda bridge would stay with Hemingway and his readers forever. It became the model for the bridge that Ernest's hero, Robert Jordan, was assigned to blow up in *For Whom the Bell Tolls*" (Wyden 303).

The offensive for which Robert Jordan is assigned to blow the bridge can also be traced to a specific offensive that took place on the Segovia front on May 31, 1937, shortly after Hemingway had left Spain for the United States. The attack was led by three Republican divisions and reached as far as La Granja before the Nationalist forces stopped them. Militarily, that offensive was a failure, due largely to the inefficiency of one of its commanders. Hugh Thomas states that "this was the offensive described by Hemingway in *For Whom the Bell Tolls*. He suggests that it was betrayed but, due to Marty's obstinacy, was allowed to continue. The action of this book covers 'the sixty-eight hours between Saturday afternoon and Tuesday noon of the last week of May, 1937'" (689n).

A much less developed but nevertheless historically significant event that Hemingway uses in the novel comes through Pilar. She tells Jordan that after capturing a Fascist town, Pablo and his band forced the entire population of Fascists to endure beatings with flails and clubs before being thrown over a cliff (102–16). Historically, this is what happened in the town of Ronda in the Malaga Province in 1936, which, according to Hugh Thomas, was not an untypical occurrence for members of the Falange (Spanish Fascist Party):

To have been a member of the Falange was almost everywhere fatal, even though many escaped through the neglect or the repentance of their captors. . . . In country districts, revolution itself often consisted primarily of the murder of the upper classes or the bourgeoisie. Thus the description, in Ernest Hemingway's novel *For Whom the Bell Tolls*, of how the inhabitants of a small pueblo first beat the male members of the middle class and then flung them over a cliff, is near to the reality of what happened in the famous Andalusian town of Ronda (though the work was the responsibility of a gang from Malaga). There, 512 were murdered in the first month of war. (Thomas 274)

A final historical event from the war that Hemingway incorporates in his novel is based upon a plot by the political group P.O.U.M. (*Partido Obrero De Unificacion Marxista* translates as "The Worker's Party of Marxist Unification") to assassinate several of the Republican leaders. P.O.U.M. was led by Andres Nin and Joaquin Maurin. Nin, a former

secretary of Trotsky, is mentioned by Karkov in a conversation at
Gaylord's hotel with Robert Jordan, as he tells Jordan about the group:

> "The P.O.U.M. It is like the name. Not serious. . . . But they made one plot you
> know to kill me, to kill Walter, to kill Modesto, and to kill Prieto. You see how
> badly mixed up they were? We are not at all alike. Poor P.O.U.M. They never did
> kill anybody. Not at the front nor anywhere else. A few in Barcelona, yes."
>   "Were you there?" [asks Jordan].
>   "Yes. I have sent a cable describing the wickedness of that infamous organi-
> zation of Trotskyite murderers and their fascist machinations all beneath con-
> tempt but, between us, it is not very serious, the P.O.U.M. Nin was their only
> man. We had him but he escaped from our hands." (247)

Nin, who had broken with Trotsky, was also politically outside the Communist power circles and was slowly being excluded from the party and from
the Catalan government. Moscow ordered that the P.O.U.M. be suppressed
and its leaders arrested. In June, 1937, Nin was arrested and tortured secretly
to obtain a confession. Most of the charges that Karkov relays to Jordan are
reflections of the rumors and facts that were circulating at the time (Beever
193–94; Thomas 701–9). Nin was, according to Hugh Thomas, murdered
in prison because he had become disillusioned with Stalinist communism
and its methods and because "he was precisely the kind of individual whom
Stalin desired dead" (704). Whether Hemingway could have known the facts
about the Nin murder and the purges of P.O.U.M. members by the Communist hierarchy is debatable. Karkov's remarks to Jordan in the light of
published information available in 1940 suggest that Hemingway was
drawing on a source of information within the higher circles of the Communist party in Spain. As one of the most powerful men in Spain, and as Stalin's
personal representative, Koltsov would certainly have known of Nin's death.
He perhaps deliberately deceived Hemingway to protect himself. In any
event, Nin did not escape, as Karkov tells Jordan, and Hemingway obviously
did not know of his death.

As a writer who prided himself on getting the facts down accurately,
Hemingway used the information he had gleaned from his own observations during his time in Spain and from what others told him. One of his
strategies was to develop friendships with people such as the guerrilla war
specialist Mamsurov, also known as Hajji. " 'At Gaylords, a Madrid hotel,
Hemingway met our army men,' recalled Ilya Ehrenburg. 'He liked Hajji,
a man of reckless courage, who used to penetrate behind the enemy lines' "
(Bolloten 293). Hajji was undoubtedly Hemingway's source for much of
the technical feats of sabotage mentioned in the novel. Irving Goff,

however, an American who fought with the guerrillas, has argued that Hemingway did not know the proper methods for explosives:

After the war, reading Hemingway's description of the action against the bridge in *For Whom the Bell Tolls*, Goff was amazed. Hemingway was supposed to have been briefed on sabotage methods in Madrid by the famous Soviet expert A. D. Mamsurov, known as Hajji. Yet Goff found that the explosion techniques in the novel were practical only for mines, and other industrial purposes, not for guerrillas—unless they were bent on suicide. The getaway time allowed by Hemingway was much too short, and needlessly so. Did literary requirements conflict with authenticity? Goff preferred to believe that Hemingway was ignorant about guerrilla warfare. (Wyden 318n)

Although Hemingway spent a great deal of his time in Spain visiting the battlefronts, he also spent considerable time in Madrid at the Hotel Florida, the headquarters for journalists, and at Gaylord's, the principal hotel for the Russian political and military advisors. At these hotels, along with many other journalists, Hemingway met or heard about most of the people and events he later wrote into his novel. With his maps, his sense of military strategy remaining from the writing and research he had done on *A Farewell to Arms*, he was both reporting the events and reshaping them in terms of characters, conflicts, and situations. Fifty years after the Spanish War, *For Whom the Bell Tolls* still speaks with an authentic sense of time, place, and history. If Hemingway would later exaggerate his own role in the conflict, his thoughts at the time of writing *For Whom the Bell Tolls* went back to Spain even as he has Robert Jordan think about writing his book after the war is over:

He would write a book when he got through with this. But only about the things he knew, truly, and about what he knew. But I will have to be a much better writer than I am now to handle them, he thought. The things he had come to know in this war were not so simple. (248)

NOTE

1. Ernest Hemingway, *For Whom the Bell Tolls* (NY: Scribner's, 1940) 229. All citations are from this edition.

WORKS CITED

Beever, Antony. *The Spanish Civil War*. NY: Peter Bedrick Books, 1983.
Bolloten, Burnett. *The Spanish Revolution*. Chapel Hill: U of North Carolina P, 1979.

Castillo-Puche, José Luis. *Hemingway in Spain*. Garden City, NY: Doubleday, 1974.

Hemingway, Ernest. *For Whom the Bell Tolls*. NY: Scribner's, 1940.

Merriman, Marion, and Warren Lerude. *American Commander in Spain*. Reno: U of Nevada P, 1986.

Thomas, Hugh. *The Spanish Civil War*. 3rd ed. NY: Harper and Row, 1986.

Wyden, Peter. *The Passionate War*. NY: Simon and Schuster, 1983.

6 "A Tiny Operation with Great Effect": Authorial Revision and Editorial Emasculation in the Manuscript of Hemingway's *For Whom the Bell Tolls*

Thomas E. Gould

The manuscript of Hemingway's *For Whom the Bell Tolls* contains a large number of revisions, but they have received surprisingly little critical attention. Although Sheldon Norman Grebstein, for example, cites some of the most obvious revisions in the appendix to *Hemingway's Craft*, he offers no analysis. The many changes in the manuscript include minor additions such as visual details, procedures, and speaking attributions; discussions of Robert Jordan's father's suicide; additions to Maria's description; additions to the depictions of death; and intensification of episodes through additions of animal imagery, writing theory, and references to the American Civil War. But the most consistently revised passages involve sexual experience and profane language. By isolating and analyzing these particular revision types, we gain a better understanding of Hemingway's creative process and the cultural conditions that influenced specific revisions.

THE MANUSCRIPT

The first draft of the manuscript confirms that Hemingway started the novel in Cuba on March 1, 1939. His diligence in recording the progress of the novel, by word counts and dates in margins, makes it possible to trace the composition of the original draft. In addition, a comparison of dates on the manuscript and the progress reported to Perkins and Hadley Mowrer indicates Hemingway's revising-while-writing process. For instance, based on a letter to Perkins, Carlos Baker finds Hemingway finished with chapter 14 on July 10 (*Selected Letters* 496). However, the manuscript reveals Hemingway still working on chapter 14 on July 31. It appears he was writing to friends about progress on the first draft while recording his progress on revisions in the manuscript margins. On July 13, 1940, he wrote Perkins that he was working on the last chapter while having the manuscript typed for Scribner's (506). He received the galley proofs in August and in early September sent the final corrections back to the publishing house.

In November, he forwarded the original manuscript to "Uncle" Gus Pfeiffer, his wife's wealthy uncle, in appreciation of his "loyalty, tolerence [sic], understanding and generosity" (Hemingway Collection). The manuscript remained in Pfeiffer's possession until his death. Afterward, it was housed in the Houghton Library at Harvard University until it was permanently deposited in the Hemingway Collection of the John F. Kennedy Library in Boston.

The 1,146-page manuscript appears variously in the writer's hand or in typescript. The pagination is consecutive until chapter 31. From this point forward, each chapter begins with page one. The revisions are either handwritten, in margins and interlinearly, or are typewritten additions inserted into the draft.

HEMINGWAY'S REVISIONS AND THE CLIMATE OF CENSORSHIP

Hemingway made significant revisions in the manuscript when dealing with sexuality and profane language. These revisions were influenced by the purpose of the novel and the historical context of its writing. In *For Whom the Bell Tolls*, we see him deliberately pushing his publisher to the limit of what, in 1940, could be said in print. Not only had other American writers been recently censored and banned for "offensive" material, but Hemingway too had been subjected to restrictions in his earlier novels.

In the years following World War I and leading up to the writing and publication of *For Whom the Bell Tolls*, publishing houses were careful about what they presented to the American public. A slow liberalization of standards was proceeding, but many authors' writings were censored. Throughout the twenties and thirties, most publishers were extremely cautious for fear of lawsuits, book bannings, and seizures. The primary crusaders in this quest for public decency were local and state vice societies, which initiated legal actions, lobbied in state legislatures for broader definitions and stricter penalties for obscenity, and encouraged confiscation of written materials from publishing houses (Hoyt and Hoyt 30–34).

Even though these societies often lost their lawsuits, the threat of costly legal battles prompted publishers to restrict publication of certain untraditional writings. Some societies had a frightening influence on local authorities' positions on censorship. For example, in Boston, the Watch and Ward Society's power was notorious: "Booksellers were warned the sale of *Elmer Gantry* would be grounds for prosecution. [The city] banned *An American Tragedy* by Theodore Dreiser. The sale of *Oil*, a novel of the Harding administration scandals by Upton Sinclair, brought about a bookseller's arrest" (Hoyt and Hoyt 37–38).

Hemingway himself was no stranger to censorship. He had been forced to make changes in the dramatic content and language in *The Sun Also Rises* and *A Farewell to Arms* before serialization and publication. Before publication of *The Sun Also Rises*, Max Perkins found himself arguing tirelessly before the editorial board that this was not an obscene book. Many of the editors who read the novel in manuscript form were shocked by the author's earthy language, and Charles Scribner vehemently objected to publishing profane words in his books.

Even Perkins felt that certain individual words and phrases, particularly profanities and unfavorable characterizations, could result in bannings and libel suits from the offended parties (Berg 97). He made a diplomatic suggestion when he wrote Hemingway:

the majority of the people are more affected by words than things. I'd even say that those most obtuse toward things are most sensitive to a sort of a *word*. I think some words should be avoided so that we shall not divert people from the qualities of this book. (quoted in Reynolds 62)

He pointed out the delicate problem of the bull's "balls" and the reference to Lady Brett Ashley as a "bitch." Hemingway responded: "I imagine we are in accord about the use of certain words and I never use a word without first considering if it is replaceable. But in the proof I will go over it all very carefully" (Baker, *Selected Letters* 211). Hemingway himself then proposed the change from "balls" to "horns." About the other suggestions for language revision Hemingway complained:

I've tried to reduce profanity but I reduced so much profanity when writing the book that I'm afraid that not much could come out. Perhaps we will have to consider it simply as a profane book and hope that the next book will be less profane or perhaps more sacred. (213)

Though most of the board's objections concerned language, the sexual content of the novel was also criticized. Perkins, too, feared there were "a

dozen different passages" in *The Sun Also Rises* that would "offend
readers' sensibilities" (Berg 97). He wrote Hemingway:

You probably don't appreciate this disgusting possibility because you've been
too long abroad, and out of that atmosphere. Those who breathe its stagnant
vapors now attack a book, not only on grounds of eroticism, which could not hold
here, but upon that of "decency," which means words. (quoted in Berg 98)

For years afterward, Hemingway referred to any censorship of his writing
as an "emasculation." But he satisfied Scribner's by changing certain
objectionable words and references. Still, the book was, not surprisingly,
banned in Boston, and Scribner's received numerous complaints from
disgusted readers asking how the company could publish such an offensive
work (Berg 100).

Hemingway's compromise indicates that even while writing *The Sun
Also Rises* he was conscious of the problems his realistic language and
sexual content could cause. At the same time, he was not interested in
challenging the censorship codes of the period. In fact, he often changed
words to avoid such a confrontation. However, he was dedicated to his
craft and to the integrity of his stories; an integral aspect of this dedication
was presenting experiences as realistically as possible. Consequently, he
felt the language and sexuality of his characters had to support and reflect
this realism. These problems with restrictions did not end with the publication of *The Sun Also Rises*.

A Farewell to Arms was not the "less profane" or "more sacred" book
Hemingway had predicted to Perkins. In fact, the profane words in *A
Farewell to Arms* were considerably stronger than those objected to in the
manuscript of *The Sun Also Rises*. The situation was further complicated
by the proposed serialization of the novel. The standards for the magazine
were even stricter than those for the book version. As a result, the magazine
omissions were considerable: "balls," "cocksucker," "fuck," "Jesus
Christ," "son of a bitch," "whore," and "whorehound." Scribner's rein-
serted "Jesus Christ," "son of a bitch," "whore," and "whorehound," but
the other deleted words were still too offensive for publication in 1929
(Reynolds 72).

Hemingway felt the exclusion of these words from his text would "kill
[its] value by emasculating it" (Baker, *Selected Letters* 297). All of his
arguments were in vain. Reluctantly, he agreed to alter certain words if
they could "not be printed without the book being suppressed" (297).
Some of the more offensive words were then eliminated by inserting
blanks in their places. The author fully recognized his lack of control over

his own words. He wrote Perkins: "I wish we could talk and you could tell me just how far you can go and what the danger is. I do not want trouble—But I want everything that can be had without trouble" (298).

Hemingway was caught in the middle. As an artist, he resented the intrusion of censorship into his work, equating it with emasculation—"a tiny operation with great effect" (300). But he was also practical about challenging standards. Suppression meant certain commercial backlash, and he depended on commercial success for his livelihood. The result was that Hemingway fought long and hard to maintain the integrity of his language but consented to alterations when faced with suppression.

Hemingway's problems with the censoring of sexual content continued with *A Farewell to Arms*. The sexuality was far stronger than in *The Sun Also Rises*, and Hemingway expected problems. First, the serialization of the novel in *Scribner's Magazine* required more cuts than the book version. Since the magazine was used in many schools, the editors wished to be cautious with the dramatic content and language. The editor of the magazine deleted Frederic's daydream of spending a weekend in bed with Catherine, edited Rinaldi's advice to Frederic on women, and deleted Frederic's seduction of Catherine in the Milan hospital (Reynolds 69, 71). The original sexual content in these scenes is tame by modern standards; in 1929, however, there was little public tolerance for any graphic sexual display. Scribner's, consequently, was wary of publishing material that might lead to banning or seizures, in which they could lose their investment or face costly legal suits.

Naturally, Hemingway remembered these previous problems when he approached the sexuality in *For Whom the Bell Tolls*. He revised both Robert Jordan's romantic encounters with Maria and the relationship between Maria and Pilar—but for quite different effects. He did not flinch when reworking the love scenes between Jordan and Maria to depict a more physical relationship. He included the sexuality in these scenes with a strength of conviction and a confidence in his talents as an artist.

For instance, in chapter 13 the love scene between Jordan and Maria is not nearly as graphic or detailed in the first draft of the manuscript as in the final text. In the scene as it was originally written, there is no explicit portrayal of the physical act of love. Initially, the love scene is quite brief: "And there was the moment when they stood absolutely still in time and he could feel the earth move out and away from under them" (Hemingway, "For Whom" MS 310). The scene then quickly shifts to the afterglow they share. Hemingway revised this section, crossing out this short, tender description. He replaced it with a page-long insert replete with a selection of strong, sexually suggestive words and a sentence arrangement that emphasizes the physical nature of the act rather than the romantic. The most explicit parts of this section read:

For him it was a dark passage which led to nowhere, then to nowhere, then again to nowhere, once again to nowhere, always and forever to nowhere, heavy on the elbows in the earth to nowhere, . . . now beyond all bearing up, up, up and into nowhere, suddenly, scaldingly, . . . and time absolutely still . . . time having stopped and he felt the earth move out and away from under them. (MS insert 310)

The earth still moves for the lovers, but the additional material, particularly the repetition, graphically and rhythmically describes the physical nature of this sexual act.

Hemingway made a similar revision later in the manuscript, in chapter 36, when Jordan and Maria make love for the third and last time. The first draft of the manuscript is heavily revised. As originally written, the scene does not contain the prolonged description of the act included in the final text. The first-draft scene leads up to the act, describes it in wholly romantic terms, and then shifts, like the earlier revision, to the two lovers in conversation afterwards. The actual lovemaking is described like this: "Robert Jordan knew then that if there is any reward, that only those have it who merit it. That it is only to be given and only by giving can it be received. He felt proud and humble and altogether happy with an ecstasy of fulfillment. There are no words for such things" (MS ch. 36, 5).

Hemingway revised this page numerous times, both interlinearly and marginally. Finally, he crossed out the whole bottom half of the page and inserted two pages of description before we find the lovers talking. Once again, the inserts are sexually suggestive in word selection and sentence arrangement. Part of this reads:

Come now, now, for there is no now but now. Yes, now. Now, please now, only now, not anything else only this now . . . always now, for now always are now; one only one, there is no other one but one now . . . going now, rising out, sailing now . . . soaring now, away now, all the way now, one is one is one, is one, is one, is one, is still one, is still one, . . . is one now on earth with elbows. (MS insert ch. 36, 6-7)

Precise and suggestive word selection, syntactical rhythms, and repetition all serve to create an explicit description of the physical act without the use of a single "offensive" or sexual word. The similarity between this revision and the earlier one is unmistakable.

Tame by contemporary cultural standards, the material in these revisions was quite explicit for 1940. Considering Hemingway's long history of censorship difficulties, why did he revise his manuscript to include this material? The purpose of the novel again had a powerful influence on Hemingway's revisions. In *For Whom the Bell Tolls*, Hemingway was seeking to create a story as true to the human experience in war as possible. His undeniable commitment to realism dominates the revised love scenes. Hemingway's painstaking revisions of the love scenes were his attempts to achieve a realistic portrayal of love in wartime. He revised these sections for sexual emphasis because that is the reality, not the romantic fantasy, of the relationship being portrayed.

During the three-day span of the entire novel, Jordan and Maria make love three times; that they make the "earth move" twice out of the three possible times indicates the emotional and physical intensity of their time together. This is no stable love relationship, no long-term affair of the heart, only two individuals desperately affirming life amid the death and destruction of war, and the emphasis on sexuality is both appropriate and necessary.

In chapter 12, another aspect of sexuality undergoes revisions that dramatically influence the audience's interpretation of the episode. In this scene, Maria, Pilar, and Jordan, as they return from El Sordo's camp, discuss the relationship between the two women. Before revision, the scene in the manuscript strongly suggests that there once existed a sexual bond between the two women.

The first draft in the manuscript implies that Maria and Pilar have shared more than a common friendship, more than a mother/daughter relationship, more than a protector/charge arrangement. In the original scene, Hemingway wrote that "Maria moved close to her [Pilar] and laid her head across the woman's big thighs" (MS 229). While not overtly sexual, this line is far more suggestive than the line the author replaced it with: "Put her arms out and folded them as one does who goes to sleep with a pillow and lay with her head on her arms" (229). This line suggests a childlike innocence on Maria's part and a protective role for Pilar. The former line is more sexual if only for the placement of the girl's head and the coarseness of the language.

Later on the same page, while Pilar still holds Maria, the final textual version reads: " 'You can have her in a little while, *Ingles*,' [Pilar] said. Robert Jordan was sitting behind her. 'Do not talk like that,' Maria said" (299). However, in the manuscript draft the speaking description continues and reads: "and stroked her head across the big woman's thighs, then patted her hands where they lay" (299). The deletion of both of these references to Pilar's "big thighs" effectively dampens any suggestion of a sexual connection between the two women.

In the first draft of the manuscript, Hemingway appears unsure in presenting the tone of the relationship. At separate times, we have the undeniable suggestion of a lesbian affair; the sudden discovery, by Pilar, of a physical attractiveness to Maria; and the intense denial of any sexual dimension to the relationship. For instance, one passage in the manuscript reads: " 'There is always something like that,' [Pilar] said. 'There is always something like something that should not be, and for me to find it now in me' " (300). But Hemingway deleted "and for me to find it now in me" and replaced it with: "But with me there is not. Truly there is not." The first draft indicates that Pilar has suddenly discovered a physical attraction to Maria. But the revision, once again, removes the sexual suggestiveness and inserts a strong denial instead.

Furthermore, in the first draft of the manuscript, Pilar's finger touches Maria "absently, but rememberingly over the line of the girl's cheekbones and over the contours of her cheeks, and over her chin and then swept three fingers down the smooth curve of her throat" (300–301). In the revision, Hemingway replaces this with "absently, but tracingly, over the line of the girl's cheekbones and over the contours of her cheeks." The change from "rememberingly" to "tracingly" is important. The earlier word selection implies that the relationship previously involved some degree of physical contact. Also, the elimination of the continuing description tempers the impression of lesbianism.

From the original draft, Hemingway also cut the line where Pilar states: "There is a darkness in us [women] that you [Jordan] know nothing of. But all have it and I say this to thee now" (301). The deletion of this statement further distances the reader from interpreting Maria and Pilar's relationship as anything but innocent. To this scene, Hemingway added Pilar's claim that "I am no *Tortillera*, but a woman made for men. That is true" (301). *Tortillera* is Spanish slang for lesbian. Also, in the margin of the manuscript page the author added Pilar's defense that "I do not make perversions. I only tell you something true" (301). These few deletions and additions dramatically change the tone of the scene from one of sexual suggestiveness to one of platonic jealousy. Hemingway's revisions struck a balance: while he deemphasized the lesbian relationship between the two women, he retained the idea of bisexuality inherent in us all.

But why did Hemingway purposely undercut the sexual aspects of the women's relationship? Censorship restrictions probably played a minor role in his decision; the author certainly could have constructed the scene to sidestep any publisher's objections. The question remained, however:

was the American public ready to read about lesbianism? Although restrictions had steadily softened, such a portrayal would have violated existing literary taboos. Hemingway was concerned over the enormous attention this aspect of the novel would receive. He already had one love relationship distracting the audience's attention from the war. He may not have wanted to chance another distraction, a controversial love relationship that would further blur his focus on war. Here, Hemingway's concern may not have been so much about censorship as about audience response.

As a result of Hemingway's careful crafting and consideration of public reaction, only two objections were raised against the material in *For Whom the Bell Tolls*. Scribner's complained that the "smell of death to come" speech by Pilar was "definitely horrifying" (quoted in Berg 379). Another scene showing Jordan masturbating before a battle was strongly objected to by the editorial board. The Pilar speech was retained while the masturbation scene was cut (379). This choice indicates that the specter of censorship over sexual material still haunted the publishing world in 1940. However, by convincingly describing graphic sexual activity without the use of sexual or "offensive" language, Hemingway successfully subverted the censorship restrictions of his day.

This subversion becomes even more evident in his use of profane language in the text. Hemingway revised two specific aspects of diction while writing *For Whom the Bell Tolls*: the Spanish and the profane language. Unfortunately, the source of the Spanish revisions is difficult to trace. With only the holograph manuscript, one cannot possibly trace the source of Hemingway's apparently faulty command of Spanish in the published text. Hemingway's less profane Spanish was heavily revised somewhere between the manuscript draft and the printed text, most probably in the galley revisions. Until we can compare manuscript, typescript, galleys, and final text, we cannot say for certain whose command of Spanish is in doubt: Hemingway's or Perkins's. But the profane language in *For Whom the Bell Tolls* presented Hemingway with the familiar problem of reconciling the "offensive" words necessary to his story with the restrictions imposed from the outside.

Hemingway was forced by his editors at Scribner's to make numerous changes in the language of his earlier novels, including the use of blank spaces for unpublishable words. He did not want a repeat performance; in *For Whom the Bell Tolls*, there would be no blanks, no "emasculation" of the story. He did not want to distract his audience or distance them from the experience in any way. Therefore, he changed the profane language to prevent objection while remaining true to the experience. The result is a word selection that adheres to social standards but still achieves

Hemingway's desired effect. In the process, Hemingway successfully subverted the restrictions that affected the published versions of his earlier novels and remained in place during the writing of *For Whom the Bell Tolls*.

When writing his Spanish Civil War novel, Hemingway feared changes to his profane language. The revisions in the manuscript indicate he recognized this threat and sought to avoid any editorial control over his words. In the revision stage of the manuscript draft, Hemingway employed various strategies to circumvent the language restrictions and maintain a vocabulary appropriate to the characters and the wartime situation. He also subverted the censorship of the period by thinly masking his profanities. His reading audience would well know the intended words, but the censors were powerless because the words were not literally in the text.

The first draft of the manuscript indicates that Hemingway was still unsure about how to present the offensive language in his story. Often in the manuscript, when one of his characters utters a profane word or phrase, the author used the vague term "obscenity." Later, in the revision stage, he substituted a more specific word. For example, in chapter 9 he changed "obscenity" to words such as "besmirch" and "vileness" (MS 198–99, 200). Also, in chapter 25, "obscenity thyself" was changed to "defile thyself" (MS 566).

Why did the author choose to substitute these words instead of more profane ones? Obviously, one reason is that their inclusion preempted any confrontation with Scribner's editors over offensive language. These words retain the harsh impact of the profanity while possessing none of the danger. Also, their uncommon, exotic sound, especially to American ears, is in keeping with the attempt to represent characters speaking a foreign language.

Another specific word revision in the manuscript reveals that Hemingway was aware of the censorship restrictions still in place as he wrote *For Whom the Bell Tolls*. Throughout the manuscript, he initially used the word "unprintable" to indicate a profane word or phrase. When revising, he often inserted another word or phrase in its place. For example, in chapter 2 he crossed out the first-draft word "unprintable" and replaced it with "obscene" (MS 36). In chapter 3, he again edited "unprintable" in favor of "obscene" a number of times (MS 71, 73). This pattern is still evident in the last chapter, when he substituted "unnameable" for "unprintable" (MS ch. 43, 80). To Perkins, Hemingway explained his motive for the revisions: "Throughout I removed unprintable as I thought it gave a literary connotation that was bad. I changed it to unnameable or some other word" (Baker, *Selected Letters* 513). The connotation is "bad" because his primary audience, the American reader, would see this word as a consequence of censorship.

Why then can the word still be found in the text? Certainly Hemingway did not just overlook it. In fact, toward the end of chapter 3 this word is the focus of a conversation between Agustín and Jordan:

> "Go to the unprintable," Agustín said. "And unprint thyself. But do you want me to tell you something of service to you?"
>
> "Yes," Jordan said. "If it is not unprintable," naming the principal obscenity that had larded the conversation. (45)

In the revision stage, the author could not have missed such a prominent use of the word. The answer can be found in Hemingway's admiration for the Spanish language, particularly the profanity.

During Sordo's last stand, the narrator states: "There is no language as filthy as Spanish. There are words for all the vile words in Spanish and there are other words and expressions that are used only in countries where blasphemy keeps pace with the austerity of religion" (318). Hemingway fully realized that as an American writer he could not hope to capture the true flavor or impact of Spanish cursing. "Untranslatable" would have been a more accurate word for Hemingway to use. The word "unprintable" serves to show both his acceptance of this inability to translate fully and the severity of the profanity. Hemingway's revisions, or lack of revisions, again strike a balance: in some instances he deleted the word so as not to confuse its intent, while he left it in place at other times to acknowledge the invective's untranslatable quality. At the same time, he reminded his American audience that full use of the language was not yet possible.

In his revisions, Hemingway also used various means to subvert censorship by presenting profane words in such a way that they could not be objected to by Scribner's or suppressed by censors. Finding himself in the same predicament that arose with his earlier novels, Hemingway knew what type of language would be censored, but he also knew this profanity was necessary to present the experience realistically. In some instances his previous battles with the censors served as a gauge of the extent he could go with his language. At one point, he changed "unmentionable unspeakable" to "whore" (MS 611), remembering, perhaps, that although "whore" was cut from the serialization of *A Farewell to Arms*, it was included in the book version. However, there was stronger language in *For Whom the Bell Tolls* that needed to be retained, so he devised various methods to prevent its exclusion.

One method was to substitute the Spanish translation for the English profanity. For example, during Sordo's stand, Joaquín steadies himself with a Communist slogan that translates as "Hold out and fortify, and you will Win" (308). Another guerilla overhears him:

> "What was the last word?" the man with his chin on the ground asked.
> "*Vencer*," the boy said. "Win."
> "*Mierda*," the man with his chin on the ground said. (309)

In the manuscript, the word "shit" is used. Somewhere in the revision stage, most probably the galleys, Hemingway replaced "shit" with its Spanish equivalent.

More pronounced is the clever use Hemingway made of the Spanish word *joder*. This word translates into English as "to fuck." From past experience, Hemingway knew there was no way "fuck" would pass the censors. But inclusion of this word was essential to the story. He decided to use *joder* both to avoid any suppression and to maintain the tone of the experience. For example, in chapter 24, Jordan and Agustín discuss Maria, and Agustín asks: "And thy care is to *joder* with her all night?" (290) Without hesitating, Jordan answers, "With luck" (290). In the manuscript, the initial wording here is "make love to her all night" (MS 544). In revision, Hemingway crossed out "make love" and wrote in "*joder*." The rest of the conversation is presented entirely in English. Agustín is portrayed as a crude peasant with a suitably filthy vocabulary. For Agustín to say "make love" instead of "fuck" would be out of character. The change from English to Spanish makes Agustín's speech all the more appropriate. Jordan's reply is equally important. Jordan certainly knows the meaning of this Spanish vulgarity. Yet, he answers this crude intrusion with a casual "With luck." He is neither offended nor outraged by this vulgar reference to his relationship with Maria. The revision of this single word also eliminates the emotionalism associated with "make love" and replaces it with a purely physical association. The conversation thus emphasizes the carnal basis of the relationship.

In revising this passage, Hemingway apparently realized that the strong, emotional connotation of "love" was inappropriate. By substituting *joder*, he was able to include the offensive word to maintain the realism without fear of deletion or suppression. The meaning of the word, even for those readers with little knowledge of Spanish, is clearly defined by the context of the conversation and the character of the speaker.

Hemingway also substituted a form of *joder* for another word in chapter 25. Here, as the guerrillas listen to the sounds of El Sordo's fight, Pilar asks Jordan how he thinks the battle is going. Jordan responds, "Bad. Very bad" (297). Pilar then asks, "He's *jodido*?" (298). In other words, she asks if Sordido is "fucked." In the manuscript, Hemingway's first word choice here was "obscenitied" (561). Because the use of the true English word was not possible, the author then resorted to the Spanish to maintain the scene's integrity.

When writing *For Whom the Bell Tolls*, Hemingway again faced the painfully familiar problem of losing his "balls" to the censors. Not wanting to risk "emasculation" of another novel, he sought to avoid the uncertainty that inevitably develops in the reader's mind when confronted with a blank space to indicate a missing word. Early in the writing, he decided to use the Spanish equivalent *cojones* to avoid this problem. Its meaning is clearly established in a conversation between Jordan and the drunken Pablo. In his confused state of mind, Pablo insists Jordan is Scottish. He asks:

"Since it is well known that you wear skirts. Even the soldiers. I have seen photographs and also I have seen them in the Circus of Price. What do you wear under your skirts, *Ingles*?"

"*Los cojones*," Robert Jordan said.

Anselmo laughed and so did the others who were listening; all except Fernando. The sound of the word, of the gross word spoken before the women, was offensive to him.

"Well, that is normal," Pablo said. "But it seems to me that with enough *cojones* you would not wear skirts." (206)

By using the Spanish, Hemingway avoided deletion or word substitution.

In *The Sun Also Rises*, the word was changed to "horns"; in *A Farewell to Arms*, the word was changed to "scrotum"; in *For Whom the Bell Tolls*, the use of the word in Spanish enabled the author to maintain the coarse, realistic language of the characters. Another example occurs during Sordo's battle on the hill with the Fascist soldiers. Hemingway wrote: " '*Me cabra*,' the captain said. 'Here there is nothing but idiots and cowards' " (MS 631). Somewhere between the manuscript and the published text Hemingway replaced *me cabra* with *cojones* and retained the gritty language of men in war.

Another technique Hemingway used to present language accurately yet avoid censorship was to alter slightly the offensive English word. For instance, while Jordan is showing the guerrillas the proper placement for the machine gun, Agustín tells him of their past difficulties with the gun. Jordan then asks, "Does it shoot now?" Agustín responds, "Yes, but we do not let the gypsy nor others frig with it" (272). In the manuscript, the initial word is "fuck" not "frig" (MS 493). His American audience obviously knew the intended word, so Hemingway lost very little with this slight change.

Another adjustment to the word "fuck" occurs in the scene after Jordan discovers Pablo's theft of the exploder and the detonators. In this scene, Jordan rants about the inadequacy of Spanish leaders. In the published text, Jordan rages on for more than a page about this leadership's lack of character. This tirade in the published text is punctuated by countless "mucks." For example:

Muck them to hell and always. Muck them before we die for them. Muck them after we die for them. Muck them to death and hell. God muck Pablo. Pablo is all of them. (369–70)

In the manuscript, this entire section is an insert into the chapter. During the first draft, before any revision, Hemingway may have felt that he could not adequately express the full force of Jordan's anger with a restricted word choice. However, in revision he realized the cumulative effect of a string of "mucks." After the first few "mucks," the reader's mind registers the intended "fuck." This one-letter alteration allowed Hemingway to avoid suppression and maintain the appropriate diction level. All of the profane language revisions have something in common: they all retain the meaning of the original or intended word but cannot be deemed unprintable by the editors.

These revisions also testify to the many obstacles Hemingway needed to overcome in order to present realistically the language of people in war. There still remain many other revision types in the manuscript of *For Whom the Bell Tolls* that deserve attention. The revisions isolated in this study, those concerned with the depiction of sexuality and "indecent" language, show the author crafting a realistic presentation of the human experience in war despite the limiting cultural standards of the period. In the process, Hemingway subverted these censoring restrictions and avoided any "emasculation" of his novel.

WORKS CITED

Baker, Carlos. *Ernest Hemingway: A Life Story.* NY: Scribner's, 1969.
———, ed. *Hemingway: The Writer as Artist.* 4th ed. Princeton: Princeton UP, 1972.
Barea, Arturo. "Not Spain but Hemingway." *Hemingway and His Critics.* Ed. Carlos Baker. NY: Hill and Wang, 1961. 202–12.

Benson, Frederick R. *Writers in Arms: The Literary Impact of the Spanish Civil War.* NY: New York UP, 1967.

Berg, A. Scott. *Max Perkins: Editor of Genius.* NY: Dutton, 1978.

Grebstein, Sheldon Norman. *Hemingway's Craft.* Carbondale: Southern Illinois UP, 1973.

Hemingway, Ernest. *Ernest Hemingway: Selected Letters, 1917–1961.* Ed. Carlos Baker. NY: Scribner's, 1981.

————. *A Farewell to Arms.* 1929. NY: Scribner's, 1957.

————. *For Whom the Bell Tolls.* First Scribner Classic/Collier Edition. NY: Macmillan, 1987.

————. "For Whom The Bell Tolls." Manuscript. John F. Kennedy Library.

————. *The Sun Also Rises.* 1926. NY: Scribner's, 1954.

Hoyt, Olga G., and Edwin P. Hoyt. *Censorship in America.* NY: Seabury Press, 1970.

Jackson, Gabriel. *A Concise History of the Spanish Civil War.* London: Thomas and Hudson, 1974.

Josephs, Allen. "Hemingway's Poor Spanish: Chauvinism and Loss of Credibility in *For Whom the Bell Tolls.*" *Hemingway: A Revaluation.* Ed. Donald R. Noble. Troy, NY: Whitston, 1983. 205–23.

Plimpton, George. "An Interview with Ernest Hemingway." *Hemingway and His Critics.* Ed. Carlos Baker. NY: Hill and Wang, 1961. 19–37.

Reynolds, Michael S. *Hemingway's First War: The Making of "A Farewell to Arms."* Princeton: Princeton UP, 1976.

Svoboda, Frederic Joseph. *Hemingway and "The Sun Also Rises": The Crafting of a Style.* Lawrence: UP of Kansas, 1983.

Thomas, Hugh. *The Spanish Civil War.* NY: Harper and Row, 1961.

Watson, William Braasch, ed. "Hemingway's Spanish Civil War Dispatches." *Hemingway Review* 7.2 (Spring 1988): 4–92.

7   Hemingway's Code: The Spanish Civil War and World Power

Charles Molesworth

It is hard to argue with W. H. Auden's assessment of the 1930s as a "low dishonest decade." The Spanish Civil War represented, in many of its aspects, some of the lowest forms of dishonesty, but it continues as well to symbolize, at least for the Left, qualities of heroic commitment and noble ideals. Ernest Hemingway's role in the war epitomizes those ideals, even as the grimmer truth about his experience faces up to some of the dishonesty.

A curious parallel obtains between Hemingway's code, the center of his vision as a novelist, and the peculiar blend of high ideals and low behavior he saw in the Civil War and embodied in *For Whom the Bell Tolls*. I would describe the code in these summary terms: the hero must not be afraid to die or to kill, but he must never delight in killing nor mistake it for anything but what it is. The dialectical balance between a rejection of fear and an equally fierce rejection of blood lust or savagery is most notoriously symbolized, of course, by the bullfight.

In the Civil War this emotional and moral balance can be applied; there can be a military and even a political version of "grace under pressure." But how can this balance be related to the larger issues raised by the Spanish conflict? Is there a possible parallel to the entangled international relations of the late 1930s? How, in short, can Robert Jordan's story be made consonant with the historical tale of the rise of fascism and its eventual (but temporary?) elimination? Can the code be applied to the political realm in any truly effective way, without devolving into defeatist individualism?

As I set out the code in a bit more detail, I want to consider, in the light of this code, two questions: why was Hemingway drawn so strongly to the

Republican cause and yet why did he never develop an extended analysis of that cause and its destiny so as to see the many historical complexities it involved?

The code Hemingway developed remains perhaps the most discussed part of the novelist's work. The formulation I offer here is not extraordinary in any sense, but it differs from the consensus version which says that "grace under pressure," an ability to be in difficult situations without succumbing to either panic, enthusiasm or indifference, is the hallmark of the hero. This is, to my mind, an essentially aesthetic model of human agency, and I would offer one that is somewhat more grounded in moral questions. Robert Jordan stands at the nexus of moral quandary; he may be taken as the moral version of Jake Barnes' essentially aesthetic stance. For Barnes, morality is measured only by whether you feel good afterwards, but Jordan must foresee the consequences of his action. The moral dimension of the code highlights much of the fictional writing Hemingway did about the Civil War, namely the play "The Fifth Column," several short stories, and the novel *For Whom the Bell Tolls*. In the newspaper dispatches he wrote from Spain during the war, the aesthetic dimension is more apparent; indeed, those dispatches are chiefly interesting because they show us how the modernist aesthetic would adapt itself to journalism. But to characterize the code sharply we can begin with a scene from the novel, where the hero, Robert Jordan, is talking to an important secondary character, the peasant Republican partisan, Anselmo.

This scene, from chapter 3, establishes Jordan's personal ethos by rooting it in his recall of American Indian customs. It also establishes the character of Anselmo, who is somewhat like the Fool in *King Lear*, apparently ineffectual but the bearer of moral wisdom. Both Anselmo and Jordan vindicate their ethos by placing it in a context of primitivism—"The gypsies believe the bear to be a brother of man." "So do the Indians in America"—a primitivism that always held great appeal to Hemingway. Anselmo tells of how the paw of the slain bear is nailed to a hut in his village, and this in turn leads to a discussion of how killing animals is different from killing men. Anselmo accepts the former, indeed can even include the trophy of the bear's paw among "all of those things [that] gave me pleasure to contemplate." Jordan agrees, but he explicitly says that nobody "except those disturbed in the head" would include killing men among these pleasures. Then, however, he adds the key qualification: "But I feel nothing against it when it is necessary. When it is for the cause." Anselmo himself has killed for the cause, but he plans to seek forgiveness for this "sin," if only self-forgiveness now that he no longer believes in God. What is clearly established here is that there are two categories of living creatures, animals and men. The first can be killed with pleasure, the second can never be. But there is a further dichotomy, for there are two conditions in which men can or can not be killed, in war or in peace. The primitive starkness of this double category will doubtless strike some as reductive, while others will see it as the cornerstone of most moral systems that eliminate a theological sanction. In either case, I believe it is the core of the moral vision in the novel.

But what I want to emphasize about this core vision is the emotional balance or mediation required to maintain it, or rather the emotional pressures entailed in accepting such a vision. The mediation is most artistically complex and interesting when the pressures are greatest, but there are several versions or temperaments for each emotion, and thus several different mediations. Jordan fails to kill an unreliable partisan, Pablo, whose treachery eventually dooms Jordan's mission of dynamiting the bridge as a crucial part of a Republican attack against the Fascists. If Jordan hadn't felt some qualms about killing, he would have executed Pablo, as he himself claims he was willing and able to do. Pilar, the woman who works for the group of partisan guerrillas, has an appetite for killing, but she is in the extenuating circumstance of not being an active full time soldier. Indeed, her account of how her fellow villagers executed the Fascist sympathizers among the village leaders is one of the great set pieces in the novel, and shows how even Pilar became disenchanted with the "pleasures" of the killing that is tolerated in war time. The young woman who becomes Jordan's lover brings into dramatic play her own vengeance, as she has been brutally raped by the Fascists, but eventually her vengeance is modulated by her essential goodness. The only person who takes unstinting pleasure in killing is the commissar, Marty, portrayed by Hemingway as depraved by his insane political purity. (This portrait earned Hemingway the scorn and vilification of the Communists, since Marty had achieved notable military success early in the war.)

In short, everyone in the novel feels a version of the pressures Jordan epitomizes, and everyone mediates them differently. Likewise with all the fictional characters created out of the Civil War context. In the play *The Fifth Column*, Philip, the protagonist (hardly heroic), fails to mediate the pressure as he becomes numbed by his role as executioner of Fascist spies. He taunts himself and his spoiled American mistress with dreams of a sensual paradise free from all conflict and fear, and when he deliberately bursts the bubble of this dream he has no mission or discipline to replace it; he is essentially defeated. In "The Denunciation," the narrator sees to it that an acquaintance, who has become an enemy informer, believes that it was he who had turned him in to the security police rather than a waiter at the cafe. The narrator does this, according to his own account, in order not to disillusion or embitter the informer. The story is cynical, and it operates without any instance of the code at work. Neither the informer nor the narrator faces death in the story, at least not in any way that the narrative itself can visualize. One rather empty gesture "faces" another, for both the denunciation and the ruse that conceals it are done covertly, with a sort of hollow formality. "The Butterfly and the Tank" is a self-reflexive story about a narrator who witnesses a pointless shooting in a cafe and decides to write a story about it. The story he plans to write will illustrate "the misunderstood gaiety coming in contact with the deadly seriousness that is here always." Here the code fails because the shooting victim has no understanding of death and killing, and he lacks the fear that he should have to struggle against in order to make the balance work.

In these stories Hemingway often deals with the subjects of betrayal and loyalty, just as he did in *For Whom the Bell Tolls* where indeed the question of Pablo's loyalty is one of the sustaining elements of suspense in the narrative. Civil War, in real life terms, turns on such issues, of course, and this was especially true in the case of Spain. The very way in which this one country became the focus of international tensions remains central to the meaning of the War, and determines that such meaning will always involve questions of ulteriority. Not only were Russia and Germany and Italy all involved for ulterior motives, but the left sectarianism that so viciously split over the priority of social revolution as opposed to a unified war effort further increased the sense of possible betrayal and bad faith. These issues may seem of paramount importance, and Hemingway does treat them, though often not very successfully. His art and his vision are more attuned to questions of individual bravery or cowardice; one often senses that for him the only true betrayal is a betrayal of one's self. But, as I will argue below, such individually conceived dilemmas have to be understood against a larger social, national, or even international frame-work. Hemingway's art does not depend wholly or even chiefly on the manipulation of nationalist "types," but neither is his fiction completely free of such dependence, either. The stories, like the novel, work in part by employing a narrator who is unmistakably American and yet who is not only partisan to Spain but privy to "her" secrets. The stories are also often about people whose destinies are determined by allegiances and identities that they don't fully control or understand.

The narrator of "Under the Ridge," perhaps the most challenging of these stories, is also a writer, and he tells a story of the need to execute deserters and malingerers. Paco, a young boy who has shot himself in the hand to escape further combat, is executed, as is a Frenchman who senses the stupidity of a hopeless attack and walks away from it "with great dignity," only to find his death at the hands of the security police. The police, by the way, are Russian and wear leather coats instead of cloth uniforms, and one soldier, perhaps an anarchist, refers to them as "representatives of tyranny." (This detail alone, by the way, seems enough to correct Edmund Wilson's claim in *The Wound and the Bow* that the Stalinists had taken Hemingway "in tow.") Poised over the impossible demands of military discipline, the story's irony is essentially unresolved, and the narrator-journalist, as he returns to the car that will carry him back to Madrid, sees the body of the executed Frenchman, "lying stretched out there on the slope of the ridge, still wearing his blanket." This final "sight" embodies the futility of death, of course, and the combination of the two executed victims—the dignified Frenchman and the young Paco—suggests only that the implacability of military discipline falls alike on the innocent and the noble.

But the story, unlike, say, Frank O'Connor's "Guests of the Nation," doesn't portray the inhumaneness of the situation with a humane feeling, nor does it suggest that such discipline is justifiable. The story is challenging because it shows the code destroyed at both poles, for neither Paco nor the Frenchman can face death, and the leather-coated police are much too ruthless in the manner in which they execute their victims. At the end of "The Butterfly and the Tank," the slain man's wife kneels over his body and cries out: "Who has done this to thee, Pedro?" The narrator grimly observes that the police "would never be able to tell her even if they had the name of the man who pulled the trigger." The same is true for the Frenchman and Paco in "Under the Ridge," for they, like Pedro, have brought about their own death on the one hand, and on the other they are simply victims of the system that is war, and by extension the existential situation, the "deadly seriousness that is here always." When the dialectical balance falters, Hemingway rather quickly slides from existential irony into nihilism.

Given such recurrent themes in Hemingway's Civil War fiction, we might easily agree with Alfred Kazin's estimation that the novelist operated with a superb art in the service of a minor vision. But we might also want to press harder and pursue an interpretive frame based on the international order against which Hemingway wrote in the later thirties. In its briefest form it might look something like this. Germany and Italy were possessed by blood-lust, enamored of death, and bent upon it on a large scale, as their use of aerial bombardment, and mechanized battle generally, amply demonstrated. France and England were temporizing, afraid to lose the stability envisioned in Chamberlain's "Four Power Pact"

(France and England combined with Germany and Italy). The Soviets were pursuing their own designs, hoping to draw England and France into the Civil War, thereby preoccupying Germany with its Western front while draining resources from its Eastern border with the Soviet Union. (Germany, of course, was skillfully allowing Italy to bear the larger share of support for Franco while it went on steadily preparing for both the Eastern and Western fronts.) This left, of course, Spain herself. The "cause" was the belief that Fascism, and its love of death, could be beaten. Hemingway, I feel certain, had little or no real stake in the Spanish social revolution as such. But the Civil War was urgent, and after the war Spain could start again to solve its problems, its tumultuous and destructive "progress" toward parliamentary democracy. But this would happen only after it had both faced its own death and refused to become enamored of it.

In *Death in the Afternoon* Hemingway argued that the artist should see the whole world, and "then any part you make will represent the whole, if it's made truly." I think that an "allegorical" reading of the international order, in such a way as to bring it in line with Robert Jordan's fate and Hemingway's code, is convincing. But obviously many will not think so. Let me try to make some other connections in the light of this reading. The single most important piece of nonfiction prose Hemingway wrote about the Spanish conflict is "The Writer and War." It was actually a speech Hemingway gave at a Writers' Congress held in New York City in 1937. Vintage Hemingway, this speech is full of his clipped rhetoric, caught in the pose of no-nonsense feeling, a feeling equally at work on the reader's presumed indifference and the author's barely concealed passion. "There is only one form of government that cannot produce good writers, and that system is fascism," he avers, and in place of any analysis he simply continues, "For fascism is a lie told by bullies. A writer who will not lie cannot live or work under fascism." Fascism is a "bloody history of murder"; it lacks the necessary part of the balance that would see death as fearsome and regrettable, no matter how necessary or justified. And while war and its killing are bad, there are worse things:

When men fight for the freedom of their country against a foreign invasion, and when these men are your friends, some new friends and some of long standing, and you know how they were attacked and how they fought, at first almost unarmed, you learn, watching them live and fight and die, that there are worse things than wars. Cowardice is worse, treachery is worse, and simple selfishness is worse.

Here the code is spelt out a bit, for those last three "sins" I would take to be ways in which the balance is not kept. Further, while Hemingway makes it apparent that Fascists are treacherous and murderers; he doesn't make it clear that they are cowards or selfish.

Now the context of the speech didn't allow Hemingway to indulge in emotional finger pointing or, with the exception of the Germans and Italians, in name calling. He was in America to raise funds for the Spanish Republicans. This was one of the few public addresses he ever gave, and the emotions he had restrained so aesthetically in his journalistic dispatches here came flowing undilutedly. But who are those guilty of cowardice and selfishness? Hemingway doesn't say, but he implies that they are the international writers and journalists of the so-called free press and those who are still trying to be objective and balanced about the war. Such putative balance might indeed mask an unwillingness to face the harder tasks.

Certainly it is more comfortable [for writers] to spend their time disputing learnedly on points of doctrine. And there will always be new schisms and new fallings off and marvelous exotic doctrines and romantic lost leaders, for those who do not want to work at what they profess to believe in, but only to discuss and maintain positions, skillfully chosen positions with no risk involved in holding them. Positions to be held by the typewriter and consolidated with the fountain pen.

The reference here, I believe, is both to fellow journalists and writers, some of whom might well have been in the audience as Hemingway spoke, and only slightly more abstractly, to those who held the position on non-intervention as developed by the British and the French. Both Leon Blum's Socialist government in France and Chamberlain's foreign ministry in England had little or no logic in their position. The English stayed out of the conflict because they feared Bolsheviks; the French feared Germany's enmity and the possible leftist seizure of France's investment in Algeria and Morocco. The two Western powers engaged in considerable skullduggery to maintain their "skillfully chosen positions," and were definitely faced "with no risk . . . in holding them."

Hemingway, despite the nearly corrosive moralizing of this speech, might have felt some hope in America's possible role in settling the war. He worked long and hard to produce a propaganda film, *The Spanish Earth*, and was able to show it to President Roosevelt. Furthermore, he raised enough money to buy twelve ambulances, but because of America's neutrality, they were never delivered. He solicited funds from the millionaires he went deep-sea fishing with, and from celebrities in Hollywood. He returned to Spain several times during the War, to serve as a journalist for the North American Newspaper Alliance, but when he left for the last time during the war, in November, 1938, he clearly knew the cause was doomed.

By this time the Republicans were in retreat from the Ebro, and Barcelona was to fall within weeks. In the meantime, Chamberlain had signed the Munich Agreement and the Russian Communists were thoroughly manipulating the last stages of the Republican government. Additionally, the suppression of the P.O.U.M., which so distressfully enlightened Orwell, was more than a year past and the Communists had effectively turned the war effort into something like a police state, jailing and executing, and often torturing, other leftist leaders. His repeated returns to Spain throughout 1937 and 1938 allowed Hemingway to see the gradual dissolution and betrayal—active and passive—of the Republican cause. The 1937 speech and the film showing with Roosevelt in attendance may be seen as the beginning of the end. Certainly, the rhetoric of the speech can be read as balanced between a deep commitment to the cause and a nearly shrill, nearly accusatory, last call for help.

"Fascism is a lie told by bullies." If we are to answer why Hemingway was drawn to the Republican cause, not only will we have to remember his deep love for the myth of the Spanish national character, but also this blunt definition of fascism. Hemingway saw war as a series of ugly necessities, but he had an inner sense that there was nevertheless a limit to the sort of lies and bullying permissible during wartime. Behind his agonized disappointment at the failure of the Republican cause lay these feelings of love for a national character and a personal standard of honesty. The Spanish character was marked for Hemingway by a simple honesty and a tragic sense of fate, combined with a capacity for tenderness that never allowed itself the rigidities of ideology or intimidation. For Hemingway, the Spanish character was based on everything that Fascism was not: a temperament capable of tenderness that was nevertheless strengthened by an unrelenting honesty.

But this is not the whole story. Hemingway, after all, had a novelist's eye for the complexities of characters and their emotional entanglements. And there is an especially important passage in chapter 31 of his novel where he speaks about the Spanish character through Robert Jordan. Jordan has just heard Maria tell of the brutal savagery of the Fascists who raped her, and he goes to sleep "pleased there would be killing in the morning." True to the code, however, he adds the line, "But I must not take any of it personally." He then launches into a meditation, part history, part psychology, part politics. I quote at length to convey the complexity of the meditation, but also because some critics stop at the line "There is no finer and no worse people in the world." I would suggest this is true of any national group (which is the main reason nationalism is so gripping and so blinding an idea), but I would also call attention to the politics at the end of the passage. But it begins with Jordan wondering how he can keep the balance and not take the killing personally:

Though how can I keep from it? I know that we did dreadful things to them too. But it was because we were uneducated and knew no better. But they did that on purpose and deliberately. Those who did that are the last flowering of what their education has produced. Those are the flowers of Spanish chivalry. What a people they have been. What sons of bitches from Cortez, Pizarro, Mendez de Avila all down through Enrique Lister to Pablo. And what wonderful people. There is no finer and no worse people in the world. No kinder people and no crueler. And who understands them? Not me, because if I did I would forgive it all. To understand is to forgive. That's not true. Forgiveness has been exaggerated. Forgiveness is a Christian idea and Spain has never been a Christian country. It has always had its own special idol worship within the Church. *Otra Virgen mas.* I suppose that was why they had to destroy the virgins of their enemies. Surely it was deeper with them, with the Spanish religion fanatics, than it was with the people. The people had grown away from the Church because the Church was in the government and the government had always been rotten. This was the only country that the reformation never reached. They were paying for the Inquisition now, all right.

The reversion to primitive feeling here as an explanation, and *almost* a justification, does not satisfy political theorists in the tradition of the Enlightenment. By calling on a "special idol worship," Hemingway side-steps the social and political complexities of Spanish history as it moved from monarchism through Rivera's dictatorship and into a very unstable parliamentarianism in the space of a generation or two. In fact we might correct this and say that the reformation did reach Spain, but too late and in conjunction with too many other, conflicting ideologies. But the part about the Church is very accurate, and the early remark about the Fascists and the far right who acted "on purpose and deliberately" in their cruelty both complicates and supports the accuracy. In a transcendent sense brutality by the powerful and brutality by the weak are equal, and equally dehumanizing and politically wrong. But this transcendent truth ignores the key fact that after its truth is enunciated there still remains the discrepancy between the powerful and the weak.

Such discrepancy is what scuttles the argument of someone like Ronald Radosh, who writes in the October 1986 *New Criterion* about how left intellectuals must be disabused of their continuing but benighted reading of the Republican "cause" as idealistic and noble. One could easily read Radosh and assume that the entire Republican undertaking was nothing but a Comintern plot to further Soviet interests. I disagree with Radosh's contention that left intellectuals fail to see that Russian motives and involvement were treacherous in the extreme. The left contends that there is a cause *despite* the Soviet betrayals. I for one am content to have Radosh rub my nose in Soviet treachery, but what then is to be said? Given the falseness of the propaganda, given the "excesses" of Spender, Auden and others, given the Moscow trials and the Hitler-Stalin pact and the pitiful chicanery of Negrin, still there were Spanish landlords and prelates and army officers who ran the country and bled the peasants and capitulated to the capitalist industrial interests. Is the solution to *that* Reaganomics or neoconservatism? Of course not, and indeed, though his notorious historical shallowness has been amply on display, in regards to Spain, Reagan has suggested that the International Brigades fought on the wrong side! Would Radosh suggest the volunteers or the American government itself should have fought to protect the rights of Spanish padrones and prelates?

To be reductive for a moment, I think there were three possible stands for an American faced with the Civil War. He or she could support Franco; support the Republicans; or take the stand of a defeatist individualism. (I am assuming that non-intervention is not in fact a principled position, but basically a refusal to take a position.) Hemingway began with the second position and moved toward the third. Such movement toward the third position is generated by the sort of critical support of the second position as it realizes that the cause is badly, even hopelessly compromised by Russian treachery. Hemingway's novel is poised between the second and third position, and this is what made it attractive to many liberal intellectuals at the time.

Such poise reverberates through the novel, not only in the character of Jordan but in the spectrum of loyalties and betrayals that is represented by the other characters as well. *For Whom the Bell Tolls* may be a flawed novel—the character of Maria is weak and drawn from sexist stereotypes, that of Pablo insufficiently motivated, the lyrical passages are not fully integrated and make some of the philosophizing sound jejune, and so forth—but as a reflection of the political forces at work it remains a fairly compelling statement. When Lionel Trilling speaks of the "essential inner dullness" of Jordan, and says his fate "is determined by the moral and political contradictions of the historical situation, but he himself explicitly refuses to recognize these contradictions, he stands apart from them," I can only demur from the aesthetic and political judgment. Jordan is not always dramatically "right" but he isn't dull, and he certainly recognizes the contradictions; he doesn't, however, *accept* them.

On the other side of the ledger there is Alvah Bessie, writing about the novel in *New Masses*, who claims that "In the widest sense [the Republican] cause is actually *irrelevant* to the narrative" (his emphasis). Bessie goes on to argue that Hemingway has "yet to expand his personality as a novelist to embrace the truths of other people, everywhere." We can hear in this the echoes of proletcult aesthetics and the Stalinist line, for Bessie adds that the Soviet "role was clear and well-defined, and so honest as to command the entire respect and adherence of the Spanish people." Both Bessie and Trilling fail to see the nature of Jordan's, and Hemingway's, commitment to the Spanish people and the "Cause," for they fail to see key elements in the novel's balance and poise.

Another way to measure the poise of the novel is to observe what happens when a reader doesn't perceive the intent of the balance it attempts to achieve. A rather egregious example of this is the argument advanced by Edwin Berry Burgum in "The Psychology of the Lost Generation." Burgum says that Hemingway's bohemian background led him into a perverse enjoyment "of the division between the laxity of the anarchist temperament" and the Communists' "hysterical insistence upon action and obedience." One would think no one but the most thorough-going Fascist would enjoy this divisiveness, especially since by most accounts it was one of the main reasons the Republicans failed militarily. But Burgum is consistent, for he actually argues that not only is the novel "sympathetic to fascism" but "the psychology of Robert Jordan is . . . strangely enough that typical of the authoritarianism of fascism." The critic arrives at this strange assessment by seeing Jordan's behavior during his mission as based on "a mystical theory that any sacrifice of life that at all hinders the enemy . . . must promote the good cause merely because it has behind it his whole-hearted enthusiasm as a subjective potential." Such a view turns Jordan into a wild-eyed fanatic, and it results either from a poor comprehension of the political complexities that were at stake or an inability to hold conflicting psychological pressures in view simultaneously.

In this Burgum resembles Radosh, for both identify the clearly pained and equivocal adherence to the Republican cause as somehow equivalent to the most brutal forms of totalitarianism. Such arguments are, to my mind, insulting to the altruistic and truly democratic ideals of the Spanish left. One can only go back to what now may seem a cliché, but what remains an irreducible and unignorable truth: for a number of years

Spanish men and women and some international volunteers were being shot at and killed by men and guns in the service of Mussolini and Hitler, while the "western democracies" did nothing.

Part of Burgum's argument is that Hemingway identifies with Robert Jordan as he does with few of his other fictional creations. Yes and no. Clearly there is much of Hemingway in Jordan, but we also know there is in Jordan the experience of Robert Merriman, an International Brigade volunteer, and that there is also much of Hemingway's love of Spain in the other characters in the book. Here the aesthetics and sensibility of the novelist as they bear upon the development and posture of his main character come most complexly into play. Hemingway has Jordan at one point debate politics with himself, and Jordan admits that it is "for others" to deal with the question of a planned society; he is a writer and a teacher of Spanish and he feels, contradictorily, that "all people should be left alone and you should interfere with no one." Such individualism is almost bound to turn defeatist. As Jordan goes on with his self-debate, he has this to say:

What were his politics then? He had none now, he told himself. But do not tell any one else that, he thought. Don't ever admit that. And what are you going to do afterwards? I am going back and earn my living teaching Spanish as before, and I am going to write a true book. I'll bet, he said. I'll bet that will be easy.

He would have to talk to Pablo about politics. It would certainly be interesting to see what his political development had been. The classical move from left to right, probably; like old Lerroux. Pablo was quite a lot like Lerroux. Prieto was as bad. Pablo and Prieto had about an equal faith in the ultimate victory. They all had the politics of horse thieves. He believed in the Republic as a form of government but the Republic would have to get rid of all of that bunch of horse thieves that brought it to the pass it was in when the rebellion started. Was there ever a people whose leaders were as truly their enemies as this one?

Prieto was a complex figure in the war, for he originally set up the S.I.M., a security force aimed at spies but concentrating on anarchists and Trotskyists, since it was essentially a Soviet organization. But he also resisted Soviet pressure in other areas; for example, he removed several Soviet-backed commissars from office and was himself eventually removed from office by Communist pressure when he became a demoralizing influence on the other cabinet members. His sense of inevitable defeat was probably fostered by his experience as minister of national defense. The events of Hemingway's novels are based on the battle of Guadarrama, which took place on March 31, 1937. A total failure, this battle was lost in part by the failure of the air force, largely staffed by Russians, to support the infantry. Thus Jordan's reference to Prieto and his equating him with Pablo is ambiguous, for in March of 1937 Prieto was probably a believer in "total victory," at least outwardly. But of course Pablo is the main voice of the defeatist politics in the novel. Hemingway, writing the book in 1939, may be taking advantage of hindsight and creating a sarcastic and cynical equation. (Lerroux was a minister who in 1934 invited the proto-fascist C.E.D.A. to join the government and who revoked much of the leftist legislation enacted in 1931–33.)

What is nevertheless established by Jordan's reflections, however, is that he has a reasoned position based on his anarchist impulses and his generally cynical reading of other people's political struggles and complexities (as when he says "the classical move from left to right, probably"). And we hear in his wry assertion "I bet that will be easy" a definite understanding of how hard it will be to tell the truth about such political complexities. Still, for all the ambiguous and cynical insights and dismissals, Jordan believes in the Republic and feels "that if it were destroyed life would be unbearable for all those people who believed in it." This is, I would suggest, the central point of the moral balance that Jordan achieves in and through the code that the novel dramatizes.

While he was writing *For Whom the Bell Tolls* Hemingway was also writing a preface to another man's novel. He had met Gustav Regler during the war in Spain, and Regler was later briefly imprisoned in a French concentration camp. Hemingway felt deeply about Regler and used the preface to ask the United States to grant him political asylum. Regler's novel, *The Great Crusade*, was seen as a book that would "give those people who are opposed to Fascism hope." But Hemingway's own novel was not written in such a hopeful vein, and indeed when he came to write the preface for Regler, he began with a very grim paragraph:

The Spanish civil war was really lost, of course, when the Fascists took Irun in the late summer of 1936. But in a war you can never admit, even to yourself, that it is lost. Because when you will admit it is lost you are beaten. The one who being beaten refuses to admit it and fights on the longest wins in all finish fights; unless of course he is killed, starved out, deprived of weapons or betrayed. All of these things happened to the Spanish people. They were killed in vast numbers, starved out, deprived of weapons and betrayed.

We can hear in the tone and undertones of this passage the feeling that would animate much of *For Whom the Bell Tolls*. The Civil War was to be a "finish fight"; about that Hemingway had absolutely no doubt. And the last two verbs of the final sentence here must apply, respectively, to the Western democracies and the Soviet Union. What I think Hemingway tried to do in his novel is to combine some of Regler's hopefulness and yet tell truly his own sense of the war. We can feel the tension required in, and consequent upon, keeping the sort of dialectical balance implicit in a sentence such as "in a war you can never admit, even to yourself, that it is lost." In a sense Hemingway created Robert Jordan so he could come to terms with what he couldn't admit, even to himself.

When he looked back on his time in Spain, Hemingway, according to A. E. Hotchner, felt that the spring of 1937 was the happiest period of his life. This period was also the beginning of a series of offensives that included Guadarrama as well as Teruel, Huesca, and Brunete, all of which ended badly for the Republicans. By describing that spring as his happiest period when he reminisced with Hotchner, and seeing it in *For Whom the Bell Tolls* as the context for Jordan's growing defeatism, Hemingway is perhaps creating a paradoxical point in time to reflect the dialectical balance of his emotional code. Lawrence Broer, in *Hemingway's Spanish Tragedy* (1973), suggests that the novel shows through the destiny of Jordan a growing fatalism on Hemingway's part, a fatalism fed by a sense that a life based on communal values is impossible. Broer further argues that the novel shows Hemingway's disillusion with the Spanish people, whom he came to see as cursed by provincialism and riddled with "emotional and psychological isolation and disunity."

Hemingway was devoted to the Republican cause not out of any explicit or complicated political stance or argument, but rather out of a cultural and empathetically nationalistic identification with the Spanish people. Never blind to the extent and consequences of Russia's involvement and ulterior motives, he nevertheless knew that the guns in the hands of his friends were supplied by the Soviet Union. He also saw that the divisions among the various left factions would prevent the war from being efficiently fought. However, he did not, apparently, see that these factions were the expression of the peculiar social divisions and historical contradictions of the Spanish experience in the first three decades of this century. Instead, he tended to look for anthropological or characterological explanations for this factionalism. His code as a novelist led him to such explanations, since they are more readily available for narrative exposition in the tradition in which Hemingway wrote. Though he was aware of the larger world order, and the increasing success of the Fascist murderousness that was threatening it, he viewed the Civil War largely in specifically Spanish terms. Robert Jordan takes up his role in that war, not as a stranger or foreigner simply, but as a partisan who is aware that it is, finally, a quarrel much like a family quarrel. It is only because fascism has interceded on one side that other forms of foreign intercession are needed on the other. As the war ended and another larger war was beginning—the most devastating of all wars, which nearly everyone saw as being forecast in Spain in 1936—Hemingway went to Cuba and wrote his novel. Considering its size, it was written very quickly, as if the tears and blood of battle were not yet dry, as if he knew that in some ways they were just beginning to be shed.

8 "The Priest Did Not Answer": Hemingway, the Church, the Party, and *For Whom the Bell Tolls*

H. R. Stoneback

> Is it [the Party] the newest and most necessary religion? . . . To hell with the Church when it becomes a State and the hell with the State when it becomes a church.
> —Hemingway to Dos Passos, 14 Oct. 1932, *Selected Letters* 375.

Hemingway biography has generally assumed that once Hemingway embraced the cause of Republican Spain his stance could be described as anti-church, due to the alliance of the Spanish Church with the Fascists (i.e., the Falangists and Traditionalists), and pro-Party, insofar as the Communists offered the best discipline for the successful conduct of the anti-Fascist war. Much of this is well documented in Hemingway's journalistic and straightforwardly propagandistic writing during the Spanish Civil War. Yet there are biographical questions, certain crucial paradoxes, involved in Hemingway's love of Spain that have been completely ignored or, at best, insufficiently examined.

First, the Spain that Hemingway loved best was not Republican Spain; the "real old stuff," the unspoiled Spain with which he was infatuated from 1923 on, was a traditional world, a Catholic society virtually untouched by Reformation and revolution. Second, his work, from 1923 until 1937, months after the Civil War was in progress, evinces at most minor concern with Spanish politics, with Republicanism, with the dictatorship of Primo de Rivera in the 1920s, with the abdication (more precisely, exile) of King Alphonso, with the establishment of the Second Republic in 1931, and so forth.

Third, Hemingway's Catholicism, which is anything but nominal (the favorite dismissive term of biographers and critics), is in some compelling sense bound up with his love of Spain. Yet he never addresses, for example, the anti-clerical rage that was a prominent feature of Spanish Liberalism and Republicanism from the early 1800s, and which grew in intensity until leftist programmatic hatred of the Church culminated first, in May 1931, when mobs burned churches in Madrid, Valencia and throughout southern Spain, and again, with greater fury, after the Popular Front took power in 1936 when hundreds of churches were burned and thousands of priests were murdered.

Finally, Hemingway's love of Spain is also bound up, of course, with the world of *toreo*, and yet Republican factions were primarily responsible for the movement to abolish the bullfight. Hemingway mentions this briefly but ominously in the penultimate chapter of *Death in the Afternoon*.

These four rubrics suggest the depth and complexity of Hemingway's relationship with Spain, with the tragic situation of the 1930s and the personal reverberations for Hemingway of that tragedy. Yet Hemingway biography and criticism has generally overlooked or oversimplified these matters; for the most part, commentary on Hemingway's political involvement with Republican Spain ignores his profound connections with traditional Spain and rests content with the facile assertion that his embrace of Republican Spain, of the collective anti-Fascist struggle, reflects what most commentators are pleased to regard as his awakening social consciousness.

I would suggest, however, that these matters contained profoundly troubling strains of bad faith for Hemingway, perhaps so troublesome that he carefully avoided examining his conscience on these matters and was somewhat relieved when he could convince himself, if he ever truly did, that the Republican cause was purely and cleanly an anti-Fascist struggle that he could embrace wholeheartedly from 1937 until the end of the Civil War.

One index to Hemingway's unspoken scrupulosity—his case of scruples—concerning all these questions may be found in certain evidence suggesting that Hemingway was far more deeply involved in specifically Communist propaganda than has been generally realized, indeed more precisely engaged in the work of the Party than he himself realized.[1] Moreover, the irreconcilable tensions in the very fabric of Spanish life were made even darker and more intractable for Hemingway by the chaos in his personal life: the breakup of his Catholic marriage with Pauline, the affair with Martha Gellhorn, and his uneasy relationship with his Church, his Catholic faith. One major thrust of this essay is to suggest that

Hemingway did not truly deal with any of this, anywhere, except in the crucible of his art, in the composition of *For Whom the Bell Tolls.*

> Now that [the Spanish Civil War] was over, he had reverted to being a writer—not a Catholic writer or a Party writer or even an American writer, but only a writer trying to tell the truth as he had personally learned it.
> —Carlos Baker 346.

By the fall of 1938, with the final Republican defeat not far off, Hemingway was disenchanted with the "carnival of treachery and rotten-ness" in Spain, was experiencing, as Carlos Baker observes, "a change in his attitude towards Spain itself."[2] And he was thinking about getting to work on his new novel, in which he would try to tell the truth of the Spanish tragedy, not as a Catholic writer, not as a Party writer, but as an artist profoundly engaged by the tragic complexity of Spain and by his own deep participation in that tragedy.

At the same time that he conceived the character of Robert Jordan, who accepted the discipline of the Party for the duration of the war, Hemingway himself relinquished that discipline, abandoned his role as propagandist for the Republican cause; also, at this time, he wrote (to his mother-in-law) that the "only way he could run his life decently was to accept the discipline of the Church" (Baker 333). Yet both disciplines, both the Party's role and the Church's role in the Spanish conflict, continued to trouble him deeply.

How, then, does Hemingway deal with these questions in *For Whom the Bell Tolls?* It is an immensely complicated affair; it seems necessary here to insist that the Church-Party conflict, the Church-Party analogies, and the imagery and resonance that issue from them, constitute a principal theme of the novel. This theme has been neglected by most observers, perhaps because commentators have had an insufficient sense of Hemingway's very personal and very Catholic anguish over the Spanish situation. Biographical awareness illuminates the question; but biograph-ical awareness need not lead to the kind of biographical criticism that violates certain critical tenets or avoids close reading of the text. For in fact the Catholic matter shapes both the texture and the deep form of the novel.

For example, Jordan identifies—in a typical passage— the "party line" as that "so mutable substitute for the apostles' creed" (164). And there are his extensive reflections on the "puritanical, religious communism" of the International Brigade, where "it was like being a member of a religious order" (234–35). He compares this feeling with "the feeling you expected to have and did not have when you made your first communion" and insists that it is as authentic as the feeling one has at Chartres cathedral. In this political novitiate, this "naive . . . state of grace" (237), the cynicism at Gaylord's, the Communist headquarters, seems thoroughly corrupt. The point here, briefly stated, is that the imagery that drives Jordan's meditations on the Party is insistently the language of the Church.

Another case in point is the role of prayer in the novel. The Republic, of course, had desecrated and closed many of the churches and passed statutes forbidding religious observance and public worship. As Pilar says, they have abolished God. It is certainly striking, then, that in a novel concerned with characters who are loyal to a government that has officially abolished God there is more praying than in most other Hemingway novels: Anselmo prays, Joaquín prays, Maria prays, Primitivo prays, even Pablo prays, and, to be sure, the Carlist Lieutenant Berrendo prays.

What all this praying suggests—especially when juxtaposed with, let us say, the pathetic and phony Sovietized media-saint La Pasionaria, who is regarded with withering contempt in Hemingway's narrative—is that the revolutionary veneer is very thin and the legislated death of God is an empty, desperate gesture. How does one pray to such a "saint of the people" as La Pasionaria? Perhaps, as the novel suggests, one contacts such a "saint" by calling long distance, calling Moscow. In any case, Joaquín, who invokes La Pasionaria and parrots her party-line rhetoric, shifts easily and naturally—when he requires some semblance of grace under pressure—to his Hail Marys (309, 321). Indeed, as Pilar puts it, "there probably still is God after all, although we have abolished Him" (88). Spain may be divided against itself, there may be two Spains—or more than two—but all of Spain continues to pray.

However, those hated foreigners who come to Spain to intervene on all sides do not pray, do not participate deeply in the Spanish litany. Here it may be useful to remember a familiar rubric in Hemingway's Spanish Civil War fiction, to recall, for example, the Extremaduran in "Under the Ridge" who hates all foreigners, has "no illusions" about them, and rejects communion with them. Paramount among such foreigners, it might be argued, is Robert Jordan who, for much of the novel, clings to his thin, dogmatic, twentieth-century version of reason, and struggles to continue to regard all forms of superstition and mystery as ignorance. But what the novel shows is far more than what Robert Jordan knows.

Yet even Jordan learns. Only when he has discovered love with Maria, when he has been initiated into "La Gloria" (380) and understood that such love and glory, such oneness is the same thing that is in San Juan de la

Cruz, when he realizes that it is ignorant to deny the mystery, the glory, only then, perhaps, has he learned to pray, to live in the permanent state of prayer of a Saint John of the Cross.

It may be, then, that Hemingway's design is to show most of the Spanish characters—and Jordan with them—moving toward a reclamation and a deeper acknowledgement of the very mystery that the Republic, and especially the Party with its fundamental, festering secular rage, had attempted to eradicate through revolutionary violence and legislation.

Another example of the ways in which the novel is constructed upon the foundations of the Church may be found in the formation of—in the very naming of—certain characters. El Sordo, whose real name is Santiago, is probably named after another distinguished Spanish horseman, St. James or Santiago, the patron saint of Spain, who in his military manifestation as Santiago Matamoros was said to appear on horseback in battle to rally the Spanish soldiers against the invading Moors, just as Santiago/El Sordo fights against the invading Moorish armies of Franco. Nor is it coincidental that Santiago/El Sordo dies in the "heart of the thunder" (322) under the attacking planes, for Santiago/St. James was, with St. John, one of the Boanerges, the "sons of thunder."

Even more obvious—yet, it seems, unnoticed by commentators—is Hemingway's secular reincarnation of Pilar, that is, Nuestra Señora del Pilar, the Virgin Patroness of Spain. As the records state, the principal miracle associated with Santiago's presence in Spain was the apparition of the Virgin Mary, standing on a stone pillar in Zaragoza. Around this pillar grew one of the most venerated shrines in Spain and, eventually, the pilgrimage cathedral of Nuestra Señora del Pilar and the famous Pilar Festivals, with processions and bullfights, which Hemingway knew well. There is also, of course, the famous Vièrge du Pilier, the cultic "Black Virgin" of Chartres, the very cathedral that figures significantly in Robert Jordan's thoughts, as in Hemingway's experience.

Thus, with his modern avatar, there is precise resonance in Pilar's first appearance in the novel, where Hemingway describes her as looking "like a model for a granite monument" (30). And, naturally, Pablo first saw her when she was living with a matador in—where else but Zaragoza? In addition, her assumption of the leadership of the guerrilla band corresponds with Pilar's role as patroness of the Spanish Army. That she is a lusty figure, more Hemingway's icon of the ultimate Spanish earth mother than a serene, otherworldly image of the Blessed Virgin Mary, is exactly Hemingway's point, and it is a specifically Catholic point.

Mere quibbles aside, Hemingway's subtle inverse transmutation of the Pilar figure is a tribute to the alchemy of his art and an index of his engagement with traditional Spain. Pilar remains, for this novel as for Catholic Spain, the symbol of maternal intercession, the Mediatrix of All Graces. And Maria, one of those graces, is yet another and more obvious avatar of the Virgin Mary as the Spanish earth, with her hair golden brown like the wheat fields.

Given the prevailing myths concerning Hemingway, and the general ignorance or indifference, disdain or presumption that is the norm in biographical and critical notice of his Catholicism, it would seem necessary to insist that he employed with great exactitude the Catholic patterns and significations in his work. For example, he certainly knew well his saints' lives and made extensive use of that knowledge in his fiction.[3] In *For Whom the Bell Tolls* still other characters, aside from El Sordo, Maria, and Pilar, figure in Hemingway's hagiological investiture of Jordan's comrades, including Andrés, Anselmo, Fernando and even Pablo—especially Pablo.

Andrés, whose principal role in the novel is messenger to the Russians, to the Soviet officers across the line, may owe something to Saint Andrew, who was a missionary to Russia (and patron saint of Russia). Anselmo, that "rare" old "Christian" (287) who thinks a good deal about the expiation or atonement that will be necessary after the war, has certain traits in common with Saint Anselm, including age and dignity and the reputation of a wise and reformist (not radical) commitment to his cause. Most striking, perhaps, is the fact that Saint Anselm's most famous work, *Cur Deus Homo*, was the most important medieval contribution to the theology of atonement, and the expiation motif in the novel centers on Anselmo. Fernando, with his heart full of duty and his mouth full of bureaucracy, may owe something to San Fernando, the successful administrator-king who liberated much of Spain from the Moors.

By far the most complex case, however, the richest figure in this gallery of comrades and saints, is that rare and complicated leader, Pablo, who like Saint Paul (as Saul) is known for his early virulent hatred and persecution of Christians. In Pilar's tale of Pablo's slaughter of the Fascists, the anger, tension, and other conflicted emotions that Pablo feels regarding the priest who goes calmly about his religious duties, his prayers in the face of death, echo Saint Paul's response to the stoning of Saint Stephen, that first Christian martyr who—at the "start of the movement"— prayed for his executioners, an act that led to Saul/Paul's conversion on the road to Damascus.

Whatever we finally make of Pablo's "conversion," there is much conversion imagery associated with him. His expressed regret over all his killing fits the pattern, as does his desertion of his former comrades. After

Saint Paul's conversion and desertion of his former comrades, the Phari-sees, the "strict Jews" planned and "took counsel to kill him" (Acts ix; Metford 193), another action paralleled in the novel. The reader who finds this far-fetched should consult the text of *For Whom the Bell Tolls* with great care, especially such scenes as the one where the guerrilla band is trying to decide what to do with the "converted" Pablo, and they speak of blinding him (219). To make certain that inattentive readers do not miss the Pablo/Saint Paul reverberations, Hemingway makes the pattern very explicit when Pablo comes back just before the blowing of the bridge. Robert Jordan ponders Pablo's return: "I didn't think you had experienced any complete conversion on the road to Tarsus, old Pablo. . . . No. Your coming back was miracle enough. I don't think there will ever be any problem about canonizing you" (392).

Does the fact that Hemingway locates Pablo's conversion on the road to Tarsus, where Paul originally came from, rather than the road to Damascus, reflect error or faulty memory on Hemingway's part? Or is it a deliberate inversion intended to suggest that Pablo has returned to what he once was? Has Pablo reversed directions so many times that the Tarsus-Damascus map no longer signifies? In any case, the Saint Paul/Pablo pattern is the richest, most complicated figure in the overall design. Pablo, Hemingway stresses, is the smartest, the most rare and complicated figure in his cause, just as Saint Paul is often similarly regarded in his. And Pablo assumes the leadership of the embattled remnant to lead them to safety at the end of the novel, just as Saint Paul finally, after much difficulty, asserts his leadership.

The novel's name-structure points finally to Jordan himself, who, as he wires the bridge, thinks "Roll Jordan, Roll!" and compares the creek in the abyss over which he is poised to the Jordan River (438). Thus Hemingway reveals explicitly the significance of his protagonist's patro-nymic, which functions implicitly as a sign from the moment the reader first learns his name. Even his given name may figure in the community-of-saints pattern outlined here as an allusion to Saint Robert of Knaresborough, who lived in a cave, who consorted with thieves and outlaws, and who died and was buried by his cave overlooking his river. Since sainthood and canonization figure in Jordan's meditations, even he may be aware of Saint Robert, and may know that in spite of his flourishing cult and the popularity of his cave as a pilgrimage site he was never officially canonized.

In any case, since the Jordan is the ancient Biblical emblem of the "achievement of purity . . . and of man's last hindrance to his final bless-edness" (Cross 743–44), the novel's iconographic design shows Jordan, through the mediation of Pilar and Maria and all the saints of the Spanish earth, achieving that blessedness. Of course for the devout some of these suggestions may amount to blasphemy; yet, as Hemingway was fond of saying, only Christians can blaspheme. More important, suggestion does not equal identity; it is Hemingway's intention, I think, to assert the oneness of Spanish tradition and contemporary Republican experience, to posit a redeeming myth of an integrated Spain beyond both revolutionary anti-clericalism and Catholic reaction.

By far the most germane and the most extraordinary sequence in the novel is Pilar's tale of "the start of the movement," of the slaughter of the putative Fascists in Pablo's village. It is, hands down, the most vivid, powerful, and memorable section of the entire novel. It has been discussed from a variety of angles, including the Party perspective; it evoked the wrath of the Communists and other leftists and earned Hemingway the stigma of betrayal of the cause. From another perspective, Hemingway was praised for doing the writer's fundamental job honestly, for telling the whole truth. But what truth does the story tell?

We should first consider the fact that Pilar, having just met Robert Jordan, is compelled to tell him this tale, that she is haunted by it, and that she chooses the "forest of boredom" as the setting for the narration. Also, it is the kind of story, Jordan says, that he wants to be able to write if he writes a book about his experiences in Spain; and it is a story that he is able to understand fully only when he has lived through the action of his last three days and nights.

It is my contention (and my experience) that we must read this story many times before we see the point, the true focus of the tale. From one reading, we may come away with an overwhelming sense of the horror of it all, from another, with an image of the pride and defiance of Don Ricardo, or the dignity and unjust death of Don Guillermo, who is seen as a Fascist because of "the religiousness of his wife which he accepted as his own due to his love for her" (117–18). In this one phrase, Hemingway expresses the facile and fatal revolutionary equation of fascism with religion and love, and the reader may well wonder if Jordan's love of Maria and her prayers for and love of Jordan would label them Fascists. Clearly, for some readers and in some versions of the Party line the answer would be yes. In another reading of the tale, we may be most struck by the carefully delineated and differentiated feelings among the Republicans who participate in the slaughter: the bloodthirsty ones, the drunken ones, the appalled ones, the dignified ones, the self-rapt anarchists, and all the others.

Yet the real focus of the tale—and it may take several readings to see this clearly—is the priest: for Pilar in the act of telling, for Pablo in the act of participating, and for Hemingway in the precisely crafted act of writing. As he is the only priest, the only figure of the Church depicted in the novel, the manner in which he is drawn is of great importance. At first we see him "complying with his duties," administering the "necessary sacraments" to the ostensible Fascists who are about to be murdered (104–5). The priest and his duties are mentioned half a dozen times in the first ten pages of the story. Then the vantage point shifts as Pilar moves to the arcade of the Ayuntamiento so that she can look in the window at Pablo and the priest and the condemned villagers, so that Hemingway can zoom in on the real picture, the formal design that centers the tale. Pablo is seen asking the priest which victim is ready to go out, but "the priest went on praying and did not answer him." Again, Pablo asks, but "the priest would not speak to Pablo and acted as though he were not there" (110). This makes Pablo angry. The angle of vision shifts again briefly as Pilar steps away from the window to watch the action in the gauntlet. Then, as the mob grows wilder, she returns to the window.

In a remarkable sequence of incremental repetition, Hemingway foregrounds Pablo and the priest. Pablo keeps saying something to the priest that Pilar cannot hear; for example, in one instance, Pablo says "something to the priest" and "the priest, as before, did not answer him but kept on praying." Again, a few paragraphs later: "I saw Pablo speak to the priest again. . . . But the priest did not answer him but went on praying."

All of the time that Pilar is watching this, the crowd grows more violent and she feels "as though the mob were on [her] back as a devil is on your back in a dream." If the Republic has "abolished" God, the reader may well wonder—indeed Pilar seems to be wondering—have they somehow failed or forgotten to legislate the devil out of existence? Once more, Hemingway writes: "I watched Pablo speak to the priest again and the priest did not answer. Then I saw Pablo unsling his shotgun and he reached over and tapped the priest on the shoulder with it. The priest paid no attention to him" (124).

This sequence of eight repetitions of the core sentence, the core image, in a few pages—four occurrences on one page—culminates with the final flat assertion, just as the door is opened to the bloodthirsty mob: "Pablo said something to the priest but the priest did not answer." Then the mob is on the priest, chopping him in the back with sickles and reaping hooks. Pilar falls away from the window onto the sidewalk that smells of spilled wine and vomit as the mob tramples over her to get inside and complete the murder.

The first question to be asked is this: what has Hemingway emphasized by omission—what is Pablo saying to the priest? Posing this question to students over the years, I have received two basic answers: (1) Pablo is asking the priest to pray for him, seeking pardon for his sins; or (2) Pablo is mocking the priest, asking him if he thinks anybody is listening to his foolish prayers, taunting him with questions about how he, the priest, is going to die. It must be some version of the latter, for in the unlikely event that Pablo were asking the priest to pray for him, the priest would have answered, would have performed his priestly duty as he was doing for the others. There is certainly nothing to the absurd notion—and this has been argued—that Hemingway here depicts a taciturn priest in order to suggest the detached or uncommunicative role of the Church in the Spanish tragedy. Indeed the priest is anything but taciturn, is talking and praying a good deal throughout the entire scene. He simply does not dignify Pablo's taunts with a response, busy as he is with the "necessary sacraments."

The point, then, is that there is nothing the priest can answer to Pablo, for the situation is unanswerable, just as the tragedy of Spain is unanswerable; and there is nothing even the best Republicans—such as Anselmo—can do in the end except pray and long for expiation, for atonement. Moreover, the thrust of the narrative is targeted not as much on what Pablo (or the priest) says as it is on what, in Pilar's eyes, the priest does, how he behaves under pressure. For Pablo, who hates priests worse than he hates Fascists, it is a great disappointment that a Spanish priest does not die with sufficient dignity. But that is Pablo's view of the matter; Pilar, a more reliable observer, thinks he had "much dignity all the time before" and that, "being chased by the mob," he died with "all the dignity that one could have" (127). In any case, even for Pablo, everything, the very essence of Spain, is at stake in the death of a Spanish priest.

It should also be noted that to do one's duty well in an impossible situation and to die with "all the dignity that one could have" exactly describes the position of Robert Jordan. Maybe this priest carries the same burden of significance, bears the same relationship to Jordan as the priest in *A Farewell to Arms* does to Frederic Henry: "He had always known what I did not know," Frederic says of that priest. Such knowledge, such exemplars, are part of Jordan's education, his growing comprehension of the Spanish situation and the human condition.

Thus Pilar's tale told in the "forest of boredom," a setting that functions as a metaphor for a condition of the soul, has many aspects, including the sense of "shame" and "wrongdoing," a spiritual hollowness and a "great feeling of oppression and of bad to come" (127). Pilar, that is, recognizes the great evil done, knows that they have all touched the web of complicity and that the consequences will reverberate infinitely. Pablo, too, recognizes the evil, and, of the people he has killed, he later says: "I would restore them all to life" (209). This may seem to be presented contextually as a sign of his unsoundness, his apostasy as true revolutionary, but it works in other ways, ways that go far beyond the mere Party line on what makes a sound comrade.

Indeed, quite contrary to those observers who for a variety of reasons assert that the famous "No man is an Iland" epigraph is not borne out in the novel, everything in *For Whom the Bell Tolls* conspires to affirm and to take the reader to the heart of Donne's meditation. The epigraph is not at all concerned with some superficial leftist vision of brotherhood, or with a Marxist vision of solidarity, or with some other mystique of collectivism, but with the core Christian vision of the oneness of humankind and the relationship of the individual soul to fate. The Marxist imperatives of history demand the sacrifice of the individual to the cause, but Jordan grows well beyond the thin, dry, rigid asseveration of the Party line. "Christ," he says in the last pages of the novel, "I was learning fast there at the end" (467). John Donne, it may be helpful to recall, was an Anglican priest; and Hemingway was, after all, a profoundly Catholic writer.

The overwhelming dramatic force of Pilar's tale, strategically placed as it is early in the book, far outstripping in its horror any account of Fascist brutality, serves to underline the subsumptive Christian truth of the epigraph: every death diminishes everyone, and the complicity, for all of Spain and for everyone involved, which spreads beyond mere knowing, demands—as that rare Christian Anselmo insists—expiation and penance. It all adds up to a vision quite distinct from the solidarity of comrades in a cause, a vision far removed from the siren song of the if-I-had-a-hammer school of love and brotherhood.

As George Orwell observed in "Arthur Koestler,": "the sin of nearly all left-wingers from 1933 onwards is that they have wanted to be anti-Fascist without being anti-totalitarian" (236). Pilar's tale demonstrates that Hemingway does not commit that sin in *For Whom the Bell Tolls*. The novel's ultimate vision approaches the profound and elusive, tragic and redemptive knowledge that declares the need for expiation in the life of communities and nations, a need that has been promulgated in and by all of the outrageous and paradoxical Tiananmen Squares of our bloody century.[4] In Madrid as in Beijing, in all places and times and most especially in our century so ravaged by politics, our epoch so devastated by statism, murderous dogmatism, and isms of every kind, the free, volitional act of resistance to the gnostic rage of ideology—of the left or of the right—must be linked, as Anselmo and Pilar and Hemingway know, as Solzhenitsyn and certain contemporary Chinese writers know, with communal sacraments of atonement.

For Whom the Bell Tolls, aside from being one of Hemingway's three or four greatest creative achievements (a judgment somewhat reluctantly arrived at by a reader whose preference, whose true love, is for the early Hemingway), is also an important chapter in the biography of Hemingway because it represents the working out of certain spiritual and political dilemmas that gave him great anguish in the late 1930s. I suspect that the spiritual dilemma was, for him, greater than the political dilemma—and I will let that stand as assertion if the evidence presented in this brief essay does not adequately testify to the fact.

Speaking of bullfighters in *Death in the Afternoon*, Hemingway wrote:

At the start of their careers all are as devoutly ritual as altar boys serving a high mass and some always remain so. Others are as cynical as night club proprietors. The devout ones are killed more frequently. The cynical ones are the best companions. But the best of all are the cynical ones when they are still devout; or after; when having been devout, then cynical, they become devout again by cynicism. (59)

At first glance, this formula may suggest the pattern of Robert Jordan's political education. In fact, however, Jordan does not "become devout again by cynicism," but by love. In any case, since Robert Jordan is most distinctly not Ernest Hemingway, I believe the most useful application of this formula here is to the spiritual education of Hemingway, moving from devotion toward cynicism, a cynicism grievously aggravated by the role of the Church and by his own propagandistic role in the Spanish Civil War, as well as by his own simultaneous betrayal and abdication of his Catholic marriage. Finally, "having been devout, then cynical," both politically and spiritually, he becomes, through the act of making *For Whom the Bell Tolls*, "devout again," not so much by cynicism as by a supreme act of the creative imagination which may, after all, be another name for love.

NOTES

1. For example, William Braasch Watson presents evidence elsewhere in this volume that Joris Ivens, the Dutch Communist who recruited Hemingway for the making of *The Spanish Earth*, was in reality serving the Party as Hemingway's "case officer," in the full sense that phrase currently conveys regarding Party and intelligence machinations.

2. In his biography, Baker inaccurately quotes Hemingway's letter to Maxwell Perkins (28 Oct. 1938) as follows: "the carnival of treachery and rottenness on both sides" (334). Baker clearly and specifically applies this passage to the Spanish situation, emphasizing this with his inserted "on both sides." However, it could be argued—as William Braasch Watson pointed out in the discussion session following my paper at the "Hemingway in Idaho" conference—that Hemingway is not specifically referring to Spain in the Perkins letter but to Chamberlain and the Munich Pact of September 30, 1938, and the general European situation of the moment. After careful reexamination of the contexts of the letter (and other Hemingway letters and statements in the fall of 1938), it seems to me that Hemingway *is* referring to Spain as well as to the general European situation on the eve of World War II—the questions are, after all, inseparable—and thus I concur with the prevailing view of Hemingway commentary, which sees the "carnival of treachery and rotten-ness" observation as a reference to the Spanish situation (see, for example, Allen Josephs).

3. For substantial evidence concerning Hemingway's Catholicism and his use of specifically Catholic imagery and patterns of meaning in his fiction, see H. R. Stoneback, "From the rue Saint-Jacques," " 'Lovers' Sonnets,' " and "In the Nominal Country."

4. This passage was written—and the Conference paper on which this essay is based was delivered—hours after the events of early June 1989, in Beijing, events that seemed to forebode civil war in China. Since what was then a timely reference continues to seem an apt touchstone for the concerns of this essay, I have chosen to let the allusion stand.

WORKS CITED

Baker, Carlos. *Ernest Hemingway: A Life Story.* NY: Scribner's, 1969.

Cross, F. L., ed. *The Oxford Dictionary of the Christian Church.* London: Oxford UP, 1957.

Hemingway, Ernest. *Death in the Afternoon.* NY: Scribner's, 1932.

———. Ernest Hemingway: Selected Letters, 1917–1961. NY: Scribner's, 1981.

———. *For Whom the Bell Tolls.* NY: Scribner's, 1940.

Josephs, Allen. "Hemingway's Spanish Civil War Stories, or the Spanish Civil War as Reality." *Hemingway's Neglected Short Fiction.* Ed. Susan F. Beegel. Ann Arbor: UMI Research Press, 1989. 313–27.

Metford, J.C.J. *Dictionary of Christian Lore and Legend.* London: Thames and Hudson, 1983.

Orwell, George. "Arthur Koestler." *The Collected Essays, Journalism and Letters of George Orwell.* Vol. 3. NY: Harcourt, Brace & World, 1968. 234–44.

Stoneback, H. R. "From the rue Saint-Jacques to the Pass of Roland to the 'Unfinished Church on the Edge of the Cliff.' " *Hemingway Review* 6 (Fall 1986): 2–29.

————. "In the Nominal Country of the Bogus: Hemingway's Catholicism and the Biographies." *Hemingway: Essays of Reassessment.* Ed. Frank Scafella. NY: Oxford UP, 1991. 105–40.

————. " 'Lovers' Sonnets Turn'd to Holy Psalms': The Soul's Song of Providence, the Scandal of Suffering, and Love in *A Farewell to Arms.*" *Hemingway Review* 9 (Fall 1989): 33–76.

Watson, William Braasch. "Joris Ivens and the Communists: Bringing Hemingway into the Spanish Civil War." Chapter 4 in this volume.

9 Pilar's Tale: The Myth and the Message

Robert E. Gajdusek

Pilar's tale of the execution of the Fascists in Pablo's town at the start of the revolution is one of the justly famed and celebrated passages of *For Whom the Bell Tolls*. It has drawn praise from numbers of critics, and some have not found the book equal to the achievement of her tale. Even critics on the far left, for whom the book was an indiscretion or an embarrassment, have praised Hemingway for the descriptive power of his prose in that section; and even Robert Jordan—to a degree a projection of Hemingway within his own work—is awed by the tale as told. Jordan, deeply moved by Pilar's description, thinks to himself:

Pilar had made him see it in that town.
   If that woman could only write. He would try to write it and if he had luck and could remember it perhaps he could get it down as she told it. God, how she could tell a story. She's better than Quevedo, he thought. He never wrote the death of any Don Faustino as well as she told it. I wish I could write well enough to write that story, he thought. What we did. Not what the others did to us. He knew enough about that. He knew plenty about that behind the lines. But you had to have known the people before. You had to know what they had been in the village.[1]

Jordan's reflections on the narrative are fascinating in and of themselves, for they well establish some of the fundamental aesthetic beliefs that were part of Hemingway's arsenal as a writer and that in part determined the composition of the tale. His commentary is intriguingly self-reflexive, for in it he stands in for the writer himself who is talking about writing the very passage he has written. Life and art come together in fascinating ways within his thoughts as he thinks of the tale that Pilar has "told" that needs

to be at some future time written, that is, of course, the written story that
we have already read. In this way, the future and the past are joined just
as effectively as the tale has joined the Fascists and the Republicans in
deadly struggle. Indeed, Hemingway has even answered his political
critics before they have begun to assail him: the need is not to know what
we have suffered, which we already too well know and will therefore teach
us little, but rather to know what we have done to *others*, which we may
not sufficiently recognize. He here simultaneously explains, as fully as he
needs to, the aesthetic basis of his vision which, he anticipates, may be
read as betrayal of the left. As Hemingway's protagonist Jordan argues for
this self-transcendence and empathic projection into the "other," he not
only defines Hemingway's own doctrine of composition, which demands
in each of his major works that he cross over to the other side to explore,[2]
but he substantiates his own position at the moment, for he, as a foreigner,
has crossed over from his side of the lines to be in the territory of the
"other."

He also defines the writer's job as making others see what they otherwise cannot see, and he suggests that a writer's craft depends upon the
accuracy of his memory, the authority of his experience, and also a measure
of luck. He even goes on to argue that if Pilar could tell that tale, it is a
tale *he* could not, for to tell it so knowingly one would have to have had
knowledge of those in the village that would depend upon a knowing
"before," a prior exposure to and familiarity with *them*. But we know as
we hear this that Hemingway has created "them," and whatever backgrounds and histories they may be inferred as having had, and that all that
Pilar knows of them is just whatever Hemingway has created to be known
of them. As he goes on to pit Pilar in her tale-telling against the writing of
Quevedo, he demands that we acknowledge the told tale as superior to
Quevedo's art. Therefore Quevedo, existing beyond any telling in the
immortality of his writing, is one of the writers Hemingway, in his writing
of Pilar's tale, has taken on and has been sparring with. He, Hemingway,
has outdone Quevedo.

When Jordan wishes that *he* might be able to write as well the tale that
has just been told, and be the agent of getting Pilar's tale finally written,
we must see that that is precisely the role Hemingway has himself already
taken, and that Pilar's tale exists through and because of his writing/telling
of it. Jordan's wishes are therefore singularly perverse, for the further we
go in the novel, the more we see that Jordan's completion of his great work
in the blowing of the bridge, and sending on those who survive the
experience over the hill, into the future, carrying inside them the memory
of his great achievement and his sacrifice to get it done, *and* the finishing

or completion of the novel become in intricate ways ever more identical until both, the author and his creature, fuse. What remains alive at the end is what he, Jordan, and he, Hemingway, have fashioned to remain alive within those who remember what they have passed through and from where they have come. Therefore Jordan's statement, of his insufficiency to this task now, exists to suggest a yet unfulfilled ideal and a journey yet to be made, but it exists against the amazing artistry he (and we) have just seen performed.

This looking back on Pilar's tale by Jordan is really a way for all Hemingway's readers to look back toward what they have received by virtue of her telling, and to reexamine it; placing Jordan's reflection here is but to follow Hemingway's directive for reconsideration of what has been received: reaction, prepared with hindsight, has become preface to what will now be examined.

Despite the great critical attention Pilar's tale has drawn, it has not yet been adequately judged the intellectual and psychological *tour de force* that it is, for in it Hemingway has written one of his most philosophical (and also Jungian) analyses of war. Pilar's tale is an intricately fashioned, deliberate, and highly particularized study of the psychic art of revolution, in which Hemingway analyzes just what is happening on the deeper mythic and psychic levels of being as a country engages in civil war, the war that he had described in *Green Hills of Africa* as the "best" kind of war for a writer (*Green Hills* 71). There he acknowledges that he "had seen a revolution . . . and a revolution is much the best if you do not become too bigoted" (71). The reader of *For Whom the Bell Tolls* is being shown a revolution by one who has seen one, and Hemingway, in the tale of the beginning of the movement and of the executions in Pablo's town, is revealing in an amazingly Jungian metaphoric structure the deeper psychic, mythic, and historical significances of just such a war.

The tale itself is rather beautifully framed against the mountain journey that the three—Maria, Pilar, and Robert Jordan—are taking in order to meet with El Sordo. It begins with Pilar's imposed suggestion that they rest, as this is phrased against Robert Jordan's imperative sense they should continue. Jordan, who wanted only to stop "at the top," has been forced by Pilar to consider an alternative. He is in a hurry, but Pilar teaches him that "there is much time." Indeed, by the time the bridge is blown, he has learned that one can live a lifetime in three days, and his typically Western zeal for attainment and completion has found moderation: he has learned how to have his cake and eat it too, that the journey need not be a sacrifice to its end, that love and war can coexist, as can time and timelessness.

As they rest by a cold mountain stream and bathe their feet, Pilar educates Jordan, and each detail as she speaks in this setting Hemingway intricately describes, is in fact a preparation for the tale of the executions she will soon tell. Hemingway tells us that it was "almost as though she were lecturing" (98). Pilar importantly insists that "the pine tree makes a forest of boredom," and that "a forest of pine trees is boredom" (97). Arguing for the character, beauty, and individuality of deciduous or cyclical forests, and against the absoluteness of pines, she similarly argues for the plains, declaring herself tired of the mountains, where "there are only two directions. Down and up." This discussion should be significantly heard against the first sentence of the novel where the reader is first given Robert Jordan lying flat on the pine-needled floor of the forest. It will be heard again against the last words of the book as Jordan's heart is described "beating against the pine needle floor of the forest" (471). Both the beginning and the end, his beginning and end for us, and his end for himself, are phrased against fallen pine needles, and one important learning stage on Jordan's final journey is this point of arrest on the mountainside where Pilar's disdain for the pines is opposed to her love of deciduous cycles. Jordan at last at his end will have learned how to accept the absolute *ever*green needles which, whatever their absoluteness, are nevertheless implicated in cycles and have *fallen* to be the base upon which he lies and on which he will die. But at this point in his journey, Pilar goes on to point out to him the water wagtail, a "ball" of a bird, "no good for anything. Neither to sing nor to eat" (97), that can only bob and jerk up and down. She observes this as she unconsciously lights her cigarette from a flint and steel lighter and before she goes on to place beauty against ugliness—"would you like to be ugly, beautiful"—ugly/beautiful—she asks Maria, and then acknowledges that she herself would have made "a good man" though she is "all woman." Speaking of relations between the sexes as a sequential and repetitive male blinding and restoration of sight, controlled by the illusion of her beauty that a woman casts upon a man that will eventually be informed by the truth of ugliness, Pilar explains the cycles of male/female fascination: "then . . . another man sees you and thinks you are beautiful and it is all to do over" (98).

This rather long introduction to the telling of the tale of the killing of the Fascists in Pablo's town is told as they have stopped half-way up the mountain and focus on the alternatives of deciduous or absolute evergreen trees, on mountains which compel ascent or descent, on the water wagtail that only goes up or down, and on the alternatives of ugliness or beauty as these relate to sight or blindness and desires for masculine or feminine identity. They talk as Pilar lights her cigarette with flint and steel. These many focused antitheses as they are skillfully linked and related by her to cycles are preparation for what follows, for the tale that Pilar now tells, however specific and historically and topically detailed, studies Fascist dialectical alternatives caught in revolution, or either/or dialectics caught in a cyclical process of renewal. Such a structure is pure myth. As given, it is so pure in its many elements that even small deviations from the mythic pattern are informative variations.

The structure that Hemingway establishes for the telling of the tale, the apparatus and technique he uses, is complex. As he essentially describes a psychic battle, he interprets his terms broadly and mythically: his major pattern associates the Fascists with the Apollonian and all that might be, either by Nietzsche, Jung, or Neumann, associated with that,[3] and he largely places the cyclical, the "revolutionary," with the Dionysian. Most details in Pilar's tale that are identified with the old order are distinguished by their Apollonian attributes, and most that are identified with the Republican cause are given as Dionysian attributes. These polar oppositions become in a broader perspective and another vocabulary masculine and feminine, and the struggle between them emerges partly as a solar/lunar battle in which male powers accept feminine control and the solar world yields to the lunar.

The geography and architecture of the main square in Pablo's town determines the action. The square is one, like the square in Pamplona in *The Sun Also Rises*, largely surrounded by arcades, and this fact in this novel, as it did in Hemingway's first, compels a basic dialectic between the area where the sun might dominate the *square* and the area under the arcades where one might, in shade and shadow, en*circle* the square. In this town the arcade covers three sides of the square; the fourth side, where there is the edge of the cliff, is still, however, in shade and shadow, being under the trees that line that edge. In *The Sun Also Rises*, as Jake walks toward his introduction of Brett to Romero during which he will lie to Romero thrice, he twice encircles the square. It is in that novel that the reader also notes that the entire fiesta is placed in jeopardy as (cyclical) rain comes to dominate the square, rain that drives people under the arcades, and also as mist from the sea comes to cut off the tops of the mountains. Such changes in landscape or scene are changes in powers and principles. The reader should not forget Margot Macomber (in "The Short Happy Life of Francis Macomber") beginning to suffer badly from the sun as Francis, bonding with Wilson in masculine rites, begins to challenge her authority, or that Brett's power is established over Jake (in *The Sun Also Rises*) preeminently when the night is dark and the moon and the river are high, and that it is in the dark lower wine cave that she is idolatrously enshrined as pagan goddess.

Crossing or circling the square are throughout Hemingway's work significant alternatives. Similarly, to accept the darkness or shadow beneath the romanesque arch of the arcade rather than submit to the terms of the sun in the square generally defines a retreat from Apollonian powers. Certainly, in Hemingway's aesthetics, as in any work of art, such basic oppositions are neither simplistic nor unvarying, while they yet serve to define a struggle between opposing forces.

One of the major controlling sub-metaphors of the tale is that of the corrida, a ritual death-dealing that usually takes place in a circular arena where *sol y sombra*, the dialectic of sun and shadow, oversees the action. However, *capeas* like the metaphoric one suggested in Pablo's town, do often take place in Spain in enclosed squares where the entering streets are closed or sealed off by carts and doors. Hemingway is superbly alert to the way the ring in Pablo's town is fashioned from a square, or is a squared circle,[4] and his metaphors reflect it. If in his tale the ring and the square seem to have become one, this is also the case with *toro* and *torero*. The Fascists readily seem to become, in the vocabulary of the life and death ritual of the bullfight, those who are to be slain, or representatives of the bull. This, however, is not simply the case in this tale, for Hemingway has deliberately complicated his symbolism by inverting its usual meaning—a frequent strategy in his work.[5] Throughout Pilar's tale the Fascists are associated with those values that are usually associated with the torero, and it is the revolution itself that is rather given—in this scene especially—to be associated with the dark wildness and ferocity of the bull in its attempt to destroy the insulting and goading codified forms that have provoked it to its attack. Although the drunkard among the Republicans will cry out "*Qué salga el toro!* Let the bull out!" establishing those in the "box" of the Ayuntamiento *as* the bulls, Don Faustino, an amateur bullfighter, who emerges like a bull from the box, is described as the torero, and is so taunted. "Don Faustino, *Matador, a sus ordenes*," mocks one in the crowd; "Come, Don Faustino. Here is the biggest bull of all," cries another; and another, after his death, declares, "He's seen the big bull now." This deliberate confusion of toro and torero and killer and killed is a major device and part of Hemingway's intellectual and aesthetic strategy here and elsewhere in his work.

Hemingway has inverted ritual terminology for specific ends.[6] The deliberate ambiguity Hemingway has attached to the Fascists and their killers can be well seen as Hemingway describes the two lines of men that connect the Ayuntamiento and the edge of the cliff where begins "the emptiness [the nada] beyond." These lines conduct those who walk between them from linear prominence and authority high above to the chaotic darkness of death in the waters three hundred feet below, and the files of men are described as standing like those who "watch the ending of a bicycle road race with just room for the cyclists to pass between, *or* as men stood to allow the passage of a holy image in a procession" (104; emphasis added). The two similes are antithetical, the cyclists or the saints, and in being joined as one and the same, merge the two principles of the flesh and the spirit, the cycle and the cross, or cycles and absolutes, that Hemingway so frequently labors to fuse. Cyclists and/or saints, toro and/or torero, and square and/or circle suggest the ideal toward which the revolution unconsciously strives, a both/and existence which might replace the rigid dichotomizing either/or dialectic which the prologue called in question as it studied Pilar's ability to be a good man while being all woman, or looked at the water wagtail, a bird of the air that is also a bird of the water that, bobbing up and down, is yet a "ball" of a bird. It is no accident that the last words of the novel are "the pine needle floor of the forest," for simultaneously Jordan's heart and the pine trees themselves accept the cycles of the nondeciduous evergreen, the fallen and changing principle of unchangedness: human and vegetable life, both internal and external nature, man and landscape, rise from, attempt to transcend and yet are caught in and ultimately acknowledge the terms of their engagement.

One of the keys to Hemingway's metaphoric structure in this novel is the fountain that dominates the center of the square, and it, at the very center of the action of the tale, is the archetype of that action. The sound of "the splashing of the water in the fountain" is one of the last details of the tale as told. The fountain is described as being apparently a statue of a lion from whose mouth protrudes a brass pipe through which water pours to fall into the bowl of the fountain below, "where the women bring the waterjars to fill them." In almost unseen but elaborate detail Hemingway describes the translation of the vivifying waters, whose source is identified as the linear masculine solar lion above, through a fall into the circular bowl beneath, where they are finally described as filling the feminine vessels. This translation is of the captive waters through the line to the circle, from the male solar principle to the cyclical feminine, and it is no accident that the action duplicates the flow of movement of the soon to be "translated" victims between the lines above and down to the watery ravine beneath, just as it is no accident that the bowl should echo toward Pablo's wine bowl where he will search for his ideas or refer back toward the bowl from which Pilar seized her stirring-spoon baton of authority. What

Hemingway is getting at is a theory of the restoration of absolutes through cycles, and of the masculine through the feminine, to create a both/and psychic base.[7]

The Ayuntamiento on the square, across from the cliff edge and in which the Fascists are imprisoned awaiting their execution, is described as a box, so emphasizing its association with the square. But landscape itself becomes the instrument of execution as those high above are cast out and down into the ravine far below. This overthrow of powers above, bringing them down, is the kind of therapeutic inversion that revolutions are meant to establish, to bring arrogant earth-and-life disdaining vanity down, to make that which is of the air, of the mind or the spirit, too abstract or elevated, acknowledge and accept the waters below, as life is coevally forced to accept death. The ravine therefore becomes heavily coded as the place of darkness, descent, the waters, death, and fear—it is also patently, in a Freudian sense,[8] a feminine metaphor—and it is a clue to Hemingway's intricate structure in this novel that the action of revolution is the enforced synthesis of that which is above with that below, the sky with the waters. The blowing of the bridge, the major action at the center of this novel, in effect destroys the barrier between sky and water, air above and ravine below, and connects them, and this successful revolutionary act brings Pablo from the roadmender's hut below to join Pilar from above so that these two bracing and reconciled surrogate father and mother figures may disappear over the crest of the hill at last, Maria between them. This new integration and synthesis is a psychic trinity for the future. It is important to so explore these relations between the height and the ravine, and a few of the meanings implicit in the blowing of the bridge, for the major irony of this novel—which has to do with each being part of the main, and no man being an island "intire of it selfe"—is that its central metaphor is the blowing and destruction of a bridge rather than the building of one. Metaphorically, it would be natural to assume that Robert Jordan, as the American who has crossed over to the other side to join others unlike himself that he may be part of their cause and share their lives, would be a bridge builder, not a bridge destroyer. It is Pilar who understands this irony, and she is the one to label his work in behalf of the common cause, as he goes on laboring below the bridge to help destroy it, masturbatory solitary and self-satisfying activity, perhaps practiced to *make* a bridge, not destroy one. And, of course, what she says is true: Hemingway's art is at once the building and destroying of a bridge.

Jordan once interrupts Pilar's tale to tell of the lynching of a Negro he had seen from the window of a house in Ohio when, at seven years of age, he had gone there to be "the boy of a pair of boy and girl" for a wedding

(116). Maria remarks that she has never seen a Negro except in a *circus*. A black man, related to cycles, raised in the air and given to fire during a celebration of a synthesis, or wedding, is patently the exact metaphoric antithesis to polarized men thrown headlong down a ravine to waters beneath during a war. Hemingway has, in almost pure Jungian dialectical terms, illustrated in Pablo's town the psychic meaning of revolution, and in Ohio demonstrated the metaphoric meaning of patriarchal Fascist control. It is exact that it should have been Jordan's mother who had pulled him away from the window, so destroying his spectatorial Apollonian disassociation.

The killing of Fascists in Pablo's town is specifically described as a destructive activity that is coevally creative. It is a fertility ritual in which fertility is assured through the separation of the chaff from the wheat, through the threshing and harvesting rituals in which the act of killing with sickle and scythe, or turning or tumbling with a wooden pitchfork, is part of a death process out of which comes renewed life. The threshing of the grain, the spilling of the blood that then waters and fertilizes the otherwise barren earth, celebrate the relations between death and birth. The killing of the old king is implicit and underwrites the fertile reign of the new successor, as destruction is seen to be implicated in creation—as the birth/death imagery and rituals of *A Farewell to Arms* tried to show. To make this point explicit, Hemingway has one of Pablo's cohorts say, "We thresh fascists today . . . and out of the chaff comes the freedom of this pueblo" (107). If, indeed, it is the blood of the Fascists that fertilizes the earth, they are nevertheless here seen as the chaff, the part that is thrown away and that has been separated from the grain, and it is out of this that freedom comes.

As the other Fascists are executed, their deaths are administered largely by the hands of peasants, men who deal with the earth, and they are killed in part by wooden instruments that relate to the crops and seasonal harvests, to fertility and its cycles: flails, herdsmen's goads, wooden pitchforks, etc. The sickles with which the priest is pursued in their very name speak of the cycles, and by their shape mythically and precisely refer to the moon and to primitive pagan fertility rites. The priest's death therefore becomes a larger victory, specifically a lunar or maternal victory, of nature religions over Christianity.

If the killings are described as a threshing, a separation of chaff and grain in a fertility ritual, in which all participate, they are also described as a feast or an eating—again, that which sustains natural process. Pilar, as the killings continue with less formality, feels she "has a bellyful," and then has a nausea "as though I had swallowed bad sea food" (119). The smell of vomit is prevalent throughout the square, and that night, Pablo, eating, is described as "having his mouth full of young goat" (127), suggesting the scapegoat sacrifice that has been served up to be eaten.

Hemingway throughout his work played with the cyclical though secondary meaning of "revolution" and "revolutionary." His short story "The Revolutionist" is a *tour de force* of such play, and in *Green Hills*, and *To Have and Have Not*, he elaborately studies the deeper ways in which revolutions are inevitably tied to cycles, and generally create them, restore them, implement them, and support them.[9] Now, at the beginning of Pilar's tale, as she begins with the story of the attack on the barracks, cyclical forces of the movement are pitted against rectilinear and static oppositions.

The techniques and strategies of Pablo's attack and the modes of execution reveal the mythos of the encounter. The Republicans *encircle* their enemies in the barracks, cut their *lines* and *wires*, and, after having destroyed the intact *form* of the building and so having brought down much of the *roof*, execute the unwounded survivors by destroying their *heads*. The exponents of the revolution throughout the tale will either destroy or be unable to maintain linear controls. The destruction or lowering of the head—or the roof—is the means toward overthrow of their enemies, and the breaking or rupturing of intact forms their need: "Open up! Open Up! and "We're going in! We're going in!" are their cries. The four men executed at the barracks are, predictably, all *tall* men who keep tight mouths, who speak, if they do, with *dry* voices, and they are described as *mother killers*. In their deaths, the patriarchal Apollonian is overthrown: the voice of one of the *civiles* is described as "grayer than a morning *without sunrise*" (101; emphasis added), while the effect of Pablo's victory and destruction is to fill the air with dust that comes down over everyone as at a threshing. As the earth and passions rise, visual and mental clarity are part of the sacrifice. The officer commits suicide with his own gun and this is then taken by Pablo and turned against the other *civiles* before it is given to Pilar who then carries it with its muzzle encircled, its "long barrel stuck under the rope" (108) about her waist. This feminine appropriation and encirclement of the male phallic linear gun is a trope that finds several variations throughout the novel as it speaks of the shift of masculine powers into feminine hands. Pablo personally executes the *civiles* with shots to the head. His act subsequently is seen as having been egoistic, and thus, for the following executions, all are formed into lines between which the victims must pass, so that all may share in the administered blows and therefore in responsibility for the deaths that follow. In this way individuality yields to commonality and integration. The killings are throughout, as they were at the barracks, described as the execution of the male principle: as one revolutionist says, "Thanks be to Christ, there are no women"; and Pilar asks, "Why should we kill their women?," suggesting that destruction is reserved for the masculine principle for male crimes.

Before the release of the first Fascist from the box to the lines, water is swept in wide sweeping arcs to moisten the ground. Hemingway carefully also establishes that the land becomes truly the peasants' land when the Fascists are "extinguished," by the verb suggesting the tale that is being told is one that recounts the struggle as additionally between light and darkness. As though to emblematize the meaning of the deaths that follow, Hemingway has Pilar discard her tricorner hat taken from the *guardia civil* so that it can be "destroyed." It is sailed far out into space to drop down into the ravine and river below. The destruction of the hat is an important metaphor for the assassination of masculine pride, vanity, identity, and power.[10] It establishes the paradigm for the deaths that follow it into the ravine, even as it establishes the values that the revolution discards.

The prototypical Fascist death is that of Don Federico González. Described as a "fascist of the first order" (109), he has been the owner of the mill and feed store, therefore proprietor/manager of the cycles and the cyclical processes of life. He is predictably tall, thin (vertical, linear), and balding (mental rather than virile), and he emerges unable to walk, "his eyes turned up to heaven. . . . his hands reaching up as though they would grasp the sky." This man who has "no legs to walk," and "no command of his legs," who seems to have no lower centers to relate to the earth but instead yearns toward the spirit and the sky, "never did open his mouth." The iconography reveals a model of what is to be overthrown. The others who die are significant variations on this model—however different, they do not contradict or challenge the paradigm—like Don Ricardo, who, equally mental and earth disdaining, "trying to walk with his head up," nevertheless is overflowing at the mouth as he verbally vilifies the effeminized principle that destroys him: "I obscenity in the milk of your fathers." He shrugs off the contamination of contact: "Don't touch me."

The failed or spurious Fascist ideal is represented in Don Faustino Rivero, who, despite his patriarchal credentials as the oldest son of his father, a landowner, and his tall height and sun-yellow hair, conceals behind his facade of masculine pride the coward who wanted to be an amateur bullfighter, who "went much with gypsies," and was "a great annoyer of girls" (112). Though he "acts" brave, and looks handsome, scornful, and "superb," when he sees the "emptiness beyond," the nada, he loses all his style, covers his eyes, "throwing himself down and clutching the ground and holding to the grass" (114). In this revelation of the failed or false Fascist ideal, Hemingway reveals the coordinates of the patriarchate. Don Faustino's apostasy—as he compromises his belief with superstition, his male insularity with uxoriousness, his authentic pride with poses and assumed and not genuine feeling, and then overthrows sight, verticality, belief, pride, and form—expresses the overthrown patriarchal pattern.

Having given these examples of the authentic and spurious Apollonian ideal, Hemingway provides the portrait of Don Guillermo, a man killed largely by the drunkards who are no longer able to distinguish or comprehend what they kill. Don Guillermo is carefully described as of medium height, as nearsighted, and as a "fascist, too, from the religiousness of his wife which he accepted as his own due to his love for her" (117–18).[11] Moderate in height, sight, in his masculinity, and in his faith which he moderates because of love, he finally nearsightedly rushes towards death "blindly," believing he is rushing towards his wife who calls his name. His final blindness is an important self-dethronement of the Apollonian world, as it speaks of the substitution of the woman for sight. The anomaly of Don Guillermo speaks to the two worlds that are in delicate balance within him.

Inside the box, Pablo sits with his legs hanging down, rolling a cigarette, while Cuatro Dedos sits in the Mayor's chair with his feet on the table. This inversion, where lower centers are emphasized or replace higher, is implicit in most revolutions; and the feet, legs, and cycling here speak of it. Outside the Ayuntamiento a drunkard lies on the one un-overturned table at the Fascist club, his head hanging down and his mouth open. The unconscious prone man with inverted head and open mouth names what has, at this point in the revolution, replaced the vertical, keen-sighted close-mouthed capitalist proprietors, and it is this state that has metaphorically been forced upon them. Overthrown, they have had their heads destroyed and brought low and into the dust and been projected down into the dark death in the ravine. In the background on the square the destroyed lines have now become a mob that chants, "Open up! Open up! Open up!"

Pilar witnesses the death of the priest. In order to see what is going on inside the "box," she has to stand on a chair to see more and higher than the heads of others, and with her face against the bars of the window, she holds on by them. A man climbs behind her on the chair and stands with his arms around hers holding the wider bars. His breath on her neck smells like the smell of the mob, like vomit on paving stones, and as he shouts "Open up! Open up!" over her shoulder, it is "as though the mob were on my back as a devil is on your back in a dream." Meanwhile the mob itself presses forward and another man hurls himself again and again against the backs of the men before him. The image and the metaphor is an image of sodomitic rape being accomplished concomitantly with the overthrow of all order and the coeval death of the priest, or the spirit. Indeed, exactly as Pilar witnesses the fatal assault on the priest, the chair she stands on breaks and she and the drunkard mounted on her back fall to roll on the pavement among the spilled wine, vomit, and the forest of legs of the mob, which is all that Pilar can now see.

Hemingway has written with keen irony a study of the almost instantaneous way a revolution, even as it is being established, creates the same competitive struggle for ascendancy and power based upon sight and visual control as existed in the capitalist world it tries to replace. As Pilar and the man on her back struggle for advantage, he pushes her head down and she hits him hard in the groin: the man tries to dethrone intimidating feminine mental supremacy, and the woman tries to castrate the man. This struggle to gain advantage over another in a competitive struggle for height and sight is pointedly at the cost of the one less advantaged. Hemingway has also suggested that erectness and verticality, sight and perception are based on a relation to spirit, and that to deprive the body of the spirit is to bring it down to the underworld of legs and leavings, to roll in the dust.

Pablo's dismay at being deprived of his belief in the manliness and courage of the priest is answered by Pilar's wisdom: "I think he died very well—being deprived of all formality." She is suggesting that to destroy the forms of life leaves it without the sacramental base through and by means of which human dignity can be maintained.

In the night after the killings, Pilar awakes and looks out at the square where the lines had been, which is now dominated by and filled with the moonlight. There she sees the moonlight on the trees, the darkness and the shadows, and hears "no sound but the falling of the water in the fountain." At the end of the executions, the once sun-drenched square is dissolved in darkness where amorphous and indistinguishable shapes and the sound of water falling seem to control the world. The solar (lion) principle has yielded to the lunar, the woman presides over the square, while Pablo, stuffed with goat, impotent after the day's deeds, lies unconscious, sleeping.

The mythic dynamics of Pilar's tale operate throughout the novel. One of the most poignant moments in this work is the exchange that, in a later chapter, takes place between Anselmo, Fernando, and Robert Jordan as they get ready to return to the guerrilla cave.

"Back to the palace of Pablo," Jordan says to Anselmo. Anselmo alters his description, "*El Palacio del Miedo.* . . . The Palace of Fear," and then Jordan caps this retort with his own, "*La cueva de los huevos perdidos.* . . .

The cave of lost eggs." Fernando, in his usual impercipience, asks, "What eggs?" and Jordan answers him, "A joke. . . . Just a joke. Not eggs, you know. The others." "But why are they lost?" Fernando asks, and Jordan replies, "I don't know. . . . Take a book to tell you. Ask Pilar" (199).

The exchange is one of the few places in a Hemingway novel where the frame is broken, and deliberately broken by a character who steps beyond his role to speak for the author and the author's controlling awareness. Another similar break in a novel's fictive frame takes place in *Across the River and into the Trees* and for approximately the same reasons. It is the moment when Richard Cantwell, having confronted a very similar recognition indeed, the significance of the green emeralds, which are the "eggs" of *that* novel, subsides to let the author intrude: "He was addressing no one, except, perhaps, posterity" (168). Here, too, the lament, the pain, if not the exasperation, show—Hemingway is now beyond exasperation—and he knows well that he cannot look for contemporary recognition of his deeper structures.

Both interpolations, in *Across the River* and *For Whom*, reveal an infinite weariness in the author, the weariness of an artist whose intricately crafted structures have created no public and scant critical awareness, who labors to establish deep patterns that meet no appreciative response, hardly a glance of recognition. When Jordan, in *For Whom*, says, "Take a book to tell you," he knows what his creator Hemingway well knows, that the intricate and detailed pattern that the writer has carefully laid down in the novel, which studies the rivalry for power within the primal cave, the eternal battle of the sexes for phallic power or authority, and the Oedipal son/father rivalries as they relate to that battle, have been studied at a level and in such depth that no explanation or speech or essay will reveal their mystery. Hemingway would need another book like the one being written to trace the many lines and ramifications he has placed in that remarkably complex story.

On the simplest of levels, the reference to the lost eggs is, of course, to lost testicular power or male potency in the struggle for power and authority that Jordan has witnessed within the cave, a battle that has culminated in Pablo's overthrow as he has been unmanned and cowed by Pilar as she, inverting her stirring spoon, has made the baton of her cyclical function the new emblem of power in the cave. On another level, the reference goes back to Jordan's two sacks which have early been carefully coded by Hemingway to develop their testicular/egg associations, and which have been packed, we are told by Jordan, "as carefully as he had packed his collection of wild bird eggs when he was a boy" (48). Those two male sacks were first studied by Hemingway in *The Sun Also Rises* when he described the driver of the stage that takes Bill and Jake up to Burguete as coming out "swinging two . . . mail [male] pouches" as they start off for their consummate male experience (106).[12] Now, again in Spain, these sacks are resurrected as the containers of Jordan's potency as a dynamiter, for in them are his exploding devices, his detonators and his bundles of explosive charges, which can allow him to fulfill his mission and himself as a male.

As Jordan heads toward the mouth of the cave with a sack in each hand, Hemingway's earlier image from his first novel is revived. Jordan's "things" are now placed in the cave. Their being there can be recognized as the provocation to the scene that ensues, in which Pablo, a surrogate but cowardly father figure, will be overthrown. Jordan's "things," now in the cave after Pablo's authority there has been called in question and stripped from him, identifies Jordan's new role with respect to Pilar and introduces new plot complications. Hemingway seems to be studying the situation that exists when a son figure takes his potency through the cave mouth, and puts it in the care and under the supervision of the maternal figure at the hearth. Such metaphors are all heavily coded with the language of sexual power dynamics and rivalries. But these are only a few of the levels of the struggle that Hemingway studies. As Jordan said, for Hemingway, "Take a book to tell you."

What is important to recognize in Jordan's remark to Fernando is that he himself is only too well aware, superlatively aware, of the sexual dynamics of the power struggle that has been going on. He has been witness to much. He has seen the shift from patriarchal authority to matriarchal power and recognized his own role in that as son-usurper. He has witnessed the subsequent humiliations of Pablo, who is now identified with a flaccidity, limpness, and inert inactivity which suggest his castration. The reader is, at this point in the narrative, not yet fully aware of Jordan's own history, one in which he has effectively lost his own father, a *cow*ardly man who was cowed, like Pablo, by Jordan's *bull*y of a mother; nor has Jordan yet suffered the assault on his sacks. In that attack, Pablo, as he takes away Jordan's potency, places slits on the sacks in the cave, apparently suggesting an attempt to effeminize that rival son and prevent the success of the action and task he hopes to perform. Hemingway has coevally let those readers who are aware of his self-reflexive mode in this novel see that Jordan's fulfillment of his task is simultaneously Hemingway's completion of his, and that the "father's" interference with its success is their shared problem. Jordan's remark to Fernando occurs on page 199 in chapter 15 of the novel, yet it was exactly 100 pages earlier, on page 99 in chapter 10, that Pilar began to tell her remarkable tale of the execution of the Fascists in Pablo's town. In order to recognize another yet more profound level of meaning behind "*la cueva de los huevos perdidos*," that tale must be carefully examined, remembered, and related to the larger patterns of mythic struggle that the novel exists to study.

NOTES

1. Ernest Hemingway, *For Whom the Bell Tolls.* (1940; NY: Scribner's, 1968) 134–35. All further page references to this novel will be given in the text.

2. This pattern, which goes far toward explaining the psychic dynamics of Hemingway's art and its philosophical/psychological concerns, is visible in each of his major works: a necessary crossover from the known country into the unknown, a binding together of two discrete and opposed worlds or modes. It may be projected as a necessary bonding of the conscious or unconscious parts of the psyche, of the masculine or the feminine aspects of the self, or of ordered realms of light with chaotic areas of darkness. I am convinced that the pattern is at once unconscious and conscious in Hemingway's work, being the compulsive need for integrated wholeness and mastery of an almost schizophrenic split (which is shared by most artists) and also his highly conscious recognition of the split that must be healed as the major dilemma of Western man in our time. Highly organized religious and mythic patterning in Hemingway's work suggests that he, like Joyce, sees the artist as the creator of the conscience of the race who forges in the smithy of his soul the coordinates for that possession. The major icon of the synthesis he proposes seems to be the "cyclical absolute," which binds natural process to ideal structures—see Robert E. Gajdusek, *Hemingway and Joyce.* And the major metaphor of the needed crossover and fusion seems to be the bridge—see Gajdusek, "Bridges, Their Creation and Destruction in the Work of Ernest Hemingway." In the details of the novels and stories, the problem may be seen in the imagery of the dephallused man and the highly sexually charged lady (*The Sun Also Rises*); the forcing of love and war together (*A Farewell to Arms* and *For Whom the Bell Tolls*); the unique relationship of the hardened old warrior and the young inexperienced Contessa (*Across the River*); or the mortal man dying of rot on the plain beneath the dream of an immortality to be achieved on the high Mountain of God ("The Snows of Kilimanjaro"). It creates a dichotomized landscape where the author studies the interrelations between the haves and the have nots, the winners and losers, and the split men—like Harry Morgan, Santiago, or Cantwell—who have had to come to terms with their betraying sides, or simply the undercover operators (Jordan or Philip Rawlings) or hunters (Francis Macomber or the Hemingway of *Green Hills*) or fishermen (Nick of "Big Two-Hearted River") who can only gain their victories by crossing into new and alien territory to explore and bind themselves to the unexplored, un-understood lands, or the psyches or internal dynamics of those "other" worlds. It demands the dynamics of *A Moveable Feast*, where the sacred and secular are joined in moments of fluid fixity, as well

as the experimentation of a *Garden of Eden* where the possibilities of androgynous male/female identity are studied. It was always Hemingway's way to empathically identify himself with and study his antagonist, and therefore boxing and war and hunting/fishing and confrontations with death were his natural fascinations. To become a man, Macomber had to learn what was inside the lion or the buffalo, to know what it was feeling—just as Richard Cantwell had to imagine the virtues of his enemies. But that self-transcendence is anathema to revolutionary commitment, and seen as apostasy to "the cause." Caught as Jordan/Hemingway was between the aesthetic need to inhabit the "other," and the political need to ignore its justifications, Hemingway has Jordan observe, shortly before his own death, "There's no *one* thing that's true. It's all true. The way the planes are beautiful whether they are ours or theirs. The hell they are, he thought" (467). The quote is a beautiful example of the two sides, whose boundaries he needs to breach, warring within the artist/warrior.

3. The binary and polar oppositions that all three use to talk about psychic dialectics readily accept a terminology which might oppose Apollonian/Dionysian, patriarchal/matriarchal, or solar/lunar, conscious/unconscious terms.

4. In one of Hemingway's high school short stories, "A Matter of Color," he describes the boxing ring as the "squared circle," giving any alert critic pause to consider the possible sophistication of this seventeen-year-old. Later in his work, the squared circle, or the absolute cycle, the mastery of time by eternity, become important concerns, concerns demonstrated in this novel by Robert Jordan's triumph as he makes time stand still and makes of seventy-two hours a lifetime and out of the "NOW" of orgasmic love an eternity.

5. When, in *Green Hills of Africa*, Hemingway relates meat on a stick to Christ on the cross, and in *A Farewell to Arms* he parodies the celebration of the mass in a scene of gross eating of pasta, and in *Across the River* he parallels blood bruised to the lips by kissing with menstruation, he is forcing carnal and spiritual, and oral and genital oppositions together. Such examples are frequent throughout his work.

6. We see this strikingly done in the "Hail nada full of nada" passage in "A Clean Well-Lighted Place," also in the profane black mass being celebrated by Frederic Henry in *A Farewell to Arms* just before his wounding, and in several inverted religious ritual moments in *Green Hills*.

7. This may help as much as anything to explain the sexual dynamics of *The Garden of Eden*.

8. In chapter 5 of *Green Hills*, Hemingway develops the ravine, in a remarkably sexual chapter, as the cleft of the feminine into which the intrepid male adventures.

9. In *Green Hills*, P.O.M., finally exasperated, breaks out, "I don't want to just hear about revolutions. All we see or hear is revolutions. I'm sick of them" (192). But Hemingway *is* concerned with them, in how they go bad, and why they do so, though to get "on that wheel" can be as disastrous as being on Pablo's Merry-Go-Round. In *To Have and Have Not*, Harry Morgan turns away from them as he asks what the "lady wrestler" Mrs. Laughton is drinking. When he is

told it is "A Cuba Libre," he says, "Then give me a straight whiskey" (134). The opposition is between revolution and straight spirits.

10. In Josef von Sternberg's film *The Blue Angel*, the stripping away and gradual destruction of the masculine hat is similarly meticulously studied as the overthrow of patriarchal authority and the eradication of masculine power.

11. Richard Gordon, in *To Have and Have Not*, is drawn as a man who sacrifices his wife to his vanities and his egocentric sense of self; in contradistinction Helen Gordon remembers her father, who "went to Mass because my mother wanted him to, and he did his Easter duty for her and for Our Lord, but mostly for her" (187). Men who sacrifice for their women, or women who do so for their men, like Maria's mother, are mostly throughout Hemingway's works contrasted with men and women insulated in their own sense of self, like the husband in "Cat in the Rain" or the young man of "Hills Like White Elephants."

12. This use of mail as male is found throughout Hemingway. One example: in *The Garden of Eden*, as Catherine begins to focus on the mail and to open the mail and David finally says farewell to the mailman, there is elaborate sexual joking taking place.

WORKS CITED

Gajdusek, Robert E. "Bridges, Their Creation and Destruction in the Work of Ernest Hemingway." *Up in Michigan: Proceedings of the First National Hemingway Conference.* Traverse City, MI: 1983. 75–81.
——— . *Hemingway and Joyce: A Study in Debt and Payment.* Corte Madera, CA: Square Circle Press, 1984.
Hemingway, Ernest. *Across the River and into the Trees.* NY: Scribner's, 1950.
——— . *A Farewell to Arms.* NY: Scribner's, 1929.
——— . *For Whom the Bell Tolls.* 1940. NY: Scribner's, 1968.
——— . *The Garden of Eden.* NY: Scribner's, 1986.
——— . *Green Hills of Africa.* 1935. NY: Charles Scribner's Sons, 1963.
——— . *To Have and Have Not.* 1937. NY: Macmillan, 1987.
——— . *A Moveable Feast.* NY: Scribner's, 1964.
——— . *The Sun Also Rises.* NY: Scribner's, 1926.

10 Once a Rabbit, Always? A Feminist Interview with María

Gerry Brenner

INTERVIEWER: It was most kind of you to agree to this interview. At your advanced age I can well imagine the difficulty of answering questions about seventy-two hours from a life long ago.

MARÍA: Perhaps. But please to proceed.

INTERVIEWER: Like other personages upon whom Hemingway based his novel's characters, you, I trust, have read his novel as a version of your Civil War experiences?

MARÍA: Truly. It is a version. And thy interview? Its purpose, if I may ask?

INTERVIEWER: Naturally. I'm interviewing marginalized women who have figured in various cultural texts—from novels to historical documents. I'm asking for their views on the experiences that male authors have recorded them as having had—to see if there might be some discrepancy between the actual and the recorded accounts. And I wish to probe for explanation of why those women conducted themselves as they did. I'll compile the interviews in an anthology.

MARÍA: The title of thy anthology, please?

INTERVIEWER: Its working title is, well, is *Backward Gazes: A Gallery of Phallocentric Women.*

MARÍA: Thy reason for including an interview with me?

INTERVIEWER: In candor, because you're one of the backward women. You represent the classic stereotype who continues to impede the cause of women's liberation. You're the nubilized princess, the fantasized dream maiden whose infantilized dependency and submissive eroticism caters to all that feminists find most reprehensible in the male gaze.

MARÍA: *Que va.* I fear thou art another Fernando. Thou hast his capacity to make a bureaucracy with thy mouth. It is thy wish, then, to abuse me for the young woman I was during those seventy-two hours?

INTERVIEWER: Quite correct. Given Hemingway's to-me unfathomable ability to endure—his unflagging popularity among readers worldwide—his chauvinistic novel about you and Robert Jordan continues to be read by benighted readers who find in you a role model, an image of a desirable type of women.

MARÍA: That image is harmful, I am to believe?

INTERVIEWER: Quite harmful. After all, María, unless male and female readers correctly see the anathema you are to actualized womanhood, they'll be misled to think of you—if they're female—as an exemplar they should emulate or—if they're male—as an ideal they should search for: they'll believe that such women—as Hemingway characterized you—really do exist.

MARÍA: Thou dost make it difficult, at my age, not to feel flattered by thy accusations of my seductive power. But should not men and women value that sexual pleasure which often attaches to the image of thy nubilized maiden?

INTERVIEWER: Indeed, indeed. But being a woman is more than clinching in a sleeping bag with a man who mutters banalities about "now . . . always now, always now . . . going now, rising now, sailing now, leaving now, wheeling now, soaring now, away now, all the way now, all of all the way now" (Hemingway 379). A woman is more than an embrace-mate in the heather to a chorus of nowheres upon nowheres, "once again to nowhere, always and forever to nowhere, heavy on the elbows in the earth to nowhere, hang on all time always to unknowing nowhere" (159). Women are for more than submissively acquiescing to a man's orders to tend the horses or to dry his feet or fetch dry stockings; for more than playing adolescent servant submitting to her dying lover's commands; for more than kowtowing to his paradoxical psychoblather that instructs her, "Thou wilt go now, rabbit. But I go with thee. As long as there is one of us there is both of us." "If thou goest then I go, too." "Whichever one there is, is both." "We both go in thee now." "Thou art me too now" (463–64). There's more to being a woman than experiencing *la gloria*, more than dissolving in the convulsive shudder of earth-moving orgasms.

MARÍA: I see. I see. Truly it is embarrassing to hear thy recitations of Roberto's love talk. Yet it doth seem rare that thou hast memorized such talk. But dost thou truly believe I know not what a woman is? Dost thou think I see not the infant I was in Mr. Hemingway's book?

INTERVIEWER: Well, María, that's precisely why I sought you out for this interview: to determine whether in the intervening years you'd gained insight on your identity as a woman.

MARÍA: Truly I did. After I recovered.

INTERVIEWER: You were injured in the war, after you left the Guadarrama mountain pass?

MARÍA: *Que va.* After I recovered from the injury of Roberto's rejection.

INTERVIEWER: You mean that you suffered from some sort of breakdown after you left him at the pass?

MARÍA: Left, nothing. Was *taken* from him at the pass. Was *led off*, forcibly, from him. Was all but *handcuffed* by the Pilar and Pablo. Was rejected by Roberto. Thou dost remember my pleas to him, as my horse was being driven away: "Let me stay! Let me stay!" Thou dost remember too his shouting, "I am with thee. I am with thee now. We both are there. Go!" (465). Many women—had they suffered at the brutal hands of the Fascist barbarians and had they gone crazy after that experience—many women might have gone crazy again after a lover's sudden rejection. That rejection: I had in no way expected or deserved it, thou canst be certain.

INTERVIEWER: I am most sorry to hear of your relapse, caused by this additional trauma. Please accept my sympathy. But, dear María, that has little to do, I'm afraid, with Hemingway's characterization of you during the seventy-two hours of the novel.

MARÍA: I beg to differ. It has everything. The Pilar was untruthful in telling Roberto, in his first hours among us, "I do not want her crazy here after you will go. I have had her crazy before and I have enough without that" (33). As if I were not still crazy during his time among us! Truly it embarrasses me to re-read Mr. Hemingway's novel and to discover what an infant I was. Dost thou believe I was such an innocent before the barbarities in our village? Dost thou believe that I, a mayor's daughter, was such an obedient, unassertive child among my family and friends before the war? Dost thou believe that a Spanish girl of my upbringing and pride would so demean herself to a stranger and to her people unless she were crazy? Surely thou canst comprehend: my traumas were responsible for those disgraceful hours with Roberto. I spit on my conduct. I behaved as an eight-year-old girl with a—how dost thou call it?—a crash?

INTERVIEWER: Crush?

MARÍA: Yes, with a crush on an older, handsome man.

INTERVIEWER: Well, María, this explains a good bit of your behavior, for it is certainly infantilized throughout the novel. But it makes your Roberto a more despicable chauvinist than I've previously regarded him.

MARÍA: What dost thou mean?

INTERVIEWER: Well, for all of his love talk to you, quite clearly you were little more than a convenient receptacle for his liquid manhood, a creature whom he spent little time finding anything about, certainly no time learning to know. He certainly left you with no means by which to contact his family in Montana, should you have needed their help after the war. And his attitude toward you—or any woman—is summed up in his nickname for you. *Guapa*! A slang-word for female genitalia! In our country it's as if he called you "cunt" or "pussy." And then to translate the term as if it meant rabbit, when *conejo* is the only correct term for rabbit (Josephs 211–12). Affectionately though he may have meant the nickname, it reeks of conventional stereotyping by reducing a woman to an animated stuffed animal, a plaything known best for its reproductive fecundity.

MARÍA: Roberto angers thee.

INTERVIEWER: That's understatement. It enrages me to listen to him commanding you what to do at the end of the novel, ordering you about, as if you were but a child, with his fancy doubletalk: "I go always with thee wherever thou goest." "Thou wilt go now. But I go with thee." "If thou goest then I go, too." "Now I put my hand there. Good. Thou art so good. Now do not think more. Now art thou doing what thou should. Now thou art obeying" (463–64). He exemplifies patriarchal ideology in its most insulting role as benevolent father. It is he, of course, who knows what's best for a woman, whose masculinity dominates speech. Like all who share your Roberto's phallocentric hegemony, he permits woman either the choice to imagine and represent herself as men imagine and represent her (that is, to speak, but to do so only as a man would speak) . . .

MARÍA: And that woman is the Pilar?

INTERVIEWER: Yes. Of course. Or he permits her the choice to be but a "gap" in the world of masculine discourse, to choose silence, becoming, thereby, the "invisible and unheard sex" (Jones, "Inscribing Femininity" 83).

MARÍA: By which thou meanst me.

INTERVIEWER: Quite so. For just how much does your Roberto let you speak? I think of your narrative of the barbershop scene in which you were brutally shorn of your hair. It is your longest speech in the novel. But what is your Roberto's refrain? "Do not tell it." "Do not talk more." "Do not tell me any more." "Do not talk of it" (350–53). Your Roberto reveals his preference for your silence when, before your recitation, he tells you, in a sentence notable for its confusion of "thee"s without "me"s: "I love thee thus lying beside thee and touching thee and knowing thou art truly there" (349). And when you are led away from his injured body at the end, he desires your obedience, not your language.

MARÍA: And thou hast more cause for thy anger against Roberto?

INTERVIEWER: Indeed. I loathe his privileging of patriarchal provincialism.

MARÍA: By which thou meanst . . .

INTERVIEWER: By which I meanst, uh, mean the ideological narrow-mindedness of his dilemma. Oh, to be caught, poor Roberto, in such a tug of war, such a mirroring civil war of imperatives. On one hand he must honor his political duty, his allegiance to his comrades and the Communist cause, for whom his bridge-blowing mission is a pragmatic means to the greater end of freeing Spain from fascism. On the other hand he must honor his ethical obligations, his responsibilities for the consequences of his political action on Pablo and Pilar's band. To bring suffering to innocent people, all in the name of right action, is as wrong as to refuse his appointed date with destiny at the bridge.

MARÍA: Doth not such a dilemma humanize him? Doth it not keep him from being an ideologue?

INTERVIEWER: But don't you see, María? That's an antiquated patriarchal dilemma. It sees issues only in terms of whether one should honor the father's call to patriotism or his call to paternalism. And what gets left out of the dilemma? It's the competing claim that you represented—the woman's call to personal obligation, an obligation of intimacy that Robert Jordan betrays when he sends you off with the band. Typical of phallocentric patriarchalists, your Roberto illustrates that ideological causes always take precedence over human beings, especially when those humans are mere women.

MARÍA: And thou hast yet more cause for thy anger against Roberto?

INTERVIEWER: Yes. But wait a minute here. I'm the interviewer. Let me ask the question of moment: have you no anger toward your Roberto?

MARÍA: None.

INTERVIEWER: Do you mean to say that you still love him?

MARÍA: By no means. But he angers me not at all. For him I feel pity.

INTERVIEWER: Pity?

MARÍA: Truly. For I have come to realize that he was a deeply confused, nay, a pathetic man.

INTERVIEWER: [Pause]

MARÍA: Thy silence, I take it, awaits some explanation?

INTERVIEWER: If you please.

MARÍA: He was no chauvinist, as thou dost call him. To tell truly, his sexuality was confused. Oh, thou hast not to worry that I will claim some overt homosexual act that only I had knowledge of. But surely thou canst understand his attraction to me with my cropped hair, canst thou not?

INTERVIEWER: Your resemblance, you mean, to a man?

MARÍA: My resemblance to a cropped-haired boy, if you will. Perhaps I resembled some playmate, brother or sister, some friend from his infancy or youth. I was someone whose uncertain sex contributed to his prompt love for me. Truly I had beautiful hair.

INTERVIEWER: Pretty plumage once?

MARÍA: Perhaps so. But for him it was tawny wheat, burned gold. Poetic compliments, perhaps. But I was no field to be harvested, no rare metal to be beaten.

INTERVIEWER: Ah! It must be your genderlessness to him, then, that explains that oddest of descriptions of your hair. It occurs on your last night together. He felt—I'm sure I can quote the sentence—"he felt the cropped head against his cheek, and it was as soft but as alive and silkily rolling as when a marten's fur rises under the caress of your hand"—now listen—"when you spread the trap jaws open and lift the marten clear and, holding it, stroke the fur smooth" (378).

MARÍA: Truly a rare comparison to make. Perhaps it shows some wish to regard me an animal, a dead one at that. Aiee, to be caught in the jaws of a lethal trap.

INTERVIEWER: Certainly it suggests his wish to detach your hair from your body, as though his lovemaking could occur with anyone with such hair, male or female. And it may explain his calling you rabbit, suggesting as that creature may, the downy fur of your mound of Venus—or of any youth's pubic area, male or female. But I'm afraid, María, willing though I am, I'm not convinced of your allegations of Jordan's confused sexuality.

MARÍA: Truly it is difficult to see, I confess. But recall thou our love scenes. Consider the language of them. Is the dark passage that he makes his incantations over, is that the entrance into my womb? Or could it be some nearby dark passage? I wish not to be vulgar or obscene. But pride in my womanhood suffers when I read those passages, whether we are lying in the heather or on his pine-bough bed, whether we are walking hand in hand or lying flank to flank. One and all, they blur my sex.

INTERVIEWER: You mean, I take it, that each of those scenes could as easily refer to the erotic pleasure of two men as of a man and a woman?

MARÍA: Truly.

INTERVIEWER: But you must remember the time in which Hemingway published his version of your story: censorship laws and public standards of decency would have prohibited any frank references to your body parts. As I recall, there was sufficient controversy over the sleeping-bag scenes anyway.

MARÍA: Thou dost misunderstand me. Mr. Hemingway's descriptions of our love reflect well Roberto's state of mind. But the language of those passages is alien to heterosexual love.

INTERVIEWER: Well, now that I think back on some of those passages, there may be some merit in what you claim. The language is curiously lacking in phallogocentricity. Hmmm. I must confess that were I to read one of the earth-moving passages out of context, I might well conclude its author was a woman:

They were having now and before and always and now and now and now. Oh, now, now, now, the only now, and above all now, and there is no other now but thou now and now is thy prophet. Now and forever now. Come now, now, for there is no now but now. Yes, now. Now, please now, only now, not anything else only this now, and where are you and where am I and where is the other one, and not why, not ever why, only this now; and on and always please then always now, always now, for now always one now. . . . [And then:] "One and one is one, is one, is one, is one, is still one, is still one, is one descendingly, is one softly, is one longingly, is one kindly, is one happily, is one in goodness, is one to cherish, is one now on earth with elbows against the cut and slept-on branches of the pine tree with the smell of the pine boughs and the night; to earth conclusively now, and with the morning of the day to come. Then he said, for the other was only in his head and he had said nothing, "Oh, Maria, I love thee and I thank thee for this." (379)

Well, now, just who is "the other" who was "only in his head"? But more, the whole passage reads like the semiotic style that Julia Kristeva associates with women—repetitive, spasmodic, rhythmic, nonstructured (Jones, "Writing the Body" 363). And the geography of the pleasure, as Luce Irigaray would say, describes *jouissance* in a diversified, complex way that borders on autoeroticism (Irigaray 101–3). Indeed, the lack of phallic regionalization in these love scenes suggests an antiphallocentric text that Hélène Cixous might well find deserving of comment (Jones, "Writing the Body" 365).

MARÍA: I beg thy pardon. Thou dost seem distracted. I know not these names. Are they other women thou hast interviewed for thy *Gallery of Backward Women*?

INTERVIEWER: Scarcely. But why not just lay your cards on the table? What else leads you to suspect your Roberto of homoerotic tendencies?

MARÍA: Surely there is his preoccupation with his father and the Pablo, a pair of men whose disgraceful acts deeply injured him. Canst thou imagine my surprise when I read of the handshake between Roberto and the returned Pablo? In that handshake is more emotion than in our sleeping bag. Surely my Roberto took great pleasure in the hard gripping and frank pressing of hands. It led him to remark to himself that "Pablo had a good hand in the dark and feeling it gave Robert Jordan the strangest feeling he had felt that morning" (404). Such words gave me cause for much jealousy when first I read them. And Roberto continued to grip "the strange, firm, purposeful hand hard." That deserved the Pilar's sarcastic question, "What are you two doing? Becoming *maricones*?"

INTERVIEWER: By which she meant homosexuals, not just sissies?

MARÍA: Truly.

INTERVIEWER: Well, there's certainly a male conspiracy between the two after your Roberto's leg was crushed. Two men, willfully asserting their medical knowledge, pigheadedly vaunting their certainty of your Roberto's imminent death, letting him play the martyr on the mountaintop.

MARÍA: But I think you confuse the scene. You release more of your anger at Roberto. You should feel pity for his confused action. He thinks his martyrdom is for the noble cause of Republican Spain. He thinks it is payment to our band in exchange for having come among us and ruined our serenity. But his sacrifice shows his love for Pablo, a redeemed father. He must have hoped that the Pablo would value his sacrifice above all other acts of male camaraderie.

INTERVIEWER: And so I suppose it would have given homoerotic pleasure to your Roberto, had he known the identity of the officer leading the cavalry to him?

MARÍA: Truly it would have pleased him to die on the field of battle with the young Lt. Berrendo. It would repeat for him his pleasure in killing the young cavalryman who came upon us in the sleeping bag on the second morning.

INTERVIEWER: Well, María, I must admit that your Roberto seems unusually fixated on male figures, strangely braids with erotic aggression his male relationships, as with Kashkin, whom he kills in an act of mercy, or with Karkov, whose lovemaking with his wife and at least two mistresses seems to reveal the *maricones'* fascination with collective sexuality.

MARÍA: Dost thou think it can be that Roberto's eyes are upon Karkov as lover, not upon Karkov's women?

INTERVIEWER: Why not? If, as alleged, there is some homosexual component in group scenes of violence, then that explains his fascination with Pilar's narrative of the extermination of the Fascists in Pablo's town, suggests that the erotic intensification of the collective sadism stirred Robert Jordan deeply.

MARÍA: *Que va*. Roberto listened in rapt attention to the Pilar's account.

INTERVIEWER: As he did to your account of the barbaric shearing of your hair in the barbershop. Yes, I see now: he desired your silence as you began telling him that event, wanting you to be the silent woman. But he desired more to hear what was done to you so that he could imagine the men whose cruel pleasure he luxuriated in, even though he would not admit to such luxury. What homoerotic delight he would have found in El Sordo's last hours I can well imagine.

MARÍA: Think you so? Can there be erotic pleasure in such a scene?

INTERVIEWER: Indeed. For is there not the pleasure of awaiting a dangerous lover's approach? Of taking with surprise the aggressive male, the Comrade Voyager, the Captain Mora of the red face and blond hair and British moustache and blue eyes? Of dropping the arrogant paternalist with the phallic spray of three shots from an automatic weapon? Yes, your Roberto would take pleasure in that violence and would enjoy his grief in the death of the young boy Joaquín.

MARÍA: Truly in Joaquín's death. For dost thou recall the episode of the Belgian boy?

INTERVIEWER: I don't believe I do.

MARÍA: Roberto remembers a boy from the Eleventh Brigade. His fellow villagers, five boys, had been killed early in the war. The boy was made an orderly. But he could do nothing without weeping or crying. All treated him very gently. Roberto resolved: "He would have to find out what became of him and whether he ever cleared up and was fit for soldiering again" (136). But why should Roberto compassionate that one young man?

INTERVIEWER: Well, his empathetic attentiveness seems commendable, to be sure. But it also smacks of sentimentality. Perhaps his humanistic, even feminized, sympathies sublimate his homoerotic interest in the orderly? Is that what you wish to imply?

MARÍA: I remark the episode because it shows a sensitivity in Roberto that was strongly at odds with his masculinity, a sensitivity that ran toward men, especially young or injured or emasculated men.

INTERVIEWER: It would seem to show that he had much in common with America's good gray poet, Walt Whitman. But to think of literary correspondence brings to mind a tradition of orderlies serving as the objects of homosexual officers, the best-known of them being one in a story by a British writer. But if I recall correctly, Hemingway has a little-read story of a homosexual proposition a major makes to an orderly. "A Simple Enquiry," it's called. And I've recently heard it reported that in an early draft of "A Way You'll Never Be" two soldiers are brought before a captain and charged with homosexuality (Smith). There are other stories of homosexuality, I am quite sure. So it should not surprise us that your Roberto was but one in a line of men whose virile masculinity should be strongly questioned and whose recurrent presence should tell something about their author.

MARÍA: Nor should it surprise thee to learn the identity of Roberto's personal hero, unnamed though he is in Mr. Hemingway's book.

INTERVIEWER: I know not to whom you refer.

MARÍA: Thou knowest not? Thou, a woman schooled in literary texts? Who else, early in our waning century, boldly put himself into the pantheon of military heroism with feats of derring-do among an alien people? What silk-robed hero legendized himself by learning strange tongues and dialects, inspired natives, and unified feuding desert tribes? Who became an explosives expert, engaged in harassing attacks on Turkish outposts, troops and supply trains, and fought guerrilla-fashion, leading a camel corps?

INTERVIEWER: You can only mean, of course, T. E. Lawrence—of Arabia. Now there's a topic for some scholar to make a name for himself with (Reynolds).

MARÍA: Truly. Roberto idolized Colonel Lawrence for his heroics. But he also found alluring the homosexuality of his personal life, ignore that allure though he tried.

INTERVIEWER: Be that as it may, María, why has this—and all of the other signs of your Roberto's homosexuality—led you to pity him?

MARÍA: *Que va.* But was he not pathetically confused, unable to reconcile to himself his homosexual longing? Did that not contribute to his yearning for death, his deliberate desire to place himself in jeopardy, as if in expiation for his tabooed desires? Did it not explain, perhaps in part, his expatriation from the American West, where there could be little tolerance for a man of homosexual leanings? What could torture Roberto more than teaching in a small-town Western university where constant contact with young men like Paco Berrendo, the Belgian boy, Joaquín, Andrés, and other cropped-haired farm youths would unbearably strain his ability to instruct them only in Spanish? Far from being thy stereotyped chauvinist, was he not deeply divided? Truly he wished to act out the patriarchal masculinity you vilify him for. But he wished, too, to indulge in the nurturing maternalism that led him to grieve over injured young boys and to pride himself on packing his explosives as carefully "as he had packed his collection of wild bird eggs when he was a boy" (48). Ah, that he wished to become a writer, but told me no such thing. Would he return to teaching or continue with war games? Would we have any domestic life without him searching out new political causes? Ahh. Many, many are the signs of my Roberto's deep confusions. They would have made life with him unendurable, I am quite sure, had he survived that agony of my country.

INTERVIEWER: And what about your life, María, since you rode away from that Guadarrama mountain pass? Did you marry? Did you have children? Why do you still live here in Gredos?

MARÍA: Such questions, I believe, exceed the scope of thy interview, do they not? Enough of my private life has been revealed already, even though it was but some seventy hours. So of thee, my interviewer: to whom dost thou turn for the next of thy interviews, thy next backward woman?

INTERVIEWER: It would not surprise you, would it, if I told you Pilar?

MARÍA: Not at all. But she has grown more irascible than she was a half century ago. She confuses herself with other women, Mr. Hemingway's mother, and that lesbian writer who held court in Paris.

INTERVIEWER: Gertrude Stein?

MARÍA: Yes. But thou knowest how to reach the Pilar, knowest the home to which she has been committed?

INTERVIEWER: Quite so. May I take along your regards to her?

MARÍA: Please to do so. And please be so kind, shouldst thou publish our interview in thy anthology, to accent properly the letter *i* in María. It would displease me to see it again anglicized, as it was by thy Mr. Hemingway, who foolishly vaunted himself on his linguistic ability, and whose errors went uncorrected by his shameless publishing house, Scrubbers.

INTERVIEWER: Scribner's, it is. Thank you, María, for so graciously and generously giving your time for this interview.

MARÍA: *Nada.* Good luck with the Pilar. Thou shalt need it. And be thou advised: do not be such a fool as to allow her to read the palm of thy hand.

WORKS CITED

Hemingway, Ernest. *For Whom the Bell Tolls.* NY: Scribner's, 1940.

Irigaray, Luce. *This Sex Which Is Not One.* Trans. Catherine Porter. Ithaca: Cornell UP, 1985.

Jones, Ann Rosalind. "Inscribing Femininity: French Theories of the Feminine." *Making a Difference: Feminist Literary Criticism.* Ed. Gayle Green and Coppélia Kahn. London: Methuen, 1985. 80–112.

————. "Writing the Body: Toward an Understanding of *l' Écriture féminine*."
    The New Feminist Criticism: Essays on Women, Literature and Theory.
    Ed. Elaine Showalter. NY: Pantheon, 1985. 361–77.
Josephs, Allen. "Hemingway's Poor Spanish: Chauvinism and Loss of Credibil-
    ity in *For Whom the Bell Tolls*." *Hemingway: A Revaluation*. Ed.
    Donald R. Noble. Troy, NY: Whitston, 1983. 205–23.
Reynolds, Michael. "*For Whom the Bell Tolls*: Colonel Lawrence Rings the
    Changes." Unpublished essay, 1988.
Smith, Paul. " 'Daffodils and Stories': The Re-writing of 'A Way You'll Never
    Be.' " Unpublished essay, 1989.

11 The Polemics of Narrative and Difference in *For Whom the Bell Tolls*

Mark C. Van Gunten

> War, indeed, is the absolute transformation of all differences into binary differences.
> —Barbara Johnson, *The Critical Difference* 106.

> The two antithetical types of narrative . . . may be labeled the *empirical* and the *fictional*. Both can be seen as ways of avoiding the tyranny of the traditional in story-telling.
> —Robert Scholes and Robert Kellogg, *The Nature of Narrative* 13.

Arturo Barea, an early critic of *For Whom the Bell Tolls* (1940), found fault with the novel for its distorted depiction of the Spanish Civil War's historical/political context and Spain's cultural and linguistic tradition (80–90). For Barea, Hemingway's alleged departure from established "fact" or "reality" rendered *For Whom the Bell Tolls* nearly worthless as a truthful record of the conflict.

More recent readers, such as Robert O. Stephens and Carlos Baker, also have pointed out that the book is not to be construed as a historical account. Stephens maintains that the language of the novel, instead of being primarily discursive, is what he terms "mythic and creative" (152). And by claiming that "the job of the artist is not to judge but to understand," Baker reads the novel as Hemingway's expert balancing-act, a tribute to the author's "obligation to truth and to art, and to humanity in its extra-political dimension," a "balance without which art may degenerate into propaganda" (240).

From these two oppositional reading strategies—exemplified by Barea, who condemns the novel for the same "literariness" that Stephens and

Baker admire—Hemingway's text seems to elevate "art" over history, either a success or failure depending upon the vested interests of the critic.

The difference between empirical and fictional in *For Whom the Bell Tolls* is enacted by the characters Robert Jordan and the gypsy Pilar. Jordan is yet another of Hemingway's painstakingly observant protagonists. As Jackson Benson notes, he "not only sees everything, but interprets everything properly" (155). Like other Hemingway heroes, Robert Jordan uses his experience, knowledge, and keen eye to assess and then act upon the problems and details surrounding his mission to blow the bridge. Pilar, on the other hand, has none of the academic or military training that Jordan has. She believes in what Jordan calls "superstition"—the gypsy folklore that allows her to read Jordan's future in his hand. Yet these two quite different modes of reading and interpretation are not incompatible, since what Pilar has seen in Jordan's hand—his death—is as literally "true" as Jordan's more empirical deduction of his probable fate.

Hemingway himself addressed this issue in a 1940 letter to Maxwell Perkins: "There is the balanceing [sic] of Jordan's good sense and sound skepticism against this gypsy crap which isn't all crap" (*Selected Letters* 508). This mediation of the opposing discourses of "good sense" and "gypsy crap" resembles the admixture of historical "reality" and fiction that makes up *For Whom the Bell Tolls*. The reader's task in encountering the novel is similar to Robert Jordan's: discerning "meaning" and "truth" in the various texts (stories, histories, dreams, superstitions, signs, and so on) that compete for attention amidst the general chaos of the war itself.

These various texts illustrate the importance of language and signification in *For Whom the Bell Tolls*; as in all of Hemingway's writings, this importance is located in the connections between things, actions, and feelings, all of which revolve around the control and power of words (Stephens 151). From Pilar's story of the massacre of Fascists in her town at the beginning of the Loyalist movement, the vividness of which makes Jordan "see it," to the lies of political propaganda on both sides, to the authority of orders and the power of those who issue them, language and writing are charged with power in *For Whom the Bell Tolls*. While their control and proper use may prevent ambiguity (as in the case of Jordan's written orders) or bad luck (as Lt. Berrendo of Franco's army feels suppressing cursing may do), all too often language, as it is passed from its source to its recipient, may propagate violence: Pilar's story "molests" Maria, and Jordan worries that if Golz fails to receive his message in time, Jordan unwittingly will "kill them all off with those orders."[1]

Issues of the power, authority, and violence of language are entwined in the novel's inherent structures of difference. One must choose sides during war, as Jordan realizes, yet the Fascist/Loyalist opposition, which seems to reduce and subsume all others into an overriding polemic, is but a variation on the truth/lies (fact/fiction) opposition that serves as *For Whom the Bell Tolls*'s primary subtext. Other binary oppositions include: the individual/the collective body; abstract ideas/concrete things; religion/politics; and Karkov's differentiation between execution and assassination. However, as a civil war, a conflict among participants who share a common history and culture, the Spanish struggle itself is an example of the subjection of differences *within* entities (the Spanish people) to those *between* entities (Loyalists and Fascists).

In effect, all distinctions between entities in the novel are undermined by their simultaneous existence as differences within: Jordan's fate is inextricably linked to that of the young Republic; his belief in "Life, Liberty, and the Pursuit of Happiness" (305) is derived from the satisfaction he receives from his work and from Maria; the guerrillas' Catholic heritage co-exists with their newfound political awareness; and Karkov's preference of the terms "execute and destroy" over "assassinate" elevates killing by the Party over "acts of terrorism by individuals" (245).

In the act of resolving this play of differences, warfare in *For Whom the Bell Tolls* becomes the pretext for a discourse preoccupied with the threat of self-destruction. Jordan is haunted by memories—mental narratives—of the deaths of his father and his predecessor Kashkin, and his own story ends in death. The simultaneous narrative of El Sordo's hilltop defense results in annihilation; similarly, if the war is lost, Jordan thinks, then so too all those things he believes in will be lost. The increasing difficulties of Jordan's bridge-blowing mission and his determination not to repeat the scripts of other doomed warriors are analogous to Hemingway's efforts in *For Whom the Bell Tolls* to "write a true book" that transcends the difficulties of historical/fictional representation and originality.

The contradictions and complexities inherent in the Spanish Civil War were apparent to Hemingway. Although his political indifference has been well documented,[2] Hemingway's sympathies lay with the Republican side. His personal interest in the war led to his involvement in the film *The Spanish Earth* and to several short stories and the play *The Fifth Column*. Nonetheless, Hemingway understood that war "is very complicated and difficult to write about truly"; in a 1939 letter to Soviet literary critic and translator Ivan Kashkin, he recalled his war experiences and discussed the difficulties in transcribing them:

For instance to take it on a simply personal basis—in the war in Italy when I was a boy I had much fear. In Spain I had no fear after a couple of weeks and was very happy. Yet for me to not understand fear in others or deny its existence would be bad writing. It is just that now I understand the whole thing better. (*Selected Letters* 480)

While hardly "bad writing," the book which resulted from that boyhood war experience in Italy, *A Farewell to Arms*, nonetheless features a very restricted narrative scope. Filtered through the narrator Frederic Henry's consciousness, the events in *A Farewell to Arms* are indeed taken on a "personal basis." Unlike Robert Jordan, Henry has no sociopolitical motives for taking up arms in a foreign country. And also in direct contrast to Jordan, Henry, instead of committing himself to getting the job done, engineers his "separate peace" by fleeing the war with the woman he loves, who is pregnant with his child.

Although their protagonists' political involvement sets them apart, the subject of war and the difficulty of re-presenting war in language binds the two novels. By setting up an opposition between abstract and concrete, between obscenity and dignity, Frederic Henry in *A Farewell to Arms* acknowledges the writer's problem of language and its possible distortion or its potential misuse. He prefers names and numbers—essentially grounded signifiers—to the abstractions and euphemisms endemic to descriptions of wartime experience. With twenty years' hindsight on his first war and a decade since his first war novel, Hemingway's approach during the 1930s to writing about war reveals how much he had learned. In the same 1939 letter to Kashkin, Hemingway discussed the technique of his most recent stories about the Spanish Civil War: "I try to show *all* the different sides of it, taking it slowly and honestly and examining it from many ways. So never think one story represents my viewpoint because it is much too complicated for that."

While both novels feature a single character and his responses to events in which he is involved, the intensely personal perspective of war that dominates *A Farewell to Arms* gives way in *For Whom the Bell Tolls* to one where simultaneous actions, though separated by distance from Jordan's guerrilla band, are presented as a means of heightening the narrative's emphasis on time. These events, coupled with the stories Jordan's band share with one another, also reveal the overwhelming complexity of differing fighting units, differing political considerations and motivations, and differing experiences of the combatants on both sides.

This complex problem of vantage point in the "truthful" or "accurate" depiction of the Spanish Civil War is dramatized in one of those short stories, "Night Before Battle" (1939). The story begins with the narrator, in Madrid as part of a film crew (much like Hemingway himself with his participation in *The Spanish Earth*), recalling the difficulty in working close enough to the battle:

At this time we were working in a shell-smashed house that overlooked the Casa del Campo in Madrid. Below us a battle was being fought. You could see it spread out below you and over the hills, could smell it, could taste the dust of it, and the noise of it was one great slithering sheet of rifle and automatic rifle fire rising and dropping, and in it came the crack of guns and the bubbly rumbling of the outgoing shells fired from the batteries behind us, the thud of their bursts, and then rolling yellow clouds of dust. But it was just too far to film well. We had tried working closer but they kept sniping at the camera and you could not work.[3]

In this passage, the narrator acknowledges the limitations of film, usually considered the most direct and accurate medium for recording events in progress. But the camera itself has inherent restrictions on distance and focus, much like the choices presented to an author concerning the presentation of his written subject matter. The narrator here has succeeded in capturing in words what his camera can not. The subjective transcription of his experience—signalled by the first- and second-person pronouns— seems to lessen the distance between that experience and its re-presentation, a distance "too far to film well."

As a metaphor for representation, then, this brief excerpt from "Night Before Battle" establishes the fundamental concern that faced Hemingway in *For Whom the Bell Tolls*. As with the bullfight, the necessity of representing a very complicated set of events in language demanded a confrontation between the subjective impressions of the spectator/partic- ipant and the more objective framework of the larger historical/political scene. In "Night Before Battle" the danger of working too closely to the action is explicitly spelled out—death from snipers. And this threat of destruction is especially evident in *For Whom the Bell Tolls*, where the stakes are even higher. In telling the "truth" of the Spanish Civil War, Hemingway's second and biggest war novel had to incorporate both texts, that of history and that of the knowledgeable participant.

Jordan's allegiance to the "truth" of his experience is expressed in terms of writing: "You have no right to forget anything. You have no right to shut your eyes to any of it nor any right to forget any of it nor to soften it nor to change it" (304). Jordan's statement may be read as Hemingway's own credo in rewriting the Spanish Civil War, what Baker regards as the "artist's obligation to truth and to art" 240.

These twin obligations are revealed in Jordan's reaction to Pilar's narrative about the slaughter of Fascists in her village at the beginning of the war. To Jordan, Pilar's story is one he "would try to write . . . and if he had luck and could remember it perhaps he could get it down *as she told it*" (134; emphasis added). In wishing to reproduce Pilar's story "as she told it," Jordan's aesthetic concern here is the faithful transcription of Pilar's words, a gesture by which he equates truth with the manner of presentation. "I will tell it truly as it was," Pilar prefaced her tale, and Jordan is impressed by her authority and narrative skill.

Her ability to make Jordan "see it as though [he] had been there" (135) points up Hemingway's own artistic efforts to re-present truthfully and realistically the impact of experience. Jordan, however, feels his skills are inferior to the task: "God, how she could tell a story. . . . He never wrote the death of any Don Faustino as well as she told it. I wish I could write well enough to write that story, he thought" (134). Jordan's authorial anxiety signals not an implied supremacy of spoken over written narrative—for both forms, like oral and written orders, are invested with authority and "truth"—but instead calls attention to writing as essentially an act of copying another story. Pilar's narrative, of course, is not the literal "truth"; it is a representation in language of certain events from her personal history. By neither adding to nor subtracting from Pilar's account, Jordan hopes to preserve—not do violence to—the implicit accuracy and explicit manner of her historical narrative.

The effects on Jordan and Maria of Pilar's story about killing the Fascists in her home town reinforce a link between violence and text. Pilar is hesitant about beginning her account for fear that it may "molest" Maria or give her "bad dreams" (99). "Molest" here is an interesting word choice given the fact that Maria's own story is one of molestation; it denotes both the sense of annoyance or troubling as well as that of sexual violence. After hearing Pilar's tale, Maria admits it "was too much" (129), but instead of molesting Jordan, the vividness of Pilar's story—"she had made him see it in that town"—stirs in him the desire to write: "If that woman could only write. He would try to write it and if he had luck and could remember it perhaps he could get it down as she told it" (134). Pilar's violent narrative does not reach an end in its transmission to Jordan and Maria, for by "molesting" Maria it propagates further violence and may possibly reconstitute itself in the form of texts authored by the unconscious—"bad dreams." For Robert Jordan, Pilar's tale deserves yet another retelling in his own text, "a true book."

Writing and rewriting are recurring structures in *For Whom the Bell Tolls*. Jordan's message to Golz to call off the planned Loyalist offensive, an order that countermands a previous order, essentially is an act of rewriting, since the faults of the already-written or previous order are evident once the "truth" of the situation has been discerned. Similarly, Anselmo's spoken vision of his postwar Republic, where "those that have fought against us should be educated to see their error" (285), is an optimistic view of the future, one in which Anselmo hopes revisionist history plays a prominent role.

This preoccupation with rewriting in the interest of "truth" also is seen in Jordan's musings over the "lies and legends" of Loyalist military leaders. Although he claims to have accepted the wartime necessity of lies and deceptions, when leaders and their reputations often need to be "manufactured," Jordan also knows that "the truth of Lister, Modesto, and El Campesino was much better than the lies and legends" (230). "[S]ome day they would tell the truth to every one" (230), thinks Jordan; yet the elevation of "fictions" over "facts" is expedient when such things as "Life, Liberty, and the Pursuit of Happiness" (305) are at stake. Lying, as Jordan terms it, is "a very corrupting business" (229), an influential transaction between text and receiver.

Maria's account of her capture, rape, and humiliation at the hands of Fascist troops painfully describes the violent molestation done to her. Her motives for telling Jordan these things also are in the interest of "truth," but they seem primarily cathartic. Maria claims that the "black thing" haunting her can be exorcised by passing her story on to Jordan. She says "that telling it to thee might rid me of it" (350), echoing Jordan's earlier notion of the cleansing powers of writing: "But my guess is you will get rid of all that by writing about it, he said. Once you write it down it is all gone" (165). The retelling of personal experiences serves to cast out the demons of violence and guilt: Jordan ponders the wartime necessity of "successful assassination," one of "the big words" standing in relation to actions: "Did big words make it more defensible? Did they make killing any more palatable?" (165)

Maria's guilt concerning her rape is lessened by sharing it with Jordan. And for Pilar, the telling of her story seems motivated by the same reasons for which she participated in the killings: "it was better for all the people to have a part in it, and I wished to share the guilt as much as any, just as I hoped to share in the benefits when the town should be ours" (119). History, language, and violence bind the characters together as much as their collective "guilt."

Maria wants Jordan to have pride in her as his wife, and therefore she wishes the truth of her struggle be known: "I would have thee know that which you should know for thy own pride if I am to be thy wife. Never did I submit to any one. Always I fought and always it took two of them or more to do the harm. . . . I tell thee this for thy pride" (350). Maria continues her story since "it affects us," she tells Jordan. In both senses of "affect," she is correct in her claim. Her history is now part of Jordan's, as their relationship is constituted as much by the past as present circumstances. But the hearing of her tale also has an effect on Jordan—it fills him with hatred and incites him to want to kill: "he was as full of hate as any man could be. . . . 'I am glad you told me,' he said. 'For tomorrow, with luck, we will kill plenty' " (353).

Later, after he has issued his orders to the guerrillas for the bridge operation, one he feels holds little chance of success, Jordan believes he "will kill them all off with those orders" (385), yet another example of the power and influence of texts in the novel. Like the identification papers carried by the guerrillas—texts supposedly guaranteeing the "truth" of their possessor and therefore safe passage—which can be imitated, forged, or misinterpreted, writing at once carries the authority of "truth" and of "fiction." In its transmission from source to recipient, writing finally becomes subjected to the authority of the reader, which delays, interrupts, or even rewrites any "truth" that might be encoded in it.

Andrés's attempts to deliver Jordan's message to Golz metaphorically illustrate this interruption of discourse. The difficulty of relaying the message dramatizes the difficulty of transmitting "truth," the author's goal in written representation. All along the dangerous route back to friendly lines, Andrés and his text are read, questioned, and treated with suspicion by various authorities. Finally, the message is intercepted by Marty, who interprets Andrés's information as a story, "using the term story as you would say lie, falsehood, or fabrication" (420). By the time Karkov recognizes the error and is able to forward Andrés and the crucial message to Golz, it is too late to stop the doomed Loyalist offensive—Jordan's message has failed to make any difference.

The issue here is one of authority. Distinctions between military and political leadership have dissolved on the Loyalist side, creating generals out of commissars, as in the case of Marty. Since there "was no one at the front with sufficient authority to cancel the attack" (423), the great "inertia" that has built up for the attack cannot be overcome. In this late section of *For Whom the Bell Tolls*, authority, while certainly equated with power, is not equated with wisdom, insight, or interpretive skill. Marty, who fancies himself a military leader, studies intently "the brown tracing of the contours" on "the map he never truly understood" (422). Like Pablo, the illiterate guerrilla leader, Marty in a sense cannot read either. As a revered and powerful member of the intricate Communist Party hierarchy, Marty, in Golz's words, has become "a symbol I cannot touch" (423), a figure whose name, reputation, and power render him invincible to error or "truth." And like Pablo, Marty's personal history, which earned him that reputation, bears little in common with his present unpredictability, abuse of power, and betrayal of his own cause. Both characters are enigmatic figures, undecipherable to their compatriots, bodies of contradictions immune to decidable reduction or interpretation.

If "truth" in writing is subject to interruption or distortion by the authority of the reader, then what becomes of writing's authority? *For Whom the Bell Tolls* seems to suggest that any supposed guarantee of authenticity, such as the impression of the rubber-stamp S.I.M. seal that Andrés's message from Jordan bears, is subject to challenge by other "authorities." As the skeptical officer tells Andrés: "Papers can be forged" (376). Since not only the message's origin and truth, but Andrés's account of the background of his mission and orders are challenged (it has become a "story—a lie, falsehood, fabrication"), the novel postulates the impossibility of writing as self-evident "truth" (i.e., not forged, copied, or invented). It is as if the message, and hence writing, are forever open to question. Their source and destination are indeterminate, resulting in the deferment and interruption of the "truth" so crucial to their transmission.

An intriguing parallel from Hemingway's life informs the connections among oral narrative, writing, and originality. In June 1941, Hemingway was served with a lawsuit that claimed *For Whom the Bell Tolls* was plagiarized from a screenplay by John De Montijo, who alleged Hemingway had attended a Hollywood party where the script was read aloud. Although Hemingway won the suit, Scribner's deducted some $1,000 from the novel's royalties to help cover Hemingway's legal fees (Meyers 339). The resemblance between this strange event and Robert Jordan's desire to transcribe Pilar's story in his own text is striking. The issue of authorial originality certainly is not restricted to Hemingway; but while *For Whom the Bell Tolls* advocates "truth" in the form of faithful transcription, it also reveals an anxiety concerning repeating historical scripts.

Jordan's awareness of historical texts and their application to his own situation is a recurring motif of the novel. Jordan "would abandon a hero's or a martyr's end gladly. He did not want to make a Thermopylae, nor be Horatius at any bridge, nor be the Dutch boy with his finger in that dyke" (164). Jordan also has "an opinion on what was wrong with everyone else's [battles], from Agincourt on down" (200); furthermore, Jordan at one point feels "that he was playing a part from memory of something that he had read or had dreamed, feeling it all moving in a circle" (212). Later, when the untimely snowfall and Pablo's disappearance with Jordan's detonators seem to have doomed Jordan's mission, he is heartened at Pablo's return: "Seeing Pablo again had broken the pattern of tragedy into which the whole operation had seemed grooved" (393). And finally, after breaking his thigh while fleeing the pursuing enemy forces, Jordan is faced squarely with the question of suicide: "I don't want to do the business that my father did" (469). Jordan's anxiety over repeating a script signals an authorial anxiety over originality—by "breaking the pattern" or refusing to conform to previous models Jordan, and hence the author, hopes to avoid (and more importantly escape the destruction of) copying his predecessors.

The repetition of the script of the death of the father is established in a darkly humorous passage wherein a comparison is made between Maria's father, shot because he was a Spanish Republican, and Jordan's father, an American member of the Republican Party who "shot himself" to "avoid being tortured," leading Maria to say to Jordan: "Then you and me we are the same" (66–67). The similarities between these two narratives recounting the death of the father, and the physical resemblance between Maria and Jordan—"You could be brother and sister by the look" (67)—generate a pattern of doubleness or repetition that merges self and other in terms of the father.

Jordan's unease with the subject of the father—"Should we talk about something else?" (67)—further underscores his anxiety. For Jordan, the loss of the father corresponds to the betrayal of authority. His paternal aggression is evident, for the "coward" and "son of a bitch" who killed himself abdicated his responsibilities toward the son—"he never had to teach me," thinks Jordan (338). The betrayal of other "fathers" in the novel—the military and political authorities—echoes Hemingway's contention that the war ultimately was lost because the Spanish people as a whole were "betrayed."[4] Yet further parallels among betrayal, authority, and suicide (along with the repetition of a previous text) are seen when Pilar tells Pablo: "Thy predecessor the famous Judas Iscariot hanged himself" (391).

Jordan, however, seems caught in a double bind. He is anxious about repeating certain scripts, but Kashkin, his predecessor, has produced a valorized narrative. Like Kashkin, Jordan is a dynamiter and a foreigner, one with a "rare name" (20) who "take[s] the place of the other blond one" (24). To the members of Pablo's guerrilla band, the incident with the train is a story retold for Jordan's benefit, effectively challenging him to duplicate its excitement and success. "Never in my life have I seen such a thing," repeats Anselmo (29), and Pilar admits that "It was the only good thing we have done" (30). Another ghost haunts Jordan's mission—Kashkin's. Jordan must work with the knowledge of his predecessor's (father's) fate and exalted story while at the same time reproducing its military success. But after he too is wounded and faced with the option of suicide, Jordan allows himself to be killed by the enemy, thus removing the stigma of cowardice that taints suicide and informs the unoriginality of repetition.

Since Jordan is engaged not only in a military mission but also a search for meaning and truth, *For Whom the Bells Tolls* insists on exposing lies and revealing truth that often is hidden or suppressed. Jordan knows the "real story" behind the leaders of the movement, and he recognizes that propaganda, mainly the party organs of both sides, cannot give "a full picture of what is happening" (246). Contrasted to Jordan is Karkov, a journalist for *Pravda*. Jordan recalls one of Karkov's stories that told of Miaja, a general in charge of Madrid's defensive positions, having to inspect the positions on his bicycle for want of motor transport. Jordan, however, "did not believe that one. He could not see Miaja on a bicycle even in his most patriotic imagination, but Karkov said it was true. But then he had written it for Russian papers so he probably wanted to believe it was true after writing it" (237).

Unlike Jordan, who questions what he has read—"Tell me, does [cyanide] smell like bitter almonds the way it always does in detective stories?" (238)—Karkov, for all his cynicism, nonetheless possesses an almost fanatical belief in the truth of writing and the power of texts to produce truth, however different it might be from historical "fact." When Jordan doubts that a communique from the Cordoba front (a serious Loyalist defeat) actually said that "Our glorious troops continue to advance without losing a foot of ground," Karkov responds: "It is in the communique" (239). Karkov also speaks of Mitchell, a British journalist, who has the "face of a conspirator. All who have read of conspirators in books trust him instantly" (242).

Moreover, Karkov is one of the very few who had read Jordan's only book, and he "said it was a good book. 'I think you write absolutely truly and that is very rare. So I would like you to know some things' " (248). And in a passage that sounds strikingly like Hemingway himself, Karkov muses on a book he hopes to author: "out of this will come a book which is very necessary; which will explain many things which it is necessary to know. Perhaps I will write it. I hope that it will be me who will write it. . . . I am a journalist. But like all journalists I wish to write literature" (244).

Karkov's distinction between journalism and literature, as with his distinction between execution and assassination, undermines itself. The "truth" of the communique and his stories for *Pravda*, like the faces from books, are essentially fictions; even when being facetious, Karkov says: "I always get my facts wrong. It is the mark of the journalist" (425). It is as if for Karkov truth is a tyranny to be liberated from—"But you will not find any such picture [of what is happening in the war] if you read twenty papers and then, if you had it, I do not know what you would do with it" (246); whereas for Jordan, truth itself is a means of liberation, in its ability to transcend not only lies—"some day they would tell the truth to every-one" (230)—but also guilt—"you will get rid of all that by writing about it" (165). Jordan's "education" consists of both personal experience and stories told to him by others, either in oral or written form. But as the various readers/authors in *For Whom the Bell Tolls* illustrate, the differ-ence between truth and text is not inherent, but a matter of interpretation.

Thus the relationship between language and truth in the novel is slippery at best. The primary polemic in *For Whom the Bell Tolls*, meaning or "truth" versus falsehood and incoherence, lies not only in the scene of civil war, but at the very heart of writing. Yet if war, as Barbara Johnson maintains, is "the absolute transformation of all differences into binary difference" (106), *For Whom the Bell Tolls* sets up its own set of differ-ences to deconstruct. Oral and written narratives, including military orders and the numerous other texts in the novel, essentially carry the same authority and perform the same functions. The guerrillas' Catholicism has been transformed into politics; both are systems invested with a dialectic between good and evil, salvation and damnation.

The fate of Joaquín, the youngest member of El Sordo's band, poignantly illustrates the faith in both religious and political texts: before he is killed by the Fascist planes, Joaquín is stiffened by the slogan of La Pasionaria, especially "Better to die on thy feet than to live on thy knees"; however, as the bombs fall, he interrupts his repetition of her slogans with the familiar "Hail Mary, full of grace" (321).

The novel furthers the comparison between these texts. As Jordan remembers the two Madrid political and military headquarters, Gaylord's and Velasquez 63, his language is laced with religious terms:

Gaylord's . . . was the opposite of the puritanical, religious communism of Velasquez 63. . . . At Velasquez 63 it was like being a member of a religious order. . . . At either of those places you felt you were taking part in a crusade. . . . You felt, in spite of all bureaucracy and inefficiency and party strife something that was like the feeling you expected to have and did not have when you made your first communion. (234–35)

By overtly identifying the politics of the struggle with Catholicism, Jordan again reveals himself as a skilled interpreter, one who embraces intertextual reading, as when he proclaims to himself: "You're not a real Marxist and you know it. . . . Don't ever kid yourself with too much dialectics. . . . But afterwards you can discard what you do not believe in" (305). Jordan's phrase "don't kid yourself" serves as a refrain throughout the novel, the motto of both the acute observer and the "honest" writer.

In order to interpret successfully, however, one must de-center the self from its restrictive egotism, merge with the text at hand, become a part of it, as Jordan does. His place in the struggle, his part in the "crusade,"

gave you a part in something that you could believe in wholly and completely and in which you felt an absolute brotherhood with the others who were engaged in it. It was something that you had never known before but that you had experienced now and you gave such importance to it and the reasons for it that your own death seemed of complete unimportance. (235)

This merger of the individual self with a cause, with humanity, with history completes Jordan's "education" at the end of the novel. After the bridge has been destroyed, resulting in Anselmo's death, Jordan recognizes the necessity of seeing it "as it was to others, once you got rid of your own self, the always ridding of self that you had to do in war. Where there could be no self. Where yourself is only lost" (447). And as he waits for the approaching enemy, the pain from his broken thigh throbbing to the point of unconsciousness, Jordan "was completely integrated now and he took a good long look at everything" (471). Faced with the choice of either killing himself or allowing himself to be killed, Jordan no longer feels as if he is playing a part—he feels "completely integrated"; it appears he has transcended the boundary between individual and society, self and other, echoing Donne's "No man is an *Iland*" theme in the novel's epigraph.

Jordan's final act of interpretive integration seems much more politically correct and less selfish than Frederic Henry's declaration of a "separate peace." Because of its emphasis on resolving a polemic of the individual versus the collective, *For Whom the Bell Tolls* affirms Jordan's desire to dismantle differences. Yet as the failure of Frederic Henry's escape into romanticism finally leads to his recognition that everyone is bound to the warlike condition of the threat of being "broken" or killed,

Jordan's "integration" is subject to its own deconstruction: in a physical sense he perishes utterly alone, cut off from the rest of his band, dis-integrated from those whose cause he dies for; the text's preoccupation with physical sensation as Lt. Berrendo unsuspectingly approaches Jordan's gunsights seems to banish any trace of spiritual or abstract thought.

But even this difference between the abstract and the concrete or physical is undermined. From his racking pain to his final appreciation of such physicalities as the sky with its white clouds and the bark and needles of the pine forest, Jordan achieves a political and spiritual transcendence. In what Frederic Henry might term "obscene," Robert Jordan obliterates the distinctions between the abstract and the concrete, thus joining in a single instant the dignity of both place and sensation and a collective awareness.

In *For Whom the Bell Tolls* Hemingway has written a subversive text, one that questions the authority of writing, difference, and truth. To read this book in either purely empirical (historical) or fictional terms, as many Hemingway critics do, only perpetuates the same sort of civil warfare enacted by history's Fascist and Loyalist counterparts; that is, to choose all allegiance to a particular reading strategy in the name of "truth" or "art" ultimately ignores Jordan's fundamental lesson—that differences *between* rely on differences *within* entities. But it also must be recognized that the freedom to choose, whether a reading strategy or a means of salvation, requires its own liberation, from the "recognition that there is nothing that is not social and historical—indeed, that everything is 'in the last analysis' political" (Jameson 20). In its connections between writing, politics, and warfare, and even how it structures the twentieth-century reader's perception of the Spanish Civil War, Hemingway's narrative—unlike Jordan's ill-fated message to Golz—certainly has made a difference.

NOTES

1. Ernest Hemingway, *For Whom the Bell Tolls* (NY: Scribner's, 1940) 385. All further page references to this novel will be given in the text.

2. See Jeffrey Meyers, *Hemingway: A Biography*; Kenneth S. Lynn, *Hemingway*; Scott Donaldson, *By Force of Will: The Life and Art of Ernest Hemingway*.

3. Originally published in *Esquire*, February 1939. Reprinted in *The Complete Short Stories* 437.

4. Hemingway, preface to Gustav Regler, *The Great Crusade* vii.

WORKS CITED

Baker, Carlos. *Hemingway: The Writer as Artist*. 4th ed. Princeton: Princeton UP, 1972.

Barea, Arturo. "Not Spain but Hemingway." *The Merrill Studies in "For Whom the Bell Tolls*." Ed. Sheldon Norman Grebstein. 1941. Columbus: Charles E. Merrill, 1971. 80–90.

Benson, Jackson J. *Hemingway: The Writer's Art of Self-Defense*. Minneapolis: U of Minnesota P, 1969.

Donaldson, Scott. *By Force of Will: The Life and Art of Ernest Hemingway*. NY: Viking Press, 1977.

Hemingway, Ernest. *The Complete Short Stories of Ernest Hemingway: The Finca Vigia Edition*. NY: Scribner's, 1987.

————. *Ernest Hemingway: Selected Letters, 1917–1961*. Ed. Carlos Baker. NY: Scribner's, 1981.

————. *For Whom the Bell Tolls*. NY: Scribner's, 1940.

Jameson, Fredric. *The Political Unconscious: Narrative as a Socially Symbolic Act*. Ithaca, NY: Cornell UP, 1981.

Johnson, Barbara. *The Critical Difference: Essays in the Contemporary Rhetoric of Reading*. Baltimore: Johns Hopkins UP, 1980.

Lynn, Kenneth S. *Hemingway*. NY: Simon and Schuster, 1987.

Meyers, Jeffrey. *Hemingway: A Biography*. NY: Harper and Row, 1985.

Regler, Gustav. *The Great Crusade*. Trans. Whittaker Chambers and Barrows Mussey. NY: Longmans, Green, 1940.

Scholes, Robert, and Robert Kellogg. *The Nature of Narrative*. NY: Oxford UP, 1966.

Stephens, Robert O. "Language Magic and Reality in *For Whom the Bell Tolls*." *Criticism* 14 (1972): 151–64.

12 "I Don't Know Buffalo Bill"; or, Hemingway and the Rhetoric of the Western

Dean Rehberger

> The annals of the mountain-desert have never been written and can never be written. They are merely a vast mass of fact and tradition and imagining which floats from tongue to tongue from the Rockies to the Sierra Nevadas. A man may be a fact all his life and die only a local celebrity. Then again, he may strike sparks from that imagination which runs riot by camp-fires and at the bars of the crossroads saloons. In that case he becomes immortal. . . . In due time he will become a tradition.
>
> —Max Brand [Frederick Schiller Faust],
> *Riders of the Silences* (1920) 61.

In 1939, Lionel Trilling outlined the central problematic of Hemingway studies that still haunts contemporary critics. He argued that Hemingway's fictions of the 1930s, particularly his play *The Fifth Column* and his novel *To Have and to Have Not*, failed because of the decade's critical pressures that mistook the "artist" for the "man." Because of Hemingway's celebrity status, leftist critics demanded that Hemingway the "man" use his status and "art" to support the correct social and political perspectives. As Trilling states, critics assumed that "art is—or should be—the exact equivalent of life" (13).

In 1985, Harold Bloom echoed Trilling when he stated, in reference to Hemingway, that "the color and variety of the artist's life becomes something of a veil between the work and our aesthetic apprehension of it" (Bloom 4). Bloom was pointing to the well-known problem of Hemingway's Byronic legend distorting a clear view of his fiction. Readers often find it difficult to separate Hemingway's adventures from the exploits of Nick Adams, Frederic Henry, Jake Barnes, Robert Jordan, and his many other artist/hunter/adventurer protagonists.

Although Bloom's focus on the problematic is slightly different, he tells, like Trilling, a tragic tale about the development of Hemingway as writer. Hemingway's tragedy was this: although the legend of the man continued to expand, Hemingway never improved as an artist. His best works, Bloom points out, are his short stories and *The Sun Also Rises*, which can be read as a series of short vignettes. His artistic talents, in short, never enlarged to encompass the form of the novel, and his late works are seen as either a parody of his early style or as an extension of his self-created legend.

Critics who have endeavored to tell an opposite tale of development and progress in Hemingway's work have tried to lift the veil of the Hemingway legend either by separating Hemingway's art from the man,[1] or by reading through the man, his biography and/or psyche, to reach a better understanding of his art.[2] Both approaches tacitly accept Trilling's distinction between the artist and his life, and the need for the critic to delineate a distinction between the two or somehow to reconcile the two. More recently, Louis Renza has tried to reconceive the problematic by exploring why Hemingway emphasizes the relations between the man and the experience of writing, and in doing so Renza draws a connection between Hemingway's early and late works. Simply stated, Hemingway's *A Moveable Feast* was an attempt to recollect the site of "original writing" that he created in the collection of short stories, *In Our Time*, a first published book that gained him the acclaim of being an "original" American writer. But like the interpretations of Trilling and Bloom, Renza's critical appraisal is a tragic tale. For Renza, *A Moveable Feast* "essentially tells the story of his fall from this original project largely as the result of his own ambition or surrender to the ideology of public literary fame" (667). Hemingway's hubris, which steadily grew over the years with his public image, was responsible for "his fall from writing 'truly' " (669).

We can, however, recast Renza's tragic plot by re-reading Hemingway's emphasis on the interrelationship between the site of writing and physical experience. This relationship can be read as a continuation and revision of an ongoing cultural debate about how adventure on the frontier could rejuvenate the ailing and fragmented psyche of modern man. The statement, "I don't know Buffalo Bill," is reputed by Carlos Baker to be Ernest Hemingway's first complete sentence, a sentence he uttered when taken to see Pawnee Bill's Wild West Show (4). The veracity of the anecdote is not as important as the fact that Hemingway was exposed at an early age to the perpetuation of the frontier myth.

Hemingway's first decade coincided with the transformation of the frontier myth's elements into forms and conventions readily used by showmen and popular novelists. The Wild West shows, performed on sports fields of cities around the country, essentially reenacted the taming of the West. Such shows as Pawnee Bill's exaggerated the skills of riding, roping, and marksmanship as the keys to success on the frontier. In general, the Wild West shows and Western novels at the turn of the century recreated in microcosm the frontier as a symbolic landscape in which the self-reliant spirit of Americans who had been overdomesticated by the urban landscape was revitalized. In an America of rapid industrialization and incorporation, the cowboy hero of the Western evolved into an image of masculine strength and honor, and his exaggerated skills and precise mastery of tasks became symbolic of his individual mastery over the undisciplined and savage other.

In the decades before and after Hemingway's birth, cultural spokespersons like Theodore Roosevelt, Henry Cabot Lodge, Owen Wister,[3] and Frederic Remington were fusing a relationship between physical activity and the aesthetic, adventure and art, so that they could revitalize with stories of frontier adventure and individual heroics a country that had moved dangerously close to dissipation and race suicide. In their writings, fact and fiction, man and legend, were combined to create a space in which the reader could share in the adventures and "feats of daring."

In their 1908 collection of sketches, *Hero Tales From American History*, for example, Henry Cabot Lodge and Theodore Roosevelt explain that their purpose is to demonstrate that the subjects of their book brought together the "stern and manly qualities which are essential to the well-being of a masterful race" and "the virtues of gentleness, of patriotism, and of lofty adherence to an ideal," so that "young Americans" who read the tales could learn that in addition to the "thrift, industry, obedience to law, and intellectual cultivation," they needed the "heroic virtues" of "energy, daring, endurance, as well as the wish and the power to fight the nation's foes" (Lodge and Roosevelt ix). They attempted, in other words, to represent an "adventure ethos" that combined middle-class values ("thrift, industry, obedience to law") with the rhetoric of adventure ("daring, endurance . . . power to fight") and theories of racial superiority to create a reinvigorated form of patriotism and nationalism.

In many ways it is possible to read the standard definitions of the Hemingway "code" as a rewriting of the adventure ethos: the taciturn character of stoic reserve who faces the presence of death in life and who always exhibits grace under pressure. Who better exemplifies this code than the stereotype of the cowboy? Think of unyielding Gary Cooper facing certain death in *High Noon*, or the restrained John Wayne facing the loss of the woman he loves in *The Man Who Shot Liberty Valance*. Or one might think of Owen Wister's classic cowboy, the Virginian, who while playing poker is called "a son of a bitch." The Virginian coolly faces the possibility of a showdown by answering with the now immortal line, "When you call me that, smile!" (29).

In this context, then, consider Robert Jordan, during the potential showdown in the cave, carefully "letting his right hand hang lower and lower" over his gun, just in case it "should be necessary" to shoot Pablo.[4] My point is that John Cawelti's description of the cowboy's "reluctance and detachment, the way in which he kills only when forced to do so, the aesthetic order he imposes upon his acts of violence . . . and finally his mode of killing cleanly and purely at a distance" describes also the primary characteristics of many of Hemingway's heroes (Cawelti, *Six-Gun* 88).

Given the terms of the adventure ethos, it becomes almost impossible—as in the cases of Theodore Roosevelt or Ernest Hemingway, who emerged as the ideal expressions of the writer/sportsman—to separate legends from lives or real actions from written adventures, precisely because the act of reading and writing evolved as the primary site of physical activity and the making of the heroic self. In order to revise the tragic tale of Hemingway's development as an artist, we need to analyze more closely how Hemingway uses and revises elements of the adventure ethos. The Byronic legend that surrounds Hemingway is not simply a veil that separates distinct realms of experience, the physical and the aesthetic, but rather it is a function of a cultural perspective that attempts to collapse the two. The problem, then, of confusing Hemingway the man and Hemingway the artist should not be relegated to the province of the literary critic, as Trilling would maintain, because this confusion is already a site encoded in Hemingway's works. That is, the heroic image of Hemingway as sportsman/athlete/aficionado/soldier/writer has deeply rooted cultural antecedents that were first brought together in the fictionalized version of the cowboy.

In this study, I want to examine the ways in which Hemingway adopts and revises elements of the adventure ethos by focusing on the way these elements developed in the modern Western at the turn of the century, particularly in the works of Owen Wister. By contextualizing Hemingway in terms of the adventure ethos, we can better understand developments in his theory of writing, his style, and his narrative strategies. And, most important, we can see—for example, in *For Whom the Bell Tolls*—the ways in which Hemingway's revisions of the adventure ethos question the

cultural work it originally performed and bring to the foreground contradictions in Hemingway's fictions.

WRITING THE ADVENTURE ETHOS IN THE WESTERN

It is possible to draw many links between Hemingway and Owen Wister,
whom many critics cite as the progenitor of the modern Western.[5] Hemingway not only enjoyed the works of Wister, particularly his immensely
popular 1902 classic, *The Virginian*, but he received from Wister encouragement, advice on his writing, and financial aid (which he returned). And
as Hemingway reminded Wister in his final telegram to him, the two were
joined by Hollywood, which had cast Gary Cooper as both the Virginian
and Frederic Henry (Vorpahl 134). And since the Western, particularly *The
Virginian*, is a compilation of conventions, we could map out many
thematic links between the two writers: the lament for the passing of the
wilderness and the desire for regeneration in "Big Two-Hearted River,"
the testing of the youth in "Out of Season," the sport and rejuvenation of
the frontier in the *Green Hills of Africa*, and the inability to reproduce in
a world strangely detached from time in *The Sun Also Rises*. Moreover,
Hemingway's main characters are rarely depicted working but, like the
cowboys in Wister's stories, they are often involved in sport, action, and
leisure.

However, we need to go beyond simply listing the conventions and
stereotypes of the Western formula that can be matched up with
Hemingway's works. Such elementary comparisons lead to a reductive
reading of both Hemingway and the popular Western, a reading that
neglects the issue of how narrative strategies used by writers inscribe the
adventure ethos. In order to historicize the Western genre and its narrative
strategies, we need to maintain a dialectical relationship between the
description of a genre and the social conditions and cultural demands that
produced it.[6]

Georg Lukács gives us insight into a dialectical conception of genre
when he explains that genres are "a peculiar reflection of reality"; that is,
"genres could only arise as reflections of typical and general facts of life
that regularly occur and which could not be adequately reflected in the
forms hitherto available" (241). For Lukács, genres are not essentialized
or static structures, but rather a heterogeneous set of narrative strategies
that are continually evolving, rupturing, and displacing outmoded forms
and conventions. Moreover, the shifts in the narrative strategies of a genre
reflect contradictions and changes in cultural practices and institutions.

Frederic Jameson extends Lukács's theory of genre by writing in terms of culture: genres are "essentially literary 'institutions,' or social contracts between a writer and a specific public, whose function is to specify the proper use of a particular cultural artifact" (*Political Unconscious* 106). For Jameson, that is, genre constitutes a performance that is acted out within a particular culture.

Reading genre as a cultural performance allows us to move away from defining the work's genre through a system of classification to defining it by its cultural function.[7] More to the point, it allows us to describe a rhetoric of genre. By this "rhetoric of genre" I mean the identification of a set of language and institutional practices adopted by particular authors as they attempt to work within the confines of established formulas and conventions.[8] Literature exists as a social institution; its various forms survive as a consequence of particular cultural practices of reading and writing. Reading and writing are always, then, forms of cultural work, and therefore, a rhetorical analysis of a text's language practices will yield insight into the kind of cultural work a genre performs.

In the case of the Western, by the turn of the century dime novels, pulp magazines, and Wister's *The Virginian* had already defined the Western as a cultural artifact. The dime novel's cultural performance, for instance, was initiated, quite simply, by the institutional form of the text, particularly its cover and title. Readers of dime novels knew by the figure(s) depicted on the cover—often a frontier character riding on horseback, exploring the wilderness, or chasing or being chased by shadowy villains or savages—and by the names and actions encoded in the titles—*Billy the Kid, the New Mexico Outlaw; or, the Bold Bandit of the West!*; *Deadwood Dick's Device; or, The Sign of the Double Cross*—what the text contained.

When readers entered the text, their expectations would usually be fulfilled by the frontier setting of the novel, by the Western hero who bridged the gap between wilderness and civilization, and by the episodic plot structure of capture, flight, and pursuit.[9] On the one hand, this description of the dime novel could double as a description of Cooper's Leatherstocking tales. But while Natty Bumppo could turn away from civilization and retreat deeper into the wilderness, the dime novel hero of the late nineteenth century combined both the refinement of Eastern middle-class morals and the values associated with the rugged individualism and self-reliance of the West (Jones 56).

The point here is that such shifts in the representation of the characters emerge out of an overdetermined relation between the publishers of the dime novels, the authors, and a constantly evolving reading public that was fast becoming more urban and imbued with the processes of consumer culture and industrialization. In other words, a dialectical conception of genre must identify both the compilation of narrative strategies and the institutional practices that endure from text to text, and also must be sensitive to the ways in which these strategies are constantly revised by market forces and cultural transformations, including changes in aesthetic ideologies.

The modern Western emerged as a recognizable genre at the beginning of the twentieth century, and although as a form it borrowed heavily from the dime novel, the modern Western revised many of its aspects, the result being, in the hands of Zane Grey and others, a serious and adult form of middle-class entertainment. In this context, the popular Western genre developed as one kind of anti-modernist response to what T. J. Jackson Lears has called a feeling of "weightlessness" brought on by the increasing industrialization of modern life. Lears argues that anti-modernists were reacting to a culture that "had narrowed the range and diffused the intensity of human existence. They longed to rekindle possibilities for authentic experience, physical or spiritual" (Lears, *No Place* 57). Many of the cultural elite, for instance, feared that the dominant class was losing its cultural authority in the face of the immigrant masses and the mechanization of everyday life. This "dread of unreality," Lears continues, created "a yearning to experience intense 'real life' in all its forms" as a way to regenerate the ailing spirit of the ruling class.

For his part, Wister was finding this revitalized sense of wholeness in a trip out West where he slept in a tent, bathed in creeks, and rode "bronchos." The experiences of rugged outdoor life reestablished a contact between the brain and the baser instincts of the animal. Visiting the West thus became a form of therapy that could save the overintellectualized Easterner. As Lears argues, the focus on a healthy mind and body that dominated the late nineteenth century materialized as a response to "the need to renew a sense of selfhood that had grown fragmented, diffuse, and somehow 'unreal' " (Lears, "From Salvation" 4, 6). In 1885, Owen Wister wrote in his journal: "I'm beginning to be able to feel I'm something of an animal and not a stinking brain alone" (*Owen Wister Out West* 32).

Owen Wister and his friend Theodore Roosevelt perhaps best epitomize the drive to reestablish the self through the adventure ethos. Both were young, frail Eastern aristocrats who went West for health reasons, and both found in their Western experience the answer to the country's ills: the frontier myth of adventure. Owen Wister recounts Roosevelt's return to health and vigor in his essay, "The Open-Air Education":

You will remember that he was not a strong boy, that physical health was one of the earliest things he set his heart upon having, that he sought it in the fields and the woods . . . and that he took many rides upon a pony in the same quest. . . . since he became a man, the Rocky Mountains have been a constant recreation—let me spell it 're-creation,' for so you will perceive the word's deep meaning—to Theodore Roosevelt. (*Owen Wister's West* 106)

In this passage, Wister intertwines the experience of the wilderness with the act of "re-creating" the self.

In his 1895 essay "The Evolution of the Cow-Puncher," he describes more explicitly how the West's powers of rejuvenation once captured in language can become the site of regenerative experience for the reader and writer. He conceives this frontier experience as being able to transform even the most effete English nobleman: the Englishman "smelt Texas, the slumbering untamed Saxon awoke in him, and mindful of the tournament, mindful of the hunting-field, galloped howling after wild cattle, a born horseman, a perfect athlete" (*Owen Wister's West* 37).

The Virginian, like the Roosevelt of Wister's essays, emerged as a symbol of the new elite that would provide a renewed political and cultural leadership desperately needed by the United States during chaotic times of labor riots and mass immigration. For men like Wister and Roosevelt, the wilderness came to symbolize a place of manly virtues, sport, and regeneration that was set at a great distance from the industrialized East. As Roosevelt noted: "Ranching is an occupation like those vigorous, primitive pastoral peoples, having little in common with the humdrum, workaday business world of the nineteenth century" (*Ranch Life* 6). Ranching—described as an occupation—is to be clearly distinguished from the alienating forms of labor that dominate the East. Like Wister's experience in the West, Roosevelt's ranching becomes a way to reestablish a more vigorous and elementary self, which is equated with wholeness.

The problem for Wister in promoting the frontier as a place for the country's regeneration is that the frontier, as Frederick Jackson Turner had argued, was already closed by the 1890s and could no longer literally function as a place to rejuvenate the spirit of modern man. Wister solved this problem by figuring the West as a timeless moment that was already past. The story of the cowboy and his moment in history takes the place of the frontier as the site of rejuvenation so that modern man, by reading the tales of the frontier, could find the spirit of the knight hidden in his Anglo-Saxon blood, thus confining the anarchic threat posed by cowboys and outlaws by introducing the Lamarckian continuity of inherited traits.

This focus on the act of reading and writing as equal to experience of the wilderness opens up a space for the development of the Western as a genre. Time and again in his writings Wister calls for a writer strong enough to represent the full significance of the West. In his book, *Roosevelt: The Story of a Friendship*, for instance, Wister exclaims:

Why wasn't some Kipling saving the sage-brush for American literature, before the sage-brush and all that it signified went the way of the California forty-niner, went the way of the Mississippi steam-boat, went the way of everything? Roosevelt had seen the sage-brush true, had felt its poetry; and also Remington, who illustrated his articles so well. But what was fiction doing, fiction, the only thing that outlived fact? Must it be perpetual teacups?[10]

This passage articulates several strategic moves to situate the genre of the Western. In naming California and Mississippi, Wister is admitting that Bret Harte and Mark Twain began the process of charting the territory for a true American literature, but also is claiming they did not go far enough, in that the territory is vanishing. And like many American writers of the 1890s—Hamlin Garland, Jack London, Frank Norris—Wister is reacting strongly against the domestic realism of writers like William Dean Howells and Henry James ("perpetual teacups") as not being able to render a literature of action that could represent the struggle inherent in "real life."

But, more important, in clearing the space for the Western, the passage emphasizes the fusion of the place with its aesthetic representation. To see the place truly is to feel its "poetry." The act of writing is not depicted as an act of the imagination but as an act of preserving, of "saving," what is already present. Interestingly, the frontier and not the writer is responsible for the creation of its own representation. As Wister explains, the fact that the cowboys'

fighting saxon ancestors awoke in them for a moment and made them figures for poetry and romance is due to the strange accidents of a young country, where, while the cities flourished by the coast and in the direct paths of trade, the herd-trading interior remains mediaeval in its simplicity and violence. (*Owen Wister's West* 50)

Wister's atavistic rhetoric emphasizes ahistorical continuity over the processes of historical change. A verbal or visual fiction that truly captures the frontier can take the place of the ever-changing and vanishing world of "fact."

This fiction of the frontier, moreover, is perceived as an expression of the self. The cowboy, for instance, was rendered in story not as the underpaid and overworked laborer that he often was, but as an adventurer—a romanticized version of the Anglo-Saxon knight. The frontier, Wister constantly reminds us, was the cowboys' "gymnasium," "playground," or "field of tournament." This version of the sporting adventurer is perceived as a function of the Western landscape. As Wister explains: "We reach the knowledge that the frontier is just ourselves expressed in unbridled terms" (*Owen Wister's West* 91). To read and write the frontier is to construct the true self, but it is a self that is clearly marked as aristocratic, Anglo-Saxon, and male.

WRITING AS SAVING IN HEMINGWAY'S FICTIONS

In describing writing as an act of transcription, Wister comes to emphasize the importance of exactitude and precision: "I value accuracy more than any other quality in such stories as I write. I don't care how effective they are, if they're false, they're spoiled for me" (*Owen Wister Out West* 223). Wister's description of his theory of writing could easily be mistaken for Hemingway's words. Like Wister, Hemingway sees a necessary connection between good writing and physical activity, a connection that shies away from intellectual activity: "If you kept thinking about it, you could lose the thing that you were writing before you could go on with it the next day. It was necessary to get exercise and be tired in the body" (*A Moveable Feast* 25). Hemingway often focuses on how good fiction writing is identical to writing "truly." As he explains: "Good Writing is true writing. If a man is making up a story it will be true in proportion to the amount of knowledge of life that he has" (*By-Line: Ernest Hemingway* 215).

Such a theory of writing inscribes several aspects of the writer's vocation. A writer cannot be a dilettante or an amateur because these are forms of incomplete knowledge that would compromise the final product. The writer must be an expert and a professional so that he may know the world "truly." Moreover, to gain knowledge of life, the writer must be immersed in it, must have the role of participant and eschew the role of spectator. In other words, how Hemingway lives his "actual" life is interwoven with his aesthetic production.

In a 1925 letter, Hemingway explains: "You see I'm trying to get the actual life across—not just depict life—or criticize it—but to actually make it alive. So that when you read something by me you actually experience the thing" (*Selected Letters* 153). His fictions strive to merge the site of reading with the site of "actual" experience. Yet for Hemingway not only does reading need to be equal to actual experience, but the act of writing coalesces into the space of physical activity: "Some days [writing] went so well that you could make the country so that you could walk into it through the timber to come out into the clearing and work up onto the high ground and see the hills beyond the arm of the lake" (*A Moveable Feast* 17).

Perhaps "Big Two-Hearted River," along with the "On Writing" section that was revised out of the story, is the best expression of the tensions in the adventure ethos between historical change and ahistorical continuity. As is well known, the story is about a soldier who has returned from the war and is trying to regenerate his spirit in the northern woods of Michigan and in the act of fishing for trout. The story fuses multiple levels of autobiography and fiction. Hemingway, the wounded soldier/expert sportsman/writer with a wife named Hadley, is writing about Nick, a wounded soldier/expert sportsman/writer with a wife named Helen.

Nick finds his renewed sense of wholeness in both his experience in the wilderness and his return to writing. Toward the end of "On Writing," Hemingway articulates the tensions between representation and actual life: "Nick, seeing how Cezanne would do the stretch of river and the swamp, stood up and stepped down into the stream. The water was cold and actual. He waded across the stream, moving in the picture" ("On Writing" 219). The aesthetic representation of the river merges with the "actual" river and sets up a tension between the act of fishing and painting, the linear and temporal movement of the narrative (stepping "down into the stream" and wading) and the stasis of the aesthetic object ("Cezanne would do the stretch of river and the swamp"). Nick is, after all, "moving in the picture."

After experiencing the landscape as representation, Nick gets an idea in his head for writing. He must hold this "something in his head" if he is to write. The act of creating a story is equated, then, with the act of capturing "something," an act not unlike the physical act of catching a trout, and one that is clearly distinguished from intellectual activity: "He was not thinking. He was holding something in his head. He wanted to get back to camp and get to work" ("On Writing" 220). Nick, not unlike Wister and Roosevelt, can return from his physical experience in the wilderness renewed and capable of doing purposeful work.

Perhaps the most telling sign of the adventure ethos is the way it works itself out on the level of style. Wister clearly sets out how the demands of describing the frontier call forth the need for a new style: "we emerge into a wider country and no more birds or rocks, or anything. This is country without eyebrows. . . . Can I apply acid to my English, tell nothing till the sharp cutting metal is left?" (*Owen Wister Out West* 99). The language of the stories must in some way be a simulacrum of the Western landscape. The "acid" is a violent gesture that one could imagine cuts away at all needless words, pares words themselves down to a minimum, and eats away at all subordination and excess description until nothing is left but plain simplicity of the landscape. The desire is to have language itself become a sharp cutting tool for the precision work of etching the landscape. Wister's desire to pare down language to its most elemental forms, of course, mirrors Hemingway's theory of style. A comparison of passages describing the labor of setting up camp from Wister's *The Virginian* and Hemingway's "Big Two-Hearted River" clearly demonstrates how the adventure ethos is encoded in the style of both writers.

The passage from Wister's text appears late in the novel, when the Virginian is making camp on a secluded wilderness island surrounded by a stream. This place is figured as a site of healing and rejuvenation for the Virginian, who has recently killed a man, Trampas, in a gunfight:

The tent was unfolded first. He had long seen in his mind where it should go, and how its white shape would look beneath the green of the encircling pines. The ground was level in the spot he had chosen, without stones or roots, and matted with the fallen needles of pines. He cut the pegs for the tent, and the front pole, stretching and tightening the rope, one end of it pegged down and one around a pine tree. When the tightening rope had lifted the canvas to the proper height from the ground, he spread and pegged down the sides and back. He cut tufts of young pine and strewed them thickly for a soft floor in the tent, and over them spread the buffalo hide and the blankets. He built the fire where its smoke would float outward from the trees and the tent, and near it stood the cooking things and his provisions, and made his first supper ready in the twilight. He had brought much with him; but for ten minutes he fished, catching trout enough. . . . All had been as he had seen it in his thoughts beforehand. (*The Virginian* 307)

The structure of the paragraph mirrors the description of the tent. Like the "encircling pines," the paragraph is closed in by sentences about the image in the Virginian's mind. The image of the tent frames the physical act of constructing the tent, setting in conflict the stasis of representation and the dynamics of the narrative.

The action proceeds primarily by simple sentences. The active agent/predicate pairings ("he spread," "he cut," "he built") emphasize the agent as actor and maker. For Wister, whose texts struggle against the mechanization of everyday life, where work is demanded by nameless agents and performed without personal satisfaction, the focus on active labor necessary for survival asserts a strong connection between the subject and his action. Because of the minimal use of subordination and the emphasis on the additive conjunction, "and," the actions appear simply to collect like a mass of items on the "level ground."

Moreover, the text minimizes temporal connections and heightens the reader's sense of spatial relations. There is only one temporal subordinator, "when," while the description of setting up the tent emphasizes the spatial relations: picking the spot, tying the rope from the peg to the tree, lifting the tent to the "proper height," building the fire so the smoke would not enter the tent, and standing the provisions by the fire. The act of building the tent, then, does not appear so much as an action, but more like a rendering, line for line, of the image in the Virginian's head. Success is found, then, when action/actuality duplicates representation.

Not only does the careful building up of details create a sense of a captured image, but the cataloging of particulars creates a sense of expertise and professionalism on the part of the narrator. The narrator knows precisely how to build a tent from materials primarily of the wilderness. This description of setting up the tent could double as a camping guide and, more to the point, it could double as a writing guide. The writer must first have the image, find the empty "level ground," the blankness of the page, and strew over it precisely those elements of the landscape ("pegs," "tufts of young pine," "buffalo hide") that have been refashioned by the writer. The paragraph echoes Wister's writing theory in that the act of writing is an act of preserving what is already present in the mind.

The passage from Hemingway's text appears as an uncanny mirror image of Wister's. The labor of making camp is a repetition of the same actions as Nick finds the right spot, cuts the tent stakes, levels the ground, and carefully erects the tent:

With the ax he split off a bright slab of pine from one of the stumps and split it into pegs for the tent. He wanted them long and solid to hold in the ground. With the tent unpacked and spread on the ground, the pack, leaning against a jackpine, looked much smaller. Nick tied the rope that served the tent for a ridge pole to the trunk of one of the pine trees and pulled the tent up off the ground with the other end of the rope and tied it to the other pine. The tent hung on the rope like a canvas blanket on a clothesline. Nick poked a pole he had cut up under the back peak of the canvas and then made it a tent by pegging out the sides. He pegged the sides out taut and drove the pegs deep, hitting them down into the ground with the flat of the ax until the rope loops were buried and the canvas was drum tight. (*Complete Short Stories* 167)

Much has been written about Hemingway's paratactic style, a style that creates a sense of dynamism and rapidity in sentences that repeatedly focus on active agent/predicate pairings. But to focus on the simplicity of the words and the sentence structures is to pass over the careful construction of the reader's perspective.

Like Wister's, this paragraph is framed. In this case, the pegs serve to close in the paragraph, which opens with the making of the pegs and finds closure in driving the tent pegs into the ground. But the actual making of the tent is further framed by two of the narrator's judgments. In the third sentence, the narrator comments on the relation between the pack and the tree: the pack is "much smaller." The fifth sentence passes judgement on Nick's work through a simile: "The tent hung on the rope like a canvas blanket on a clothesline." The job is not yet complete and is therefore imperfect and more like the products associated with doing laundry in the domestic sphere. In order to make it right, the tent must be pegged firmly to the ground. When he has done so, the tent becomes almost a perfect object, "taut" and "drum tight." The fourth sentence, which describes the actual hanging of the tent, is a piling up of actions.

As in Wister's prose, the emphasis is on spatial relations and the cataloging of details, which is enhanced by the polysyndetonic use of the additive "and." It is as if Hemingway has honed Wister's style to its barest elements, finding simpler words and making the reflections of the narrator and character less intrusive. As Wister explains, after he read Hemingway his own style became "tighter and more frank than anything he wrote before" (Vorpahl 136).

Like Wister's, Hemingway's paragraph focuses on the tension between static representation and narrative action. And both paragraphs resolve the tension by making the actions one of creating a static object. Nick reflects that "he wanted [the pegs] long and solid to hold in the ground," articulating his desire for stasis. The sharpened pegs, like a sharpened pencil, become the tools to make the tent into an aesthetic object. But the act of finishing the tent, as well as closing the paragraph, is a violent act.

The violence of the act is made manifest in both the actions of Nick and the words of the final sentences. Nick pokes and "pegs deep," hitting the pegs with "the flat of an ax." This violence of making is enhanced by alliteration of the hard "p" in "poked," "pole," "peak," "pegging," "pegged," and "pegs." Like Wister, Hemingway figures the act of creating the perfect object, the aesthetic object, as necessarily violent. It is always an act of tearing and closing off the actual image from time. And finally, Hemingway's focus on the details and sequence of actions emphasizes the narrator's skill and precision.

In both cases, the writers foreground an adventure and the necessary sequence of events, but they both, likewise, attempt to wrest the story from time by giving it mythic and dreamlike qualities. The style, then, of the sentences and paragraphs recapitulates in microcosm the narrative strategy of each entire work: the attempt to find in physical activity the whole and complete image. Both works cut away at language so that they can somehow "truly" preserve the image, and yet this is by no means a communal yearning for a true language. After all, Wister was not attempting to heal the masses, but only to regenerate the ailing aristocracy. Thus, while Wister's passage does demonstrate the desire for stasis and wholeness, it is figured as an image already completed in the mind: "All had been as he had seen it in his thoughts beforehand." Similarly, critics have commented that Nick's fishing trip is an interior one, "from the dreaming and remembering part of the mind of the protagonist" (Adair 265). The landscape of "Big Two-Hearted River" is the landscape of Nick's mind; it is as if the story is a rendering of the "something" in Nick's head. In other words, both Hemingway and Wister internalize the process of writing so that it becomes not only a process of preserving but a process of recovering the self.

REVISING THE ADVENTURE ETHOS: *FOR WHOM THE BELL TOLLS*

In considering how Hemingway revises the adventure ethos, what should be stressed is how that ethos not only exists as an antidote to the alienation of modern life, but also performs, for men like Wister and Roosevelt, the cultural work of justifying the subjugation of minorities and women while simultaneously promoting a particularly virulent strain of nationalism. As Wister writes, "to survive in the clean cattle country requires the spirit of adventure, courage, and self-sufficiency; you will not find many Poles or Huns or Russian Jews in that district; but the Anglo-Saxon is still forever homesick for out-of-doors" (*Owen Wister's West* 37). For both Roosevelt and Wister the cowboy was a symbol that was able to bridge and displace the contradictions created between East and West, civilization and primitive savagery. The cowboy was a marriage of Eastern aristocracy and Western adventurer. The Virginian, for example, was both a rugged, uneducated outdoorsman and a Southern aristocrat. The cowboy was likewise figured as the wild vagabond and the obedient soldier. As Roosevelt noted: "In all the world there could be no better material for soldiers than that afforded by these grim hunters of the mountain, these wild rough riders of the plains" (*Rough Riders* 15). In the stories told by Wister and Roosevelt, the rejuvenated Eastern aristocrat emerged as the natural leader, and the focus on the military ideal of order, combined with the contradictory impulses of the wild frontier, worked to displace the feminized domestic sphere and the crowded, chaotic urban landscape.

In his youth, Hemingway was imbued with the nationalism inherent in the adventure ethos. As Michael Reynolds explains, the health craze and the adventurism of Roosevelt was a great influence on young Hemingway, because the people of Oak Park were saturated by the "progressive conservatism" of Teddy Roosevelt. The Western-ranching, rough-riding President—whose image expressed the ideal leisure-class adventurer and promised that "a man of moral fiber and physical endurance can do whatever he can imagine himself doing" (Reynolds, *Young Hemingway* 25)—was an important role model for the young Hemingway in that Roosevelt was not only the consummate outdoorsman but also a prolific writer.

In many ways, Hemingway's *The Green Hills of Africa* is a rewriting of Roosevelt's *African Game Trails*. In his book on the American adventure narrative, Martin Green draws this connection between the ideology of Hemingway and Roosevelt more tightly when he argues that in the *Green Hills of Africa*,

It was an aristo-military, an imperial hunt that Hemingway engaged in; hunting was important to him just because it 'was' imperial in that sense. The hunt was an alternative to revolution and war, an avocation for a writer, and Hemingway, as hunter-writer, represented in Africa and Cuba and elsewhere the great American empire. Only Americans were rich enough, relaxed enough, big enough (physically and morally) to live such a life. (Green 171)

In other words, for Green the public image of Hemingway as adventurer/sportsman/writer is a re-presentation of the legend surrounding Roosevelt.

At important junctures, however, Hemingway rewrites the adventure ethos and turns away from the racist concepts of nationalism and the need for an aristocracy that are inherent in the works of Wister and Roosevelt. In the well-known passage from *A Farewell to Arms*, Frederic Henry explains, "I was always embarrassed by the words sacred, glorious, and sacrifice and the expression in vain. . . . There were many words that you could not stand to hear and finally only the names of places had dignity" (177–78). It is as if he is taking Wister's theory of fiction to its logical conclusion: only using words that have a definite place as a referent can constitute writing "truly." *A Farewell to Arms* attempts to destroy the linkages between the individual actions of soldiers and the all-encompassing concepts of patriotism and heroism. Although in Hemingway's works there are strong vestiges of racism, his fictions often attempt to destabilize simple readings of motive. In this way we can read *For Whom the Bell*

Tolls as an extended attempt to subvert and destabilize an important empowering myth of the frontier—Custer's Last Stand, a myth that has often been used to fortify American patriotism and nationalism.

Hollywood, as mentioned, provides a surface connection between the *For Whom the Bell Tolls* and the popular version of the cowboy, since it cast Gary Cooper as the gun-toting, laconic Robert Jordan from Montana. But the text itself also supplies many references to the modern Western and the American frontier. Jordan is a figure who is both an expert in the outdoors and well educated, not unlike Wister's Specimen Jones, who is noted as the best horseman in New Mexico and who sings German opera when he rides. Jordan's memories return to the frontier when he thinks of his grandfather, the Indian fighter, who could have saved Custer if he were there "that day" (337). The sense of the West is created by the rugged wilderness terrain, the primitive living conditions, and continual focus on horses. The white man other pairing of Jordan and Anselmo is a standard trope of the frontier, beginning with Natty Bumppo and Chingachgook and continuing through to the Lone Ranger and Tonto. At one point in the novel, Jordan attempts to explain the Homestead Act to Agustin and Primitivo (207). As Henry Nash Smith has noted, the Homestead Act as symbol is central to American conceptions of frontier settlement (Smith 163–73).

As in Wister's *The Virginian*, the primary narrative strategy of *For Whom the Bell Tolls* is to foreground a love story in a world that seems strangely mythic and romanticized—one cut off from the larger social and political worlds that intrude into the narrative. As many critics have noted, Hemingway's novel is torn between a realistic portrayal of the war and politics and a romantic adventure. This is not unlike many westerns that similarly try to negotiate between the real-life struggle for survival and the mythic adventures of their cowboy heroes. Christine Bold argues, for instance, that Wister attempts to create a sense of narrative closure that displaces the passing of time in order to protect the West and the cowboy from the ravages of history and to create a cyclical sense of closure that wrests the story from the linear progression of time (Bold 67).

Earl Rovit and Gerry Brenner have made the same argument about *For Whom the Bell Tolls*. As they explain, "Hemingway's first strategy in attempting to create an illusion of suspended time was to isolate the novel temporally and spatially" (Rovit and Brenner 119). Hemingway's novel, like the Western, seeks a cyclical sense of closure. Another common narrative strategy of the Western is to have the hero find a woman, who has been physically or psychologically wounded, remove her to a secluded place —a place constantly threatened by outside forces —and fall in love with her. Interestingly, in Zane Grey's *Riders of the Purple Sage*, one of the heroes of the tale, Venters, finds the man he has shot is a woman. He takes her to live among the caves in Surprise Valley, where he brings her back to health and falls in love with her. Their idyllic love is threatened by Venters's obligations that he must fulfill outside of Surprise Valley and by a local band of cattle rustlers. Not only does Grey's novel set in conflict the romance and the fight against the rustlers, but the woman is figured, like Jordan's Maria, as both male and female.

Upon entering Hemingway's novel, we are led by a native guide into a frontier caught between the need for order and the potential for violent disorder. As Cawelti points out, a Western does not need to take place in the American West "but near a frontier, at a point of history when social order and anarchy are in tension," and the story must involve pursuit and possible capture (Cawelti, *Six-Gun* 57). As we continue in the novel, we move into a landscape filled with warring guerrilla bands who when not fighting the Fascists fight among themselves.

In case we miss an allegorical reading of American Indian tribes attempting to displace the white invader, Hemingway clues us in early by having Jordan detect a similarity between the mythology of the bear produced by gypsy culture and the "Indians in America" (40). During the course of the novel, we are continually brought back to stereotypical images of the American Indian. Pilar, for example, is described as having a "heavy brown face with high Indian cheekbones" (298) and her bed "smelt stale and sweat-dried and sickly-sweet the way an Indian's bed does" (360).

John Teunissen has rightly pointed out how *For Whom the Bell Tolls* makes use of the Custer myth. He argues that the novel is a mythic narrative that stands above the bickering of critics who want either to embrace the novel for its realism and historical accuracy or condemn it for its romantic falsifications and stereotypical characterizations. As Teunissen argues, "the archetypal action demands iconographic representation, and the icon makes no historical judgments. Custer and the Sioux and Cheyenne are locked topocosmically together forever in the landscape, the memory, and the collective unconscious" (228). The legend of Custer's Last Stand, however, has always been a potent and politically charged myth, that has helped America down the path to Wounded Knee more than once.

Roland Barthes has argued that "myth is constituted by the loss of the historical quality of things" (129). In forgetting what made the myth, we transform the contradictions of history into something that appears natural. This process allows the complex politics and cultural needs that motivate myth to remain concealed. In other words, the myth of Custer's Last

Stand—if perceived as an ahistorical icon of the American consciousness—conceals a complex cultural drama that combines elements of the frontier myth with social problems of the late nineteenth century. As Richard Slotkin has meticulously argued in his book, *The Fatal Environment*, both the mythologizing and politicizing of the Last Stand have been present since the very first newspaper reports.

The Custer myth—best developed in Frederick Whittaker's 1876 *Complete Life of Gen. George A. Custer*, which remained popular up to the 1930s—creates Custer as a version of the soldier-aristocrat who goes to the frontier to become a "buckskin" hero and "who finally perishes in a complex confrontation with the forces of both primitive savagery and Metropolitan corruption" (Slotkin 502). Not only was he done in by the Indians, but the corruption of the Grant administration was greatly to blame. As in Wister's ideology, the forming of the Custer myth relies heavily on the racial purity of Custer in the face of the savage other. Custer and his death became a perfect symbol for the need to destroy the Native American populations, clearing an area for expanding capital. And more important, as Slotkin chronicles, immediately after the Battle of Little Big Horn the need to subjugate the Indians was tied directly to the need to uproot and displace both radical labor groups and Communists.

With this in mind, we need to return to the "chancre" upon which El Sordo made his last stand to see how Hemingway subverts the Custer myth. Hemingway is very explicit in the way he brings up Custer and then turns against the standard heroic image. Perhaps the best example of how Hemingway figured Custer appears in *Across the River and into the Trees*:

George Armstrong Custer. That beautiful horse-cavalry-man. I guess it is fun to be that way and have a loving wife and use sawdust for brains. But it must have seemed like the wrong career to him when they finished up on that hill above the Little Big Horn. . . . and nothing left to him for the rest of his life but that old lovely black powder smell and his own people shooting each other, and themselves, because they were afraid of what the squaws would do to them. (169)

This description helps us to better understand Kashkin's fears, to which the narrative continually returns. If injured, he would rather be killed or commit suicide than be captured, not unlike the men with Custer. The fear, of course, is of the savagery of the Fascists, the same Fascists who mutilate the bodies of El Sordo's men.

In Hemingway's retelling of the Custer myth the savagery is displaced to the side of military order and technological superiority. Moreover, a version of Sitting Bull is placed on the hill for the last stand. El Sordo is described as a commanding figure who is "a man of few words," with a "thin-bridged, hooked nose like an Indian's" (141). He speaks in the clipped, verbless or subjectless Hollywood version of Indian speak: "When blow bridge?" and "Heard last night comes English dynamiter. Good. Very Happy. Get Whiskey. For you. You like?" (156). What is being martyred is not civilization and order, as in the Custer myth, but the last vestiges of the noble savage. Whether intentionally or not, Hemingway has reversed the power of the myth in that the "other" is not the communist forces but the Fascists. Yet the novel is only beginning, and the last stand will be reprised one more time.

Before we get to the moment of Jordan's last stand, we need to look more closely at how Hemingway repoliticizes the Custer myth. Christine Bold has noted the importance of codes to the Western genre (26–28). Cowboys and their guides are always attempting to read signs and decipher both human and natural codes. Bold argues that this is, in part, a self-re-flexive gesture used by the Western writers to comment on the particular system of signs and conventions that bound them within certain formulas.

In *For Whom the Bell Tolls*, the reading of signs and the making of codes dominate a great deal of the action and provide an important commentary on the myth of Custer's Last Stand. From Pilar reading Jordan's palm to the seal used by Andrés to pass through the lines with greater speed, the interpretation of signs plays an important part in the movement and direction of the plot. But perhaps the code that is most highlighted is the one Jordan explains to Anselmo to mark down military movement on the road.

The code is doubly highlighted since when it breaks down the narrator intrudes with one of his rare reflections:

Anselmo did not distinguish between Fords, Fiats, Opels, Renaults, and Citroens of the staff of the Division that held the passes and the line of mountain and the Rolls-Royces, Lancias, Mercedes, and Isottas of the General Staff. This was the sort of distinction that Robert Jordan should have made and, if he had been there, he would have appreciated the significance of these cars which had gone up. But he was not there and the old man simply made a mark for a motor car going up the road, on the sheet of note paper. (192)

The code fails. The signifiers created by Jordan cannot transmit a sense of hierarchy, so the signs lose their value. The signs that Anselmo makes conceal the full significance and power of what is signified. Jordan is perceived to have the power to distinguish hierarchy in the military world, where hierarchy matters, while Anselmo, who lives outside of this world, does not have this power. Jordan, in other words, can determine the relationship between signifiers and their signified.

This failure of the code prepares us for the proper reading of the image of Custer presented to us in the text. Jordan's first encounter with Custer is to see his heroic figure "in buckskin shirt, the yellow curls blowing, [as he] stood on that hill holding a service revolver as the Sioux closed in around him in the old Anheuser-Busch lithograph that hung on the poolroom wall in Red Lodge" (339). The young Jordan could only feel "resentment" at finding out that the sign of heroism presented in the advertisement displaced the stupidity of Custer and his military blunder. As Jordan's grandfather explained, "George Custer was not an intelligent leader of cavalry. . . . He was not even an intelligent man" (339).

This blindness to the full impact of signs is highlighted by Custer's inability to read signs. Jordan thinks: "How could he ever not have seen the smoke nor the dust of all those lodges down there, must have been a heavy morning mist? But there wasn't any mist" (338). Jordan desires a heroic image of Custer who was only blinded by the "morning mist," but the desire is negated by his knowledge that the signs were present but simply not read. The failure of signs and codes highlighted in the text force us to call into question the larger codes and myths invoked by the text and its narrative strategies. In this case, the text forces us to call into question the heroic image of last stands.

The discursive and historical intrusions, such as the views presented at Gaylord's or the description of Comrade Marty, also play an important role in subverting the mythology invoked by the novel. They help to create a tension between the romanticized world of Maria and Jordan, and the historical and political world of the war. We do not have to look far back in the Western to see where writers use the narrative strategy of combining romantic elements with social commentary.

Zane Grey's 1918 *U.P. Trail*, for example, develops a plot based on a hero who saves the heroine several times from captivity while he exposes the political intrigues behind the building of the transcontinental railroad. The simplicity of the romance clashes with the ambiguity of the politics. As Christine Bold points out, in many of Grey's works from 1918 to 1925 there is a "basic incompatibility" between the mythic level, "which seem designed to confine his fiction to an unchanging formula" and "his introduction of social criticism and complex plot, which involve a sense of causality and development" (Bold 85–86).

For Hemingway, on one level, the intrusion of the historical allows him to repoliticize the myth of Custer's Last Stand in terms of the Communist cause. On another level, the intrusion of the political into the romanticized world of Maria and Jordan destroys the simple opposition of good and evil that is often created by myth. In the many digressions of the novel we find that the enemy is not so bad and that the allies can be savages. And Jordan is shown in his education at Gaylord's the ways in which the myth of the peasant leader is deliberately constructed. The education is another demonstration of how mythic reading is destabilized, and another reason we should be suspect of the Custer presented in the Anheuser-Busch lithograph. The war, as Jordan points out, is "not so simple" (248).

There still remains the last stand of Jordan. Slotkin points out that "from the ashes of that terminal battle of the last Frontier the shape of a hero for the new age arises: a soldier, a commander of men, a youth vested with the authority of age, a technocrat, a natural aristocrat" (531). Perhaps the best version of this new hero to arise in the twentieth century was Theodore Roosevelt, but Jordan is also a young soldier and an expert in explosives. He readily connects the world of sport and arenas with war when he makes a direct connection between the sport of bull fighting and the Indian fighting that his grandfather had done (338).

At the end of the novel, Jordan, like Custer in the lithograph, is left waiting on a hill—frozen in a timeless moment before the inevitability of his death. In one way, then, we can look at the end of the novel as a form of exorcism that cuts away a remaining vestige of the Custer myth by making us skeptical of the heroics and mythic qualities of last stands. The destabilizing of Custer's Last Stand makes it difficult to equate Jordan's death with concepts of patriotism or nationalism. Or, more to the point, the sign of the heroic last stand can no longer perform the cultural work of being an unambiguous sign of national unity.

In a rambling passage from the *Green Hills of Africa*, Hemingway articulates his own confusions about the possibility of recapturing a frontier:

Our people went to America because that was the place to go then. It had been a good country and we made a bloody mess of it and I would go, now, somewhere else and as we had always gone. You could always come back. Let the others come to America who did not know that they had come too late. Our people had seen it at its best and fought for it when it was worth fighting for. Now I would go somewhere else. We always went in the old days and there were still good places to go. (*Green Hills of Africa* 285)

The passage articulates the confusions of the adventure ethos, in which movement is always a contradiction: to venture out into the frontier is to venture back to the self and to find the frontier is to find it is already gone.

For Owen Wister, the writing of the Western was a way to preserve the frontier. For Ernest Hemingway, the possibility of preserving the frontier is not so certain, but he leaves open the possibility of finding "good places," or, in other words, of finding new fictions. Obviously, the fictions of Hemingway are overdetermined. His writing, in all likelihood, was influenced by many sources, including those aesthetic ideologies most often cited by critics such as journalism, modernism, and realism; but unless we consider the western and its articulation of the adventure ethos, it is difficult to understand why the writer's "life" becomes so much like the writer's "art."

NOTES

1. There are numerous studies that warn against the folly of confusing Hemingway's life and his works of fiction. As the biographer and critic Michael Reynolds warns: "To read any of Hemingway's fiction as biography is always dangerous, but to read *A Farewell to Arms* in this manner is to misread the book" ("Going Back" 56). Roger Whitlow outlines the problems of autobiographical criticism, and registers the general frustration of critics who believe that too much emphasis is placed on "autobiographical similarities," when he says: "Hemingway . . . must be read with the same respect that freshman literature students are taught to offer any author. They learn to ask, 'What does the story say?' " (112).

2. Many recent works on Hemingway have focused on psychoanalytical approaches to his fiction. Kenneth S. Lynn's recent biography *Hemingway* concentrates on analyzing the "conflicted, haunted man" behind the myth and how his "torments" produced his fiction. Perhaps the most compelling analysis of Hemingway's psyche read through his art is Gerry Brenner's *Concealments in Hemingway's Works*. He argues that Hemingway is a much more "artistically deceptive" and "crafty" writer than he seems to be when we consider his fictions as simple autobiography. Brenner is led to these conclusions by exploring the ways in which Hemingway's literary experimentation is a "conscious conceal-ment" of his "repressed obsessions."

3. The most recent discussion of the relationship between Hemingway and Wister is by Alan Price.

4. Ernest Hemingway, *For Whom the Bell Tolls* 53. All further references to this novel will be given in the text.

5. Many critics of the Western cite Owen Wister's *The Virginian* as the first instance of the popular modern western. See Christine Bold (37–45), Cynthia S. Hamilton (11), and John Cawelti's *Adventure, Mystery, and Romance* (215–30).

6. Fredric Jameson argues for a similar conception of genre when he explains in *The Political Unconscious* that we need an "increasingly vivid

apprehension of what happens when plot falls into history, so to speak, and enters the force of the modern societies" (130).

7. In traditional genre criticism, the critic often finishes the critical act with naming and classifying. For example, the genre critic might argue that *For Whom the Bell Tolls* is a "classical epic," or a " 'positive' tragedy," or a "pastoral idyll." These analyses are useful in that they yield an explanation of Hemingway's particular writing practices. But often the genre critic's aim seems to subsume an entire text under one genre title in order to specify the text's "fit" within the essential limits of the genre. For the examples cited, refer to genre readings of *For Whom the Bell Tolls* in Gerry Brenner's *Concealments in Hemingway's Works*, Wirt Williams's *The Tragic Art of Ernest Hemingway*, and Earl Rovit and Gerry Brenner's *Ernest Hemingway*.

Now a dialectical approach to genre that sees texts as heterogeneous compilations of narrative strategies will readily admit that a consciously literary writer like Hemingway would and did encode the rhetoric of many genres in his texts. Such confusing genre signals would explain why critics have such a difficult time confining Hemingway's texts to a single genre without modifying the genre's definition or viewing the text as a failure. Traditional genre criticism focuses, in other words, on static definitions, while a dialectical view of genre must be sensitive to both stasis and change, continuity and contradiction. A study of the dialectical relations between Hemingway's text and the Western, then, will not nullify earlier genre critiques nor will it claim that Hemingway primarily adopted the rhetoric of the Western; it will investigate the traces of Western rhetoric found in some of Hemingway's works and the way in which the texts encode and transform these traces of a distinctive cultural artifact.

8. In establishing a rhetoric of genre, we never leave far behind the problematic of how genres encode history. For as Jameson has argued in *Marxism and Form*, we must "imagine a dialectical 'Rhetoric,' in which the various mental operations are understood not absolutely, but as moments and figures, tropes, syntactical paradigms, of our relationship to the real itself, as, altering irrevocably in time, it nonetheless obeys a logic that like the logic of language can never be fully distinguished from its object" (374).

9. For a more detailed analysis of Western dime novels and pulp magazines, refer to Daryl Jones, *The Dime Novel Western* and Christine Bold, *Selling the Wild West* (1–36).

10. Wister, *Roosevelt: The Story of a Friendship (1880–1919)* 29. The title and structure of the book emphasize the idea that a life can only be captured in narrative.

WORKS CITED

Adair, William. "Landscapes of the Mind: 'Big Two-Hearted River.' " *Critical Essays on Ernest Hemingway's "In Our Time."* Ed. Michael S. Reynolds. Boston: G. K. Hall, 1983. 260–67.

Baker, Carlos. *Ernest Hemingway: A Life Story.* NY: Scribner's, 1969.

Barthes, Roland. "Myth Today." *Mythologies.* Trans. Annette Lauers. NY: Hill & Wang, 1982. 109–59.

Bloom, Harold, ed. *Modern Critical Views: Ernest Hemingway.* NY: Chelsea, 1985.

Bold, Christine. *Selling the Wild West: Popular Western Fiction, 1860 to 1960.* Bloomington: Indiana UP, 1987.

Brand, Max. *Riders of the Silences.* NY: Dodd, Mead, & Co., 1986.

Brenner, Gerry. *Concealments in Hemingway's Works.* Columbus: Ohio State UP, 1983.

Cawelti, John. *Adventure, Mystery, and Romance: Formula Stories as Art and Popular Culture.* Chicago: U of Chicago P, 1976.

————. *The Six-Gun Mystique.* Bowling Green, OH: Bowling Green UP, 1984.

Green, Martin. *The Great American Adventure.* Boston: Beacon Press, 1984.

Hamilton, Cynthia S. *Western and Hard-Boiled Detective Fiction in America: From High Noon to Midnight.* Iowa City: U of Iowa P, 1987.

Hemingway, Ernest. *Across the River and into the Trees.* 1950. NY: Macmillan, 1978.

————. *By-Line: Ernest Hemingway: Selected Articles and Dispatches of Four Decades.* Ed. William White. NY: Scribner's, 1967.

————. *The Complete Short Stories of Ernest Hemingway: The Finca Vigia Edition.* NY: Scribner's, 1987.

————. *Ernest Hemingway: Selected Letters, 1917–1961.* Ed. Carlos Baker. NY: Scribner's, 1981.

————. *A Farewell to Arms.* 1929. NY: Scribner's, 1957.

————. *For Whom the Bell Tolls.* NY: Scribner's, 1940.

————. *Green Hills of Africa.* 1935. NY: Macmillan, 1987.

————. *A Moveable Feast.* NY: Scribner's, 1964.

————. "On Writing." *The Nick Adams Stories.* NY: Bantam, 1973.

Jameson, Fredric. *Marxism and Form: Twentieth-Century Dialectical Theories of Literature.* Princeton, NJ: Princeton UP, 1971.

————. *The Political Unconscious: Narrative as a Socially Symbolic Act.* Ithaca, NY: Cornell UP, 1981.

Jones, Daryl. *The Dime Novel Western.* Bowling Green, OH: The Popular Press, 1978.

Lears, T. J. Jackson. "From Salvation to Self-Realization: Advertising and the Therapeutic Roots of the Consumer Culture, 1880–1930." *The Culture of Consumption: Critical Essays in American History, 1880–1980.* Ed. Richard W. Fox and T. J. Jackson Lears. NY: Pantheon, 1983. 1–38.

————. *No Place of Grace: Antimodernism and the Transformation of American Culture, 1880–1920.* NY: Pantheon, 1981.

Lodge, Henry Cabot, and Theodore Roosevelt. *Hero Tales From American History.* NY: Century, 1908.

Lukács, Georg. *The Historical Novel*. Trans. Hannah and Stanley Mitchell. Lincoln: Nebraska UP, 1962.

Lynn, Kenneth S. *Hemingway*. NY: Simon and Schuster, 1987.

Price, Alan. " 'I'm Not an Old Fogey and You're Not a Young Ass': Owen Wister and Ernest Hemingway." *Hemingway Review* 9.1 (Fall 1989): 82–90.

Renza, Louis A. "The Importance of Being Ernest." *South Atlantic Quarterly* 88 (Summer 1989): 661–89.

Reynolds, Michael. "Going Back." *Ernest Hemingway's "Farewell to Arms."* Ed. Harold Bloom. NY: Chelsea, 1987. 49–59.

———. *The Young Hemingway*. NY: Basil Blackwell, 1986.

Roosevelt, Theodore. *Ranch Life and the Hunting Trail*. NY: Winchester, 1969.

———. *The Rough Riders*. NY: Scribner's, 1899.

Rovit, Earl, and Gerry Brenner. *Ernest Hemingway*. Boston: Twayne Publishers, 1986.

Slotkin, Richard. *The Fatal Environment: The Myth of the Frontier in the Age of Industrialization, 1800–1890*. Middletown, CT: Wesleyan UP, 1986.

Smith, Henry Nash. *Virgin Land: The American West as Symbol and Myth*. Cambridge: Harvard UP, 1950.

Teunissen, John J. *"For Whom the Bell Tolls* as Mythic Narrative." *Dalhousie Review* 56 (1976): 52–69. Rptd. in *Ernest Hemingway: Six Decades of Criticism*. Ed. Linda W. Wagner. East Lansing: Michigan State UP, 1987. 221–37.

Trilling, Lionel. "Hemingway and His Critics." *Modern Critical Views: Ernest Hemingway*. Ed. Harold Bloom. NY: Chelsea, 1985. 7–15.

Vorpahl, Ben Merchant. "Ernest Hemingway and Owen Wister: Finding the Lost Generation." *Library Chronicle* 36 (Spring 1970): 126–37.

Whitlow, Roger. *Cassandra's Daughters: The Women in Hemingway*. Westport, CT: Greenwood, 1984.

Whittaker, Frederick. *A Complete Life of Gen. George A. Custer, Major-General of Volunteers, Brevet Major-General U.S. Army, and Lieutenant-Colonel Seventh U.S. Cavalry*. New York: Sheldon & Co., 1876.

Williams, Wirt. *The Tragic Art of Ernest Hemingway*. Baton Rouge: Louisiana State UP, 1981.

Wister, Owen. *Owen Wister Out West*. Ed. Fanny Kemble Wister. Chicago: U of Chicago P, 1958.

———. *Owen Wister's West*. Ed. Robert Murry Davis. Albuquerque: U of New Mexico P, 1987.

———. *Roosevelt: The Story of a Friendship (1880–1919)*. NY: Macmillan, 1930.

———. *The Virginian: A Horseman of the Plains*. 1902. NY: Signet, 1979.

Selected Bibliography

HEMINGWAY'S WORKS

Novels

The Torrents of Spring. NY: Scribner's, 1926.
The Sun Also Rises. NY: Scribner's, 1926.
A Farewell to Arms. NY: Scribner's, 1929.
To Have and Have Not. NY: Scribner's, 1937.
For Whom the Bell Tolls. NY: Scribner's, 1940.
Across the River and Into the Trees. NY: Scribner's, 1950.
Islands in the Stream. NY: Scribner's, 1970.
The Garden of Eden. NY: Scribner's, 1986.

Short Story Collections

In Our Time. NY: Boni & Liveright, 1925.
Men Without Women. NY: Scribner's, 1927.
Winner Take Nothing. NY: Scribner's, 1933.
The Fifth Column and the First Forty-nine Stories. NY: Scribner's, 1938.
The Fifth Column and Four Stories of the Spanish Civil War. NY: Scribner's,
    1969.
The Nick Adams Stories. Ed. Philip Young. NY: Scribner's, 1972.
The Complete Short Stories of Ernest Hemingway. NY: Scribner's, 1987.

Nonfiction

Death in the Afternoon. NY: Scribner's, 1932.
Green Hills of Africa. NY: Scribner's, 1935.

The Spanish Earth. Introd. Jasper Wood. Cleveland: J. B. Savage, 1938.

"Introduction." *Men at War: The Best War Stories of All Time.* Ed. Ernest Hemingway. 1942. Rpt. NY: Bramhall House, 1979.

A Moveable Feast. NY: Scribner's, 1964.

By-Line: Ernest Hemingway, Selected Articles and Dispatches of Four Decades. Ed. William White. NY: Scribner's, 1967.

Ernest Hemingway: Selected Letters, 1917–1961. Ed. Carlos Baker. NY: Scribner's, 1981.

The Dangerous Summer. NY: Scribner's, 1985.

Dateline Toronto: The Complete "Toronto Star" Dispatches, 1920–1924. Ed. William White. NY: Scribner's, 1985.

SECONDARY SOURCES: *FOR WHOM THE BELL TOLLS*

Adair, William. "*For Whom the Bell Tolls* and *The Magic Mountain*: Hemingway's Debt to Thomas Mann." *Twentieth Century Literature* 35.4 (Winter 1989): 429–44.

————. "*For Whom the Bell Tolls* as Family Romance." *Arizona Quarterly* 41.4 (Winter 1985): 329–37.

————. "Hemingway's Debt to *Seven Pillars of Wisdom* in *For Whom the Bell Tolls*." *Notes on Contemporary Literature* 17.3 (May 1987): 11–12.

Alinei, Tamara. "The *Corrida* and *For Whom the Bell Tolls*." *Neophilologus* 56 (1972): 487–92.

Allen, Mary. "Hail to Arms: A View of *For Whom the Bell Tolls*." *Fitzgerald-Hemingway Annual 1973*. Ed. Matthew J. Bruccoli and C. E. Frazer Clark, Jr. Washington, D.C.: Microcard Editions Books, 1974. 285–93.

Allen, Michael J. B. "The Unspanish War in *For Whom the Bell Tolls*." *Contemporary Literature* 13.2 (1972): 204–12.

Brenner, Gerry. "Epic Machinery in Hemingway's *For Whom the Bell Tolls*." *Modern Fiction Studies* 16 (1970): 491–504. Rptd. in Brenner, *Concealments in Hemingway's Works*. Columbus: Ohio State UP, 1983. 124–47.

Broer, Lawrence. *Hemingway's Spanish Tragedy.* Tuscaloosa: U of Alabama P, 1973.

Capellán, Angel. *Hemingway and the Hispanic World.* Ann Arbor: UMI Research P, 1985.

Cass, Colin S. "The Love Story in *For Whom the Bell Tolls*." *Fitzgerald-Hemingway Annual 1972*. Ed. Matthew J. Bruccoli and C. E. Frazer Clark, Jr. Washington, D.C.: Microcard Editions Books, 1973. 225–35.

Cheney, Patrick. "Hemingway and Christian Epic: The Bible in *For Whom the Bell Tolls*." *Papers on Language and Literature* 21.2 (Spring 1985): 170–91.

Conrad, Barnaby. *Hemingway's Spain.* San Francisco: Chronicle, 1989.

Cooper, Stephen. *The Politics of Ernest Hemingway*. Ann Arbor: UMI Research P, 1987.

Crozier, Robert D., S.J. "For Thine is the Power and the Glory: Love in *For Whom the Bell Tolls*." *Papers on Language and Literature* 10 (1974): 76–97.

————. "The Mask of Death, The Face of Life: Hemingway's Feminique." *Hemingway Review* 4.1 (Fall 1984): 2–13. Rptd. in *Ernest Hemingway: Six Decades of Criticism*. Ed. Linda W. Wagner. East Lansing: Michigan State UP, 1987. 239–55.

Davison, Richard Allan. "The Publication of Hemingway's *The Spanish Earth*: An Untold Story." *Hemingway Review* 7.2 (Spring 1988): 122–30.

Delaney, Paul. "Robert Jordan's 'Real Absinthe' in *For Whom the Bell Tolls*." *Fitzgerald-Hemingway Annual 1972*. Ed. Matthew J. Bruccoli and C. E. Frazer Clark, Jr. Washington, D.C.: Microcard Editions Books, 1973. 317–20.

Elliott, Gary D. "*For Whom the Bell Tolls*: Regeneration of the Hemingway Hero." *CEA Critic: An Official Journal of the College English Association* 38.4 (1976): 24–29.

Fleming, Bruce. "Writing in Pidgin: Language in *For Whom the Bell Tolls*." *Dutch Quarterly Review of Anglo-American Letters* 15.4 (1985): 265–77.

Fleming, Robert E. "Hemingway's Treatment of Suicide: 'Fathers and Sons' and *For Whom the Bell Tolls*." *Arizona Quarterly* 33 (1977): 121–32.

Gajdusek, Robert E. "Pilar's Tale: The Myth and the Message." *The Hemingway Review* 10.1 (Fall 1990): 19–33.

Gladstein, Mimi R. "Ma Joad and Pilar: Significantly Similar." *Steinbeck Quarterly* 14 (1981): 93–104.

Grebstein, Sheldon Norman, ed. *The Merrill Studies in "For Whom the Bell Tolls*." Columbus, OH: Charles E. Merrill, 1971.

Gunn, Giles B. "Hemingway's Treatment of Human Solidarity: A Literary Critique of *For Whom the Bell Tolls*." *Christian Scholar's Review* 2 (1972): 99–111.

Hansen, Erik Arne. "Ernest Hemingway's the Fall of Troy in Spain." *Dolphin* 16 (1988): 54–87.

Hodson, Joel. "Robert Jordan Revisited: Hemingway's Debt to T. E. Lawrence." *Hemingway Review* 10.2 (Spring 1991): 2–16.

Josephs, Allen. "Hemingway and the Spanish Civil War: Or, The Volatile Mixture of Politics and Art." *Rewriting the Good Fight: Critical Essays on the Literature of the Spanish Civil War*. Ed. Frieda S. Brown et al. East Lansing: Michigan State UP, 1989. 175–84.

————. "Hemingway's Poor Spanish: Chauvinism and Loss of Credibility in *For Whom the Bell Tolls*." *Hemingway: A Revaluation*. Ed. Donald R. Noble. Troy, NY: Whitston, 1983. 205–23.

Kastely, James L. "Toward a Politically Responsible Ethical Criticism: Narrative in *The Political Unconscious* and *For Whom the Bell Tolls*." *Style* 22.4 (Winter 1988): 535–58.

LaPrade, Douglas E. "The Francoist Censorship of Hemingway's Works About Spain." *Journal of Interdisciplinary Studies/Cuadernos Interdisciplinarios de Estudios Literarios* 1.2 (Fall 1989): 277–90.

Larsen, Kevin S. "Rounds with Mr. Cervantes: *Don Quijote* and *For Whom the Bell Tolls*." *Orbis Litterarum* 43 (1988): 108–28.

Laurence, Frank M. *Hemingway and the Movies.* Jackson: UP of Mississippi, 1981.

Lee, Robert A. " 'Everything Completely Knit Up': Seeing *For Whom the Bell Tolls* Whole." *Ernest Hemingway: New Critical Essays.* Ed. Robert A. Lee. London: Vision Press, 1983. 79–102.

Lewis, Robert W., Jr. *Hemingway on Love.* NY: Haskell House, 1973.

Martin, Robert A. "Hemingway's *For Whom the Bell Tolls*: Fact into Fiction." *Studies in American Fiction* 15 (1987): 219–25.

McClellan, David. "Is Custer a Model for the Fascist Captain in *For Whom the Bell Tolls*?" *Fitzgerald-Hemingway Annual 1974.* Ed. Matthew J. Bruccoli and C. E. Frazer Clark, Jr. Englewood, CO: Microcard Editions Books, 1975. 239–41.

Meyers, Jeffrey. "*For Whom the Bell Tolls* as Contemporary History." *The Spanish Civil War in Literature.* Ed. Janet Perez and Wendell Aycock. Lubbock: Texas Tech UP, 1990. 85–107.

Miller, R. H. "Ernest Hemingway, Textual Critic." *Fitzgerald-Hemingway Annual 1978.* Ed. Matthew J. Bruccoli and Richard Layman. Detroit: Gale Research, 1979. 345–47.

———. "*For Whom the Bell Tolls*: Book-of-the-Month Club Copies." *Fitzgerald-Hemingway Annual 1979.* Ed. Matthew J. Bruccoli and Richard Layman. Detroit: Gale Research, 1980. 407–9.

Molesworth, Charles. "Hemingway's Code: The Spanish Civil War and World Power." *Salmagundi* 76–77 (Fall-Winter 1987–88): 84–100.

Monroe, H. Keith. "Garbo as Guerilla: Queen Christina and *For Whom the Bell Tolls*." *Fitzgerald-Hemingway Annual 1978.* Ed. Matthew J. Bruccoli and Richard Layman. Detroit: Gale Research, 1979. 335–38.

Moses, Carole. "Language as Theme in *For Whom the Bell Tolls*." *Fitzgerald-Hemingway Annual 1978.* Ed. Matthew J. Bruccoli and Richard Layman. Detroit: Gale Research, 1979. 214–23.

Nakjavani, Erik. "Ernest Hemingway's Robert Jordan and Carlos Fuentes's Lorenzo Cruz: A Comparative Study." *Selected Proceedings of the Pennsylvania Foreign Language Conference.* Ed. Gregorio C. Martin. Pittsburgh: Department of Modern Languages, Duquesne U, 1988. 127–35.

———. "Intellectuals as Militants: Hemingway's *For Whom the Bell Tolls* and Malraux's *L'Espoir*: A Comparative Study." *Rewriting the Good Fight:*

Critical Essays on the Literature of the Spanish Civil War. Ed. Frieda S. Brown et al. East Lansing: Michigan State UP, 1989. 199–214.

———. "Knowledge as Power: Robert Jordan as an Intellectual Hero." *Hemingway Review* 7.2 (Spring 1988): 131–46.

Nibbelink, Herman. "The Meaning of Nature in *For Whom the Bell Tolls.*" *Arizona Quarterly* 33 (1977): 165–72.

Orlova, Raisa. "*For Whom the Bell Tolls.*" *Soviet Criticism of American Literature in the Sixties.* Ed. and trans. Carl R. Proffer. Ann Arbor, MI: Ardis, 1972. 116–48.

Phillips, Gene D. *Hemingway and Film.* NY: Ungar, 1980.

Pohl, Constance. "The 'Unmaking' of a Political Film." *The Modern American Novel and the Movies.* Ed. Gerald Peary and Roger Shatzkin. NY: Ungar, 1978. 317–24.

Reynolds, Michael. "Ringing the Changes: Hemingway's *Bell* Tolls Fifty." *Virginia Quarterly Review* 67.1 (Winter 1991): 1–18.

Rodenberg, Hans-Peter. "The Moment of Truth—Hemingway, Spain, and the Civil War 1936–1939: A Study in the Psychoanalysis of Adventurism." *The Spanish Civil War in British and American Literature.* Ed. Bernd-Peter Lange. Braunschweig: Technische Universität Braunschweig, 1988. 46–75.

Rudat, Wolfgang E. H. "Hemingway's Rabbit: Slips of the Tongue and Other Linguistic Games in *For Whom the Bell Tolls.*" *Hemingway Review* 10.1 (Fall 1990): 34–51.

———. "Jacob Barnes and Onan: Sexual Response in *The Sun Also Rises* and *For Whom the Bell Tolls.*" *Journal of Evolutionary Psychology* 9.1–2 (March 1989): 50–58.

———. "The Other War in *For Whom the Bell Tolls*: Maria and Miltonic Gender-Role Battles." *Hemingway Review* 11.1 (Fall 1991): 8–24.

———. "Robert Jordan and Hamlet's Conflicts: *For Whom the Bell Tolls* as Family Romance Once More." *Journal of Evolutionary Psychology* 12.1–2 (March 1991): 65–78.

Shulman, Jeffrey, ed. "Hemingway's Observations on the Spanish Civil War: Unpublished State Department Reports." *Hemingway Review* 7.2 (Spring 1988): 147–51.

Slatoff, Walter. "The 'Great Sin' in *For Whom the Bell Tolls.*" *Journal of Narrative Technique* 7 (1977): 142–88.

Stanton, Edward F. *Hemingway and Spain: A Pursuit.* Seattle: U of Washington P, 1989.

Steinberg, Lee. "The Subjective Idealist 'Quest for True Men' in Hemingway's *For Whom the Bell Tolls.*" *Literature & Ideology* 13 (1972): 51–58.

Stephens, Robert O. "Language Magic and Reality in *For Whom the Bell Tolls.*" *Criticism* 14 (1972): 151–64.

Stradling, R. A. "The Propaganda of the Deed: History, Hemingway, and Spain." *Textual Practice* 3.1 (Spring 1989): 15–35.

Teunissen, John J. *"For Whom the Bell Tolls* as Mythic Narrative." *Dalhousie Review* 56 (1976): 52–69. Rptd. in *Ernest Hemingway: Six Decades of Criticism.* Ed. Linda W. Wagner. East Lansing: Michigan State UP, 1987. 221–37.

Thorne, Creath. "The Shape of Equivocation in Ernest Hemingway's *For Whom the Bell Tolls.*" *American Literature* 51 (1980): 520–35.

Von Ende, Frederick. "The Corrida Pattern in *For Whom the Bell Tolls.*" *Re: Arts and Letters* 3.2 (1970): 63–70.

Wagner, Linda W. "The Marinating of *For Whom the Bell Tolls.*" *Journal of Modern Literature* 2 (1972): 533–46.

Waldmeir, Joseph. "Chapter Numbering and Meaning in *For Whom the Bell Tolls.*" *Hemingway Review* 8.2 (Spring 1989): 43–45.

Watson, William Braasch, ed. "Hemingway's Spanish Civil War Dispatches." *Hemingway Review* 7.2 (Spring 1988): 4–92.

———. " 'Humanity Will Not Forgive This!' The *Pravda* Article." *Hemingway Review* 7.2 (Spring 1988): 114–18.

———. "In Defense of His Reporting from Spain: A Hemingway Letter to NANA." *Hemingway Review* 7.2 (Spring 1988): 119–21.

———. "Investigating Hemingway." *North Dakota Quarterly* 59.1 (Winter 1991): 36–68. Parts 2 and 3 of this article forthcoming in *North Dakota Quarterly* 59.3 (1991) and 60.1 (1992).

———. "Joris Ivens and the Communists: Bringing Hemingway into the Spanish Civil War." *Hemingway Review* 10.1 (Fall 1990): 2–18.

———. "A Variorum Edition of Dispatch 19." *Hemingway Review* 7.2 (Spring 1988): 93–113.

Zehr, David E. "Bourgeois Politics: Hemingway's Case in *For Whom the Bell Tolls.*" *Midwest Quarterly* 17 (1976): 268–78.

Index

About the Editor and Contributors

GERRY BRENNER has taught for the past twenty-two years at the University of Montana, where students recently voted him the most inspirational teacher of the year. He has also taught in Skopje, Yugoslavia, as a senior lecturer in American Literature under the Fulbright Program. He is the author of *Concealments in Hemingway's Works* (1983), *The Old Man and the Sea: Story of a Common Man* (1991), and co-author with Earl Rovit of *Hemingway*, revised edition (1986). His articles on Hemingway have been featured in journals and anthologies, including *Hemingway's Neglected Short Fiction: New Perspectives* (1989), edited by Susan Beegel. In addition to a forthcoming glossary to *A Moveable Feast*, he is completing a book of essays, *"Each Age a Lens" : Essays in Fictive Criticism*.

ROBERT E. GAJDUSEK is professor of English at San Francisco State University, where he was awarded the Outstanding Professor in Humanities Award. He has written two books on Hemingway: *Hemingway's Paris* (1978; paperback 1982); *Hemingway and Joyce: A Study in Debt and Payment* (1984). He has been working for some time on two works, *Hemingway in Key West and Cuba* and *Hemingway's Italy*. His literary criticism has been featured in scholarly journals, and several of his articles have been anthologized since the 1950s, with two additional articles on Hemingway accepted for publication in the near future.

THOMAS E. GOULD is currently a visiting lecturer at North Carolina State University. Under the direction of Michael Reynolds, he recently completed a comprehensive cataloging and analysis of the revisions in the manuscript of *For Whom the Bell Tolls*.

ROBERT A. MARTIN, after teaching for a number of years at the University of Michigan, Ann Arbor, is currently professor of English at Michigan State University in East Lansing. He is the editor of *The Theater Essays of Arthur Miller*; *Arthur Miller: New Perspectives*; *The Writer's Craft*; and (with others) *Rewriting the Good Fight: Critical Essays on the Literature of the Spanish Civil War*. His essays on F. Scott Fitzgerald, Hemingway, Faulkner, Heller, Vonnegut, William Gaddis, and Arthur Miller, among others, have appeared in numerous leading journals and collections. He is a frequent reviewer of critical and biographical studies of American literature and American culture.

CHARLES MOLESWORTH is chairperson of the Department of English at Queens College, City University of New York, where he also teaches at the Graduate Center. He is one of the editors of *The Heath Anthology of American Literature*, and he is the author of *Marianne Moore: A Literary Life* (1990), the first full-length critical biography of this poet. In addition, he has published books on Gary Snyder, Donald Barthelme, and contemporary American poetry. Currently he is working on a study of the roots of cultural criticism in the 1920s.

DEAN REHBERGER teaches at Michigan State University. He is presently working on a book-length study of frontier adventure literature, 1885 to 1935.

MICHAEL REYNOLDS teaches at North Carolina State University. He has written five books on Hemingway: *Hemingway's First War* (1976; 1987); *Hemingway's Reading, 1910–1940* (1981); *"The Sun Also Rises": A Novel of the Twenties* (1988). For several years, he has been preparing what is sure to become the definitive biography of Hemingway. The first volume, *The Young Hemingway* (1986), was a nonfiction finalist for the American Book Award, and it was nominated for the 1986 Pulitzer Prize in biography. The second volume, *Hemingway: The Paris Years*, appeared in 1989, and the final volume is scheduled for publication in 1993. In addition, Professor Reynolds has edited *Critical Essays on Ernest Hemingway's "In Our Time"* (1983). His numerous articles on Hemingway have been extensively anthologized.

RENA SANDERSON, a visiting assistant professor at Boise State University, teaches American literature and women writers. Her current research interests include Hemingway, immigrant and expatriate writings, and autobiographies by women of the Lost Generation. She organized and directed the "Hemingway in Idaho" conference, June 1989.

H. R. STONEBACK teaches at the State University of New York, New Paltz. He has published extensively on modern American, British, Chinese, and French literature, including numerous essays on Faulkner and Hemingway. He has also published fiction, poetry, and songs. His books include a Chinese edition of the *Selected Stories of William Faulkner* and *Cartographers of the Deus Loci*, a volume of poetry. Professor Stoneback has lectured on Hemingway and Faulkner around the world, for the United States Information Agency, the British Council, and other organizations. He has been a Senior Fulbright Professor at Peking University, and a Visiting Professor at the University of Paris. He is presently completing a book dealing with Hemingway's major fiction.

MARK C. VAN GUNTEN wrote his dissertation on Hemingway, under the direction of Matthew J. Bruccoli. He has taught as visiting assistant professor at the University of South Carolina, and his current research interests include the modern American novel and critical theory. Presently he teaches American literature and world Literature at Hammond Academy, Columbia, South Carolina.

KURT VONNEGUT is the author of numerous short stories, essays, and satirical novels, including the best-selling *Slaughter-House Five* and *Cat's Cradle*. He has taught at the University of Iowa Writers Workshop, Harvard University, and the City College of New York. A member of the National Institute of Arts and Letters, he has in recent years become known as a champion of the environment and of freedom of expression. His most recent books include *Hocus Pocus* (1990) and *Fates Worse Than Death: An Autobiographical Collage of the 1980s* (1991).

WILLIAM BRAASCH WATSON teaches history at the Massachusetts Institute of Technology. He is a specialist on the history of the Spanish Civil War. Since 1981 he has been investigating the participation in that war of John Dos Passos, Ernest Hemingway, and the Dutch documentary film maker, Joris Ivens. He has edited and published various Hemingway manuscripts of this period. In 1982, he discovered and published an unknown polemical article that Hemingway wrote for *Pravda* in 1938, and in 1988 he edited all of Hemingway's Spanish Civil War dispatches for *The Hemingway Review.* Professor Watson's article on the writing of Hemingway's "Old Man at the Bridge" was recently included in *New Critical Approaches to the Short Stories of Ernest Hemingway,* edited by Jackson Benson.

Recent Titles in
Contributions in American Studies

Abortion, Politics, and the Courts:
Roe v. Wade and Its Aftermath
Revised Edition
Eva R. Rubin

The Secret Constitution and the Need for Constitutional Change
Arthur S. Miller

Business and Religion in the American 1920s
Rolf Lundén

Modular America: Cross-Cultural Perspectives on the Emergence of an American Way
John G. Blair

The Social Christian Novel
Robert Glenn Wright

The Urbanists, 1865–1915
Dana F. White

In the Public Interest: The League of Women Voters, 1920–1970
Louise M. Young

The Rhetoric of War: Training Day, the Militia, and the Military Sermon
Marie L. Ahearn

Restrained Response: American Novels of the Cold War and Korea, 1945–1962
Arne Axelsson

In Search of America: Transatlantic Essays, 1951–1990
Marcus Cunliffe

Prophetic Pictures: Nathaniel Hawthorne's Knowledge and Uses of the Visual Arts
Rita K. Gollin and John L. Idol, Jr., with the assistance of Sterling K. Eisiminger

Testing the Faith: The New Catholic Fiction in America
Anita Gandolfo